SUCCESSION PLANNING
IN THE LIBRARY

Developing Leaders, Managing Change

PAULA M. SINGER with GAIL GRIFFITH

AMERICAN LIBRARY ASSOCIATION
CHICAGO 2010

Paula M. Singer is president of the Singer Group, through which she maintains a heavy consulting schedule on human resources topics, including compensation studies, leadership development, strategic planning/implementation, organization design and development, performance management, and board development. Since publication of the first edition of *Developing a Compensation Plan* (2002), she has cowritten *Winning with Library Leadership* (2004, with Christi Olson), *Human Resources for Results* (2007, with Jeanne Goodrich), and the second edition of *Developing a Compensation Plan* (2009, with Laura Francisco). She has also coauthored articles in *Public Libraries*, *Bottom Line*, and *Library Journal*. Singer holds a BS in industrial design and labor relations from Cornell University, an MS in administrative sciences from Johns Hopkins University, and an MS in organization development and a PhD in human and organization systems from the Fielding Institute.

Gail Griffith has enjoyed a thirty-five-year career in libraries, with over twenty-five years as a public library administrator responsible for public services, organization development, and human resources. In 2008 she retired as deputy director of the Carroll County (Md.) Public Library. Since 1992, Griffith has consulted with library, local government, and nonprofit clients. Her areas of expertise include strategic planning and organization design, and she is also a skilled trainer, particularly in the areas of leadership development and team building. She holds a BA in sociology from Otterbein College, an MS in applied behavioral science from Johns Hopkins University, and an MLS from the University of Maryland.

The paper used in this publication meets the minimum requirements of American National Standard for Information Sciences—Permanence of Paper for Printed Library Materials, ANSI Z39.48-1992. ∞

Library of Congress Cataloging-in-Publication Data
Singer, Paula M.
    Succession planning in the library : developing leaders, managing change / Paula M. Singer with Gail Griffith.
        p.   cm.
    Includes bibliographical references and index.
    ISBN 978-0-8389-1036-8 (alk. paper)
    1. Library administration. 2. Manpower planning. 3. Library planning. 4. Library employees. 5. Organizational change. 6. Library administration—United States. 7. Manpower planning—United States. 8. Library planning—United States. 9. Library employees—United States. I. Griffith, Gail. II. Title.
Z678.S57 2010
025.1—dc22

2009046233

ISBN-13: 978-0-8389-1036-8

Printed in the United States of America
14 13 12 11 10   5 4 3 2 1

CONTENTS //

ACKNOWLEDGMENTS

WE THANK the public library directors, human resource directors, and training coordinators who contributed their time, best practices, and examples to make this book so much richer. In particular, we thank Karen Bosch Cobb and Camille Turner, Fresno County (Calif.) Public Library; Charles Brown and Rick Ricker, Public Library of Charlotte and Mecklenburg County (N.C.); Melinda Cervantes, Santa Clara County (Calif.) Library; Margaret Donnellan Todd, County of Los Angeles (Calif.) Public Library; Thomas Galanate, Queens Borough (N.Y.) Public Library; Donna Lauffer and Tiffany Hentschel, Johnson County (Kans.) Library; Patrick Losinski, Columbus (Ohio) Metropolitan Library; Jean Mantegna, Baltimore County (Md.) Public Library; George Needham, OCLC; Pat Olafson, Sno-Isle (Wash.) Libraries; Neel Parikh, Pierce County (Wash.) Library System; Terri Schell, Harford County (Md.) Public Library; Tracey Strobel, Cuyahoga County (Ohio) Public Library; and Patty Wong and Gina Duncan, Yolo County (Calif.).

We also want to show our appreciation to Linda Saferite and Shauna McConnell of Tulsa City County (Okla.) Library for sharing their thoughts and programs about succession planning and leadership development, as well as Lynn Wheeler, director of Carroll County (Md.) Public Library, for helping us solicit best practices. Finally, many thanks to our editor, John Thomas, for keeping us jargonless, comma and capital letter appropriate, and free of redundancies.

Paula offers special thanks to Gail, without whom this book would not have left my Mac in this decade; our clients, who often coexperiment in creating new best practices; Jeanne Goodrich, with whom early thoughts, presentations, and articles were created; my brother Ezra Singer, who shared some of his own best practices from corporate America; and of course my supportive husband, Michael Pearlman. Without Michael's encouragement (as well as shopping and cooking), writing would not be an option.

INTRODUCTION ///////////////////////////////

WHEN WE began to write this book, the plan was to focus only on succession planning—that is, why to have a plan and how to design a succession planning program. We saw a great need for this topic to be addressed in the library community for a variety of reasons. Beyond that, as we traveled around the country working with clients and offering workshops on human resources and related topics, not only were we asked for information about succession planning, but our eyes told us more dramatically than a graph or chart could—more than three-fourths of our clients and workshop participants were older than 50. This isn't shocking; just look around.

We can see that a change is coming, but are we planning for it? Do we have the capacity? Libraries will need to manage this change to serve their communities effectively as great numbers of experienced workers retire. In the past few years, we have seen several publications lamenting the statistics and forecasting upcoming baby boomer retirements. We realized that most of the how-tos didn't quite address the situation facing *libraries*, so we agreed to write one.

However, as we began to write, reflect on our own experience, and conduct research, we recognized that to be really useful we needed to broaden the topic of succession planning, especially beyond succession planning for the top jobs. This book therefore includes information on how to retain employees so they are motivated and stay, and how to develop high-quality performers so you have successors at all levels where and when they are needed at your library. We also help you assess your current workforce, not only to identify those ready for retirement but to rejuvenate midcareer staff and capitalize on the knowledge, skills, and abilities of those contemplating retirement and soon-to-retire members of your workforce.

This book also includes a chapter devoted to planning for the succession of the library director, designed for both new and potential library directors and library boards of trustees or commissions.[1] Planning for the succession of the library director is simply a different situation. In addition, the transition surrounding the departure of a library director and installation of a new recruit is another topic that warrants attention. The way this transition is managed can be an opportunity for learning and growth or one marked by divisiveness and trauma. How libraries can make the most of this situation is a topic we determined needed to be addressed.

The first three chapters of this book deal with succession planning for all positions below that of library director and are designed to help you develop a plan that fits your library. Chapter 1 explains why libraries need to attend to succession planning and how to make the case for it. Chapter 2 gives you a framework of what you need for a successful program and how to put one into place, and chapter 3 dives deeper to help you determine which positions are key at your library and develop the competencies that are foundational to an effective succession plan.

Chapters 4 and 5 speak to retention. One of the most important aspects of succession planning in this day and age in libraries of all types is "growing our own"—and keeping them. Younger new hires want growth, experience, a social environment, challenges, and more. Long-service workers are the bearers of institutional history and a great deal of knowledge. Many are able and willing to work past retirement. Is that a good thing? Research shows that members of Generation Y leave their jobs at the drop of the hat (e.g., they want vacation time they haven't yet earned and you need them to cover the desk), and it is not unusual for these workers to have seven jobs by the age of 35. Money is part of it, but certainly not the only contributing factor. In these chapters you can explore a variety of ways to help retain the employees you want to keep—at least for longer than the norm.

Chapter 6 focuses on planning for the succession of a new leader, the library director. In this chapter we discuss why succession planning should begin long before the leader decides to retire and needs to continue after the new leader joins the library; we also provide steps for doing this, as well as an emergency process—the "God forbid the library director gets hit by a truck or resigns abruptly" process. Needless to say, there is also a process for when you have the time to do it right and plan in advance. This discussion is also of importance to governing boards who are responsible for recruiting and hiring the directors. Making the right selection is *the most important job* that library trustees have. This responsibility includes doing whatever is needed to ensure a smooth transition for the new leader.

This book has many stories and cases—most from peer libraries. Library directors and their human resource directors from around the country have been generous in sharing their stories with us; we have woven some throughout the book, and others are offered in chapter 7.

We hope this book provides you with a lot of material and ideas to think about and struggle with. Not every idea will fit your library; not every plan will be appropriate for your culture. Pick what you think will work and adopt it if useful, tailoring it to meet your needs for succession.

What is unique about this book? Several things. First, it is for and about libraries. You are not offered cases about Microsoft or asked to adopt processes that work for organizations with tens of thousands of employees. Because this book is tailored for the library world, many of the choices we made and our recommendations are focused to be pertinent and useful for much smaller organizations with limited human resources staff and a leadership team that is already on overload.

One of our colleagues (OK, it was Paula's cousin Rachel) is a deputy of a large government organization. In preparation for (yet another) succession planning meeting, she and other members of the management staff were given a questionnaire of about twenty-seven pages to complete. She did not have the time, nor did most of her cohort, to invest in this elaborate process. Some of her peers, she shared, declined to complete the paperwork in the scrupulous manner that usually marks their work; rather, she said with a sly smile, several copied the work of another.

We do not think the library management population would do that, *and* we want you to know that we actively sought to streamline the process to the fullest extent possible. You will find agendas, forms, and processes that are easy to use.

This book is geared to libraries of all sizes, from small rural to large urban, and should also be useful to similar public, private, and not-for-profit organizations. It includes examples of public and academic libraries and their cultures.

Realizing the active role that both leadership and employees need to take as libraries push or fly through to 2020, we refer to the process holistically as *succession planning and development*. We need to plan for succession, and in collaboration with our staff we need to focus on employee development and retention.

Finally, we wrote this book to be useful to library managers and leaders as well as trustees.

Good luck with succession planning and development. Do send us your stories.

Note

1. For the purpose of simplicity, unless referring to a specific person we use the title *library director* to refer to the person responsible for running the library, though realizing that many libraries use other titles including *dean, CEO, executive director, county librarian, chief librarian,* and more. In addition, we write *she* and *her* throughout for simplicity and ease of reading; this is not in any way to discount the hes and hims in libraries.

SUCCESSION PLANNING AND DEVELOPMENT
Ensuring the Library's Future

[Succession management is] more than "replacement planning," or simply filling openings as they occur. Comprehensive succession management integrates talent management with organizational strategic planning. It anticipates changes in management. . . . A strategic business plan can only be realized when the *right people* are in the *right place* and at the *right times* to do the *right things*. Having the necessary intellectual capital to compete is a given in today's fast-paced world.

—William J. Rothwell, *Effective Succession Planning*

HAVING THE right people in the right place and at the right times to do the right things—this happens only when the library has engaged in an ongoing process of identifying, assessing, and developing talent to ensure leadership and management continuity throughout the organization. It is more than *replacement planning*, although finding backups to fill key vacancies, especially for senior-level positions, is certainly a part of the process. *Succession planning* goes further and is broader. It is about developing talent, so that individuals have the capacity to assume greater responsibilities, do their jobs better, and take on an expanded management or leadership role in their work. Every time a manager makes a work assignment, she is preparing the employee for the future by building on her ability. Work experience builds competence, and different kinds of work experiences build different kinds of competence. The library with a succession planning process understands this and continually works to build its bench strength by developing staff at all levels.

Succession planning, for the purposes of this book, is defined as a systematic effort by the library to ensure continuity in key positions, retain and develop intellectual and knowledge capital for the future, and encourage individual advancement. It is designed to be ongoing, owned by leadership. It encourages a focus on aligning staff and leadership with the library's strategic goals and objectives.

We read the stories in newspapers and the business press: an organization with tremendous influence and clout goes from leading edge to leaderless in one horrible stroke of fate. Not too long ago, McDonald's Corporation announced the sudden death of its chairman and CEO, Jim Cantalupo. Yet the company continued, hardly skipping a beat, announcing just twenty-four hours after the tragedy a new chairman and CEO. Investors barely responded to the news, and the $40 billion multinational purveyor of Big Macs and supersize fries survives better than most of our waistlines.

Or consider these organizations with iconic leaders: Dave Thomas of Wendy's, Sam Walton of Walmart, or Habitat for Humanity founder Millard Fuller. Each of these organizations lost a founder who was its public face, yet each manages to live on without missing a beat, and even thrive. Though you might be hard pressed to name their current CEOs (in the case of Walmart, Mike Duke is the *third* CEO to follow Sam Walton), Wendy's, Walmart, and Habitat for Humanity all worked hard to ensure that new leadership would be ready. In addition, they developed and prepared new leaders who would not be carbon copies of those they succeeded—rather, they would have the talent, understanding, and skills to help their organizations progress through the unique challenges the future would present. How did these companies make such smooth transitions? What can libraries learn from them?

The saving grace for each one was succession planning. They were prepared for a leadership change and could handle a crisis if, and when, one occurred.

Succession planning is a common program in most large corporations. Leaders of these organizations understand that they are obliged to stakeholders to ensure a successful transition. Without plans for replacing top leadership talent, whether the departure is sudden or not, the organization will suffer.

// DO THE RIGHT THING

Many library leaders understand that they, too, have enormous responsibilities to stakeholders—the members of the public who rely on their libraries for education, Internet, storytime, research, enrichment, and enjoyment—as well as to the library's employees. Libraries have adopted what William J. Rothwell calls comprehensive succession planning, which anticipates changes in management and creates a strategic plan that puts "the right people . . . in the right place . . . at the right times to do the right things." These libraries are prepared for whatever comes down the road.

Succession planning is more than planning for contingencies like the proverbial Mack truck wiping out your management team (God forbid). It means assessing the *key positions* (not just top management positions, but all specialties and areas of expertise) that could become vacant in the near future and providing training, mentoring, special assignments, and other developmental opportunities so that staff members are ready to move into them when the time comes. This development of "bench strength" (skilled backups for key positions at all levels) is important in small and large libraries alike. Forward-thinking libraries are doing just this.

At the root of the issue is the appreciation that the library's most important, most valuable asset is its people. With the large cohort of baby boomers on the cusp

of retirement, most perceptive managers understand that there is not a huge cadre of trained, skilled workers ready to step into their places. Other factors are also shrinking the available labor market for libraries, particularly in some areas of the country. Populations continue to shift to the Sunbelt for better weather, to the southern states for a lower cost of living, or west for the Promised Land, where at the time of this writing housing is more affordable than ever even though state and local governments are struggling financially. Traditional sources of labor—new college and library school graduates—will be highly sought as their cohort shrinks. The labor market is becoming more ethnically diverse, with more individuals for whom English is a second language. All of this means that libraries have to redefine the attributes of their top candidates, learning to value multiculturalism, older part-time workers, employee attributes other than advanced education, and employees who value their leisure time to the extent that they refuse to work more than forty hours a week.

As your library tries to address people issues, talent supply, and succession, there are several trends you can count on. We are sure you will recognize many of them in figure 1.1.

The public sector, where many of our public, academic, and school libraries live, has additional burdens that private employers may resolve by requiring management degrees. In private industry most managers possess MBAs and formal management training, but in the library world managers come from the ranks of librarianship. Although this situation is changing, library managers rarely receive formal instruction on how to develop strategic plans and achieve goals, negotiate effectively, motivate staff, prepare budgets, manage buildings, or maximize employees' potential. Even in a tight economy, library managers are usually paid less than those in the private sector and often receive promotions to management positions in lieu of higher pay, bonuses, or other perks simply not available to their library bosses as ways to award their achievements.

What do the numbers say? The demographics tell us that in the United States there are about 72 million baby boomers, born between 1946 and 1965. The According to the Department of Labor, 11,000 Americans turn 50 every day, and projections based on the U.S. Census indicate that an average of 4.6 adults turn 65 each minute.

This older population will increase dramatically from 1995 until 2025, a period in which members

FIGURE 1.1
A CHECKLIST OF TRENDS TO COUNT ON

Aging. The average age of employees will continue to rise, and the workforce will become more multigenerational. Proportionately, mature workers are the fastest-growing age segment, and large employers can expect to double their percentage of workers over 55 during the next five to ten years.

More ethnic diversity. By demographic standards, the racial and ethnic mix is changing very rapidly, with minorities now accounting for one-third of younger workers. But fewer and fewer are going to library school as other opportunities have opened up for people of color, people who speak other languages, and so on.

Increasing lifestyle/life-stage variety. People are no longer "acting their age." Their life plans are no longer linear and predictable. They differ wildly in how they integrate work and other pursuits into their lives.

Tightening labor markets. As the rate of labor force growth plummets to 2 to 3 percent per decade, labor markets will tighten and competition for talented people will intensify. Of course, this competition for the best and the brightest will affect not only libraries. There will be a lot of competition for government workers at all levels, as well as workers in the business world, education, nonprofits—anywhere that talent and skills are needed.

Shortages of skills and experience. As the baby boom generation reaches retirement age, organizations face a potentially debilitating brain drain of skills and experience.

Shortages of workers. Overall demand for workers is already beginning to exceed supply. The gap is projected to grow to millions, perhaps tens of millions, of workers, with potentially profound effects on economic output and standard of living. The current economic climate, with its high unemployment rate, will slow this demand in the short term. But the overall shortfall is inevitable as the population ages.

Shortages of educated candidates. Despite continuing progress in average educational achievement, colleges will graduate too few candidates to fill the technical, information-intensive, judgment-intensive jobs five years from now.

Pressure on training and development. Employers must not only encourage employees' continuing education but also provide that education directly to maintain needed skills levels.

Tension around HR policies and practices. The whole range of management practices—compensation, benefits, and especially work arrangements—must appeal to the new workforce and accommodate the expanding variety of workers' needs and preferences.

Strain on organizational coherence. As the workforce diversifies and disperses—adopting flexible schedules, telework, and other technology-enabled arrangements—leaders must find new ways to cultivate and nourish organizational culture and identify.

Source: Adapted from Ken Dychtwald, Tamara J. Erickson, and Robert Morison, *Workforce Crisis: How to Beat the Coming Shortage of Skills and Talent* (Boston: Harvard Business School Press, 2006), 26–27.

Note: We eliminated one of the trends to watch for: that of an increasing number of women entering the workforce. We did not find it pertinent to this discussion.

of the populations ages 35–44 and 45–54 actually decrease, especially the former (figure 1.2). In the years between 2005 and 2020, this younger population actually decreases by 15 percent (figure 1.3). The talent pool following the baby boomers is a shrinking traditional leadership pool.

Such numbers are sobering for those of us working in and with libraries. In landmark research conducted using 1990 census data, the ALA Office for Research and Statistics estimated that 40 percent of all U.S. librarians would be eligible to retire at age 65 with their baby boomer colleagues by the end of 2014. Recently, using updated census data, Mary Jo Lynch and others found that these numbers have shifted and provide a brief reprieve—but *only* a brief one. These findings indicate that retirements are likely to peak between 2015 and 2020, when more than 45 percent of librarians will reach retirement age. It is now expected that "the greatest estimated retirement wave will occur between 2010 and 2020, creating a potential deficit of library and information science graduates between 2015 and 2019."[1]

Lynch and her colleagues also pointed out a related trend: between 1990 and 2000 the number of working credentialed librarians grew by 22 percent. Much of this growth came from people who entered the field as a second career or who had delayed entry into the workforce—most often women in their late thirties or early forties, who will soon approach retirement age; this is the factor that has provided the brief reprieve mentioned above but will result in an even larger pool of retirees. Because library workers are disproportionately middle-age and older, the percentage of younger workers, in their twenties and early thirties, is comparatively quite small. In 1999, ALA estimated that only 7 percent of the library workforce was ages 20–29.[2] As you can see in figure 1.4, the 2000 census data show that the smallest cohort of librarians will reach age 65 between 2040 and 2044; these are the people born between 1975 and 1979, who at this writing are 30 or under. "Young talent" is not entering the library workforce in great numbers.

As if that weren't frightening enough, ALA's "Diversity Counts" study points to the difficulty of retaining

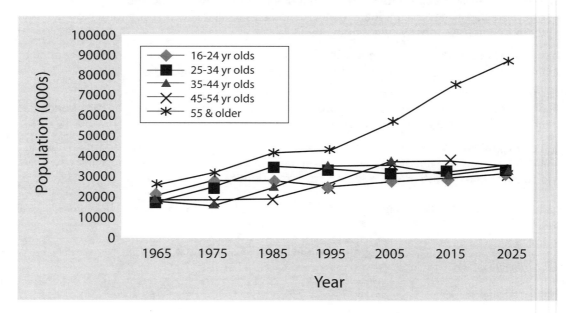

FIGURE 1.2
U.S. POPULATION BY AGE, 1965–2025

Source: Stacy Poulos and Demetra Smith Nightingale, "Employment and Training Policy Implications of the Aging Baby Boom Generation," (Washington, D.C.: Urban Institute, June 1, 1997; www.urban.org/url.cfm?ID=407145). The report was prepared for the U.S. Department of Labor, Employment and Training Administration, under Contract No. F-5532-5-00-80-30.

library workers *at all levels* under the age of 45. This includes those who entered the library workforce as career changers in their thirties or forties. Attrition rates for both credentialed MLS librarians and library support staff are so high that they suggest a lack of opportunities and structure for staff who might be recruited into professional practice or promoted into more responsible positions within libraries. The study points to a

> revolving door effect where individuals are compelled by competing workforce opportunities or by delayed access to managerial leadership to leave the library for greener pastures elsewhere. More so than a matter of not having enough individuals in the pipeline to fill . . . positions, these numbers point to what can be foreseen in the LIS field as a crisis of leadership.[3]

There will be even more data coming with completion of "The Future of Librarians in the Workforce" study (www.libraryworkforce.org), conducted by Dr. José-Marie Griffiths and funded by the Institute of Museum and Library Services. One of the study's goals is to identify the nature of anticipated labor shortages

in the library and information science field that may result from retirement of current workers over the next decade.

Libraries are experiencing labor shortages now, and many have for several years. But as these charts show, the severest deficit is yet to come. Libraries must accelerate their planning and consideration of how they will deal with this reality. Even though the recession's impact may force some older workers to delay retirement in the short term, the long-term shift in population is inevitable.

Before moving away from the numbers, we want to mention that this material is pertinent to our colleagues across the border in Canada as well as halfway around the world in Australia. The Canadian Library Association's 8Rs 2003 study, "The Future of Human Resources in Canadian Libraries" reports that 50 percent of Canadian library professionals were over the age of 45 and that, after 2006, there would be double the number of librarians turning 65 than there had been in the previous two years.[4] Jenny McCarthy, in "Planning Future Workforce: An Australian Perspective," writes that 53 percent of Australian librarians are over age 45 and 20 percent over 55, whereas only

FIGURE 1.3

SHRINKING OF TRADITIONAL LEADERSHIP POOLS: 35- TO 44-YEAR-OLDS IN THE UNITED STATES

Source: Paula Singer and Jeanne Goodrich, "Library Leadership: The Next Generation," presented at ALA 2004, Orlando, Fla.

12.2 percent of the total Australian workforce is over 55. In her own library, the Queensland University of Technology Library, the average age of staff is 43, with 34 percent of them over 50. Of staff holding senior management roles, 80 percent are over 50, and a large portion of supervisory staff are also over 50.[5] It is no surprise that the profession worldwide is asking, Who will run the libraries when this talent leaves?

Who will run the library? Individuals identified by current staff and managers as qualified and trainable, and who are given the right opportunities to develop into next-generation library leadership, will run the library.

Planning for an orderly succession is the right thing, ensuring continuity for all constituents, including members of the community who rely on library pro-

---

TRENDS: THE NUMBERS

1. Aging Workforce: By 2010 . . .

- 35–44 year old group will decline by 10%.
- 45–54 year old workers will grow by 21%.
- 55–64 year olds will expand by 54%.
- 64 million (40% of the workforce) could retire.

2. Shortage of Qualified Candidates

- Workers between the ages of 26–35 have less education than those 36–45 years old. By 2020, only 32% of the workforce will have a college degree.
- The continuing shift toward a knowledge-based economy (and certainly libraries) requires higher levels of education; costs increased by 63% at public schools and 47% in private schools.
- The Employment Policy Foundation projects that the U.S. will need 18 million college graduates by 2012, a shortage of 6 million.
- New entrants to the workforce will be less prepared to take on higher levels of responsibility.
- The time available to experience and acquire knowledge is diminished.
- The size of the workforce is slowing—a 0.6% growth rate is projected for the next several decades.

3. Free Agent Workforce

- Job-hopping, tech-savvy, fulfillment-seeking, self-reliant, independent workers.

- Length of time employees stay with an organization:

  Employee tenure: 4 years (BLS)

  Executive tenure: 3 years (HR Magazine)

  CEO tenure: 3.6 years (Spencer Stuart)

- The average 38-year-old has already held 10.2 jobs! (BLS)

4. Four Generations Working Side by Side

For the first time in history, 4 generations are working together side by side. Each generation is defined by:

- Social events and life/family circumstances
- Different needs, motivators, work/communications styles
- Life plans that are no longer linear and predictable
- People no longer acting their age

5. Our Multigenerational Workforce

- 150 million employees:

  Schwarzkopf (before 1946; 1 million over 75 still working), 6.5%

  Baby boomers (1946–1964), 41.5%

  Generation X (1965–1977), 29.5%

  Generation Y (1978–1990), 22.5%

- 6–7 million entering the workforce over the next 3 years

Source: Denise Kruse and Patrick Magers, Emerging Leader Focus Group Results, presentation February 2008.

grams and services. A rigorous system of succession planning provides a source of strong in-house candidates who can compete effectively for the key positions that become available. Providing high-potential employees with developmental challenges helps retain them. And it does even more: it also prepares them to step into new challenges and future leadership positions. Succession planning also provides for the orderly transfer of knowledge from the skilled, highly experienced employees to the new generation of leadership and others in key positions without the loss of critical information.

Ultimately, succession planning is a plus for any organization. Lost productivity and lost expertise are minimized. Costs are controlled because internal talent with in-depth knowledge of the institution can be developed rather than recruited from the outside. It can also be useful for recruitment. A library with a visible succession planning and development program is more attractive to external candidates. And when the process recognizes talent from nontraditional candidates, diversity can be celebrated and leveraged to the library's advantage.

Succession planning is proactive. You do not wait for the talent and those in key positions to leave; you are ahead of the curve, anticipating, developing, and ensuring that the key work is accomplished by top-flight staff, and that knowledge is shared and transferred in a healthy, collaborative way. Succession planning is a vital tool for implementing your library's strategic plan.

Are you convinced yet?

What else do you need to make a case that embarking on succession planning is a good use of your time and energy? What are the arguments you need to make to your library director or board? Here are some additional ideas; use those that fit your situation.

1. As has been written and said so often, succession planning is not an end in itself. It is a means to an end.[6] Succession planning is an important step to achieving your library's goals and strategic plan. It is a way to ensure that you have the right people, in the right place, at the right time, doing the right work. Having a human resources plan that supports the library's strategic plan (along with facilities, technology, budget, and other supporting plans) is a way to ensure that this happens.

2. Succession planning and development help you systematically identify and develop employees with high potential for key positions. From traveling the country talking to clients and colleagues, we know that one outcome of budget cuts, new technology,

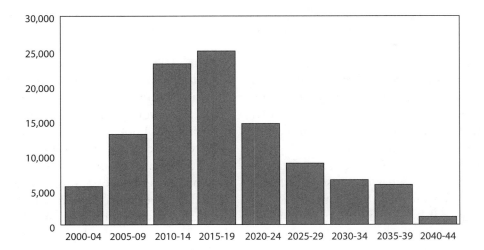

FIGURE 1.4

NUMBER OF LIBRARIANS REACHING AGE 65 (2000 CENSUS BASE)

Source: Mary Jo Lynch, Stephen Tordella, and Thomas Godfrey, "Retirement and Recruitment: A Deeper Look," *American Libraries* 36, no. 1 (January 2005): 26.

streamlined work processes, and empowered staff is fewer middle managers in libraries. Until recently, these members of the workforce were the ranks from which leadership came. Thus it becomes increasingly important to identify, reward, and develop high-potential staff—at every key level for every key job.

3. Baby boomers who leave us take with them a tremendous store of organizational knowledge and history. It is important to transfer that intellectual capital, because once it disappears it cannot be recovered.

4. Recruitment is not going to be as easy as it once was. Librarians have more choices of jobs to take in far more lucrative positions and industries. As the economy recovers, it will be become evident that we are facing a seller's market. Employees are increasingly selective about where they go to work. This holds true even for library directors and other senior members of leadership. Not only is competition stiff for the well-qualified candidates in these roles, many of them are also quite content where they are. How can you keep yours, grow yours, *and* plan in case/when your key leadership says good-bye?

5. Not only is it important to develop staff to meet the difficulties of replacing employees in key positions, but, as good stewards of public funds, we must also consider the cost of turnover, which is a cost you should be able to avoid in many cases. The cost of turnover can easily add up to as much as twice the salary and benefits of the person leaving. First is the staffing cost—that is, the actual cost to hire. This can include fees for a search firm or advertisements and the cost of time to screen résumés, identify and train interview panels, serve on a panel, and so forth. But these are not the only costs. There is also the lost productivity created by a vacancy, the training costs to prepare a new employee, and "acting pay" if your union contract or HR policies require that you pay the employee filling a higher-level position additional salary. You also need to consider the costs of work actually not getting done: projects unfinished, priorities not met, and the actual money spent on substitutes and temporary employees whose value added is limited to keeping the doors open and desks covered rather than moving library strategy and projects forward. And there is, of course, the impact on colleagues who often are asked to pick up extra work (or just do it because it is the right thing, although it too takes its toll). Finally, there are the training costs of time in orientation and bringing the new employee up to speed—the new hire's time along with the time of her supervisors, colleagues, and subordinates. This is the time required to get her up to speed on the technical aspects of the job and what is happening at your library, as well as on the library's culture and how things are done in the new environment.

6. Regardless of your attention to succession planning at the leadership level, you will still be stymied without a succession planning program that incorporates talent development at all levels, including the creation of a culture that fosters employee development and retention. Look around your library. How many, or what percentage, have been employees in your institution for more than twenty years? fifteen years? ten years? You won't be seeing such high numbers in the next decade. There has been a significant change in the psychological contract between an organization and the members of its workforce—any organization, any workforce, not just libraries. Loyalty, for the most part, is a thing of the past.[7] Staff members in generations X and Y have more loyalty to their profession than to their employer (and even more to their family, friends, and other activities). The rewards, opportunities for growth and challenge, and team leadership roles that come with succession planning also help keep your high-potential, high-performing employees in place.

/// BRINGING IT ALL BACK HOME

What do your numbers tell you?

If these arguments in the previous section do not make the case, pull out the data and take a look at your own demographics. Most library directors and boards respond to hard data. Start by taking a snapshot of your workforce by age. Figure 1.5 provides an example of what it might look like.

Then take it further. An important new step in this research is to look at who is eligible for retirement. This isn't too hard to do and the information, whatever HR/payroll system you are using, should be readily available. Look at the age of each member of the library's workforce. See who they are and when each will be eligible for retirement. Do it for a rolling three-year period. Then look at this information with a focus on different positions and levels. For example, conduct such an analysis for those in the position of librarian, branch manager, and departmental leader for each branch and your central facility, plus other key positions in your library. (Needless to say, you will have to adjust these numbers as you learn of retirements and review your employee turnover statistics.) Showing your library director or board of trustees this information just might do the trick.

Sno-Isle Libraries in Washington State went through this exercise. We show you the process and form they used in chapter 3 and give the full Sno-Isle story in chapter 7.

/// EVERY PICTURE TELLS A STORY

We worked with a large East Coast urban library that realized it was time to begin a succession planning process. The first thing we did was analyze the status at the time. This is what we found:

Leadership (director and deputies, department and assistant department heads)
Total: 24
ages 55+   10 (42%)
ages 50–54   5 (21%)

These demographics included public service as well as all other members of leadership (e.g., finance, HR, marketing, IT). Of the nine remaining members

FIGURE 1.5
WORKFORCE SNAPSHOT EXAMPLE

POSITION	AGE RANGE									
	20-24	25-29	30-34	35-39	40-44	45-49	50-54	55-59	60-64	65+
Clerk I	10	12	10	5	5	6	5	4	2	1
Clerk II				3	5	2	1	1		
Clerical Manager						8	1	1	2	
Paraprof I		2	10	12	10	6	5			
Paraprof II		3	6	5	12	10	1			
Librarian I			2	6	6	2	2			
Librarian II				4	4	3	5			
Branch Mgr					1	2	3	5	1	
Division Mgr								2	1	1
Asst Director								2	1	
Director									1	

of leadership under the age of 50, none were in public services. That raised a red flag: it meant that all fifteen members of the senior leadership over the age of 50 were in public services—vital areas, of course, to meeting community needs.

What about the next level down, the talent pool to follow? How did this client fare when it looked at its branch and division managers? Would there be ready replacements from this group for the members of senior leadership? No, these demographics were even worse:

Branch and Division Managers
Total: 63

ages 55+	29 (46%)
ages 50–54	16 (25%)

Even if this client were doing a perfect job of preparing branch and division managers to step up, many of them might retire with—or before—the senior leadership group.

Would the talent pool at the next level down be ready to move up to senior leadership? In most organizations, this is not very likely. And it is scary when you think about the impact of recruiting for so many key positions on the commitment you make every day to your stakeholders. What would Habitat for Humanity or Wendy's be thinking about if it seemed likely that 45 percent of their key leaders and managers would be able to retire within five years? Certainly they would be looking at ways to keep their organizations viable.

In addition to looking at the demographics of your library, ask the following questions to see if your library needs to worry about talent:[8]

1. Do key positions have weak bench strength, that is, are only a few employees *ready now* to assume the positions? Do managers complain that they have trouble finding employees ready or willing to take a promotion as vacancies occur?

2. Has your library experienced a long-term vacancy in a key leadership position (large branch manager or department head and above) in the past year? Did you have to go outside to fill the position? What was the cost to the library?

3. Are key positions filled—but with less than full confidence? Has the library had to compromise on experience or leadership quality to fit certain positions?

4. What percentage of your leaders would be selected if they were applying today for their current positions?

5. What does turnover look like at your library? Do employees at all levels leave the library to advance professionally or to meet their personal or career goals? How many people who are ready or being groomed for promotion *at any level* typically leave the library before they get that promotion?

6. Is *critical turnover* high? Critical turnover is the percentage or number of high-potential workers who leave the library as compared to average or fully successful employees. Does your library

LOCAL GOVERNMENT TAKES ACTION

Local governments seem to be a bit ahead of the library world in this arena. The HR department of Henrico County, Virginia, recognized the looming demographic crisis and developed its *Succession Management Program.* This local government, which includes the state capital, Richmond, was concerned with the impending loss of intellectual capital and the projected dearth of "traditional" job candidates. Acting on these concerns, the county created a systematic approach to sustaining the workforce. This program consisted of five well-thought-out, integrated activities: (1) identifying key positions for succession planning; (2) identifying the desired competencies associated with top performance in those positions; (3) developing employees as ultimate position candidates; (4) assessing development results against needs; and (5) evaluating program success. Implementation was a collaborative process, engaging upper management support to set specific, measurable objectives and provide a structured, creative learning environment in which to develop future leaders. Leadership was provided with distinct developmental strategies targeted to address specific competency gaps. The HR department received its thirty-first Achievement Award from the National Association of Counties to recognize the innovation. This program further supports one of the county's value statements: *We recognize that our employees are a valuable resource to be treated with equality, fairness and justice.*[9]

have a plan to retain high-performing and key employees (see chapters 4 and 5)?

7. Have the business challenges faced by your managers and leaders changed significantly during the past five to ten years? Does your library have the bench strength to staff its strategic and other plans for the changes that will come in the next five to ten years?

8. Is the time to fill positions too long, or perceived by managers to be too long?

9. Do employees or managers complain that decisions about who to promote or transfer are made on criteria other than best qualified, such as friendship and favoritism?

10. Is there a process to respond quickly to sudden, surprise losses of key talent? How long would it take to replace a key member of your workforce who resigned, retired, or died?

If the answers to these questions make you nervous, or if you do not know the answers, it is time for management, and in some cases (pertaining only to the position of library director) your board of trustees, to become increasingly invested in this topic.

In your library system, which are the most important issues and concerns from the list above that you are facing? Do you have any "horror stories?" For example, are you staffing some key positions with retirees from other libraries because your bench strength is weak—the result of a training and development hiatus for too many years? Did you have such a difficult time recruiting a deputy director that you had to promote from several levels down to fill the gap? If a large branch or regional manager left next week, could you quickly think of at least three employees ready to take her place, and three others ready to take the place of the one promoted into the new job? One of our clients *is* this fortunate. This client has been working on leadership development and succession planning for several years. Her library has developed employees via leadership classes, webinars, community exposure, committee experiences, and job rotation. She is not only lucky but smart. Her investment in planning has paid off.

Think about the situations in your library, your own best practices and horror stories. These will also help you make a case to library leadership about moving the agenda for succession planning and development forward.

The future is around the corner. As the builders of great library systems, you have invested heavily in creating lasting organizations. What you do now ensures the viability of your organization going forward.

In summary, figure 1.6 shows the major reasons for succession planning and development. Which are the most pressing to you?

Now that you have assessed your needs, take some time to think through your answers to the following questions:

- What are our library's particular goals in developing a succession management program?
- How does our program contribute to helping the library achieve its mission and strategic plan?
- What outcomes and results will we measure to assess success?
- What shall we name the program?

Now you have a picture of why to engage in succession planning in your library and the information to build a case. Chapter 2 takes you through the steps to make it happen.

FIGURE 1.6
REASONS TO DEVELOP A SUCCESSION PLANNING PROGRAM

REASON	SIGNIFICANT FOR OUR LIBRARY?	IMPACT/NOTES
Provide source of in-house replacements		
Retain key talent		
Prepare individuals for future challenges		
Increase library's human capital by providing for critical/timely knowledge transfer		
Accelerate development of key individuals		
Provide challenging, growth-oriented, and rewarding career opportunities		
Ensure continuity of management culture		
Avoid lost productivity (new person's learning curve)		
Control costs—developing internal talent is less expensive than hiring from the outside		
Make organization more attractive to job candidates		
Support diversity goals		

Notes

Parts of this and subsequent chapters are adopted from Paula Singer, Jeanne Goodrich, and Linda Goldberg, "Your Library's Future," *Library Journal* 129, no. 17 (October 15, 2004): 38–40.

1. Mary Jo Lynch, Stephen Tordello, and Thomas Godfrey, "Retirement and Recruitment: A Deeper Look," *American Libraries* 36, no. 1 (January 2005): 26. Study details are available at www.ala.org/ala/research/librarystaffstats/recruitment/recruitretire-adeeperlook.pdf and www.ala.org/ala/research/librarystaffstats/recruitment/recruitretire-adeeperlook-figures.pdf.

2. Mary Jo Lynch, Age of Librarians, www.ala.org/ala/research/librarystaffstats/librarystaffstudies/ageoflibrarians.cfm.

3. Denise M. Davis and Tracie Hall, Diversity Counts Report (2006). See www.ala.org/ala/aboutala/offices/diversity/diversitycounts/divcounts.cfm for report and associated data.

4. The Future of Human Resources in Canadian Libraries, University of Alberta, www.ls.ualberta.ca/8rs/8RsFutureofHRLibraries.pdf. The original study was designed to be 3Rs—recruitment, retention, and retirement. The additional Rs—remuneration, restructuring, reaccreditation, repatriation, and rejuvenation—emerged from the data.

5. Jenny McCarthy, "Planning a Future Workforce: An Australian Perspective," *New Review of Academic Librarianship* 11, no. 1 (April 2005): 41–56.

6. See, for example, Jeanne Goodrich and Paula Singer, *Human Resources for Results: The Right Person for the Right Job* (Chicago: American Library Association, 2007).

7. Ibid., 91.

8. Adapted from Audrey Smith, William Byham, and Matthew Paese, *Grow Your Own Leaders: How to Identify, Develop, and Retain Leadership Talent* (Upper Saddle River, N.J.: Prentice-Hall 2002), 4.

9. Henrico County Virginia Succession Management Program, www.co.henrico.va.us/departments/hr/employee-development---training/succession-management-program/.

A FRAMEWORK FOR BUILDING BENCH STRENGTH

The time to repair the roof is when the sun is shining.
　　　　　　　　　—John F. Kennedy

THIS CHAPTER can help you create a succession and development plan that fits your library's needs and culture. Since there is no one-size-fits-all plan and we wish to create a useful model for many types of libraries, we offer a framework, suggestions, and questions to ask as you create a plan that fits your library, its culture and environment.

Unlike typical succession or replacement planning that concentrates only on a few senior leadership positions, we propose a system that develops a broad range of high-performing members of the workforce. The focus is on building bench strength, the library's ability to fill a wide range of vacancies from within. This bench strength should be built throughout the library rather than on a few potential replacements for a few leadership positions. In addition, we believe the library has to plan for the future of several key positions that are not in leadership roles but contribute significantly to the library accomplishing its strategic goals or are difficult to recruit: government documents librarian, archivist, faculty/liaison librarian, head cataloger, circulation supervisor, security supervisor, to name a few. Doing this helps build the long-term success of the library.

It is in this context that we recommend a variety of methods to build the library's bench strength. We elaborate on these models in chapter 5.

/// SUCCESSION PLANNING AND DEVELOPMENT: WHAT IT TAKES TO SUCCEED

Succession planning and development happen only when the right ingredients are there at the start. They are

- commitment from top management
- ownership
- vision of what the library needs
- snapshot of present conditions

- openness to nontraditional sources of talent
- culture
- training and development programs
- objectivity

Commitment from Top Management

Leadership has to see the planning and development program as an important endeavor, one that requires focused attention and dedicated resources. The development needed to improve a library's overall bench strength must come from *all* managers and leaders in the organization, not just a few who are exceptionally skilled at developing their staffs.

In most organizations it is easy to spot the highly skilled leaders and managers; they are the people whose staffs step up to volunteer for stretch assignments, team leadership, and promotion. They may also be the people to whose departments employees who "need a little work" are transferred, because senior leadership has confidence in their ability to help someone get on a good track and realize her potential.

There will always be managers and leaders who have exceptional development skills, but an organization that depends on only a few people to develop its entire bench strength will fail. Managers and leaders must first understand the need to devote time, energy, and resources to developing staff; many of them must also strengthen their own skills and abilities in this area; and they must also encourage the managers they supervise in their long-term efforts. Managers and leaders must understand that building bench strength is a key part of their job, not a set of new tasks that takes away from their "real work." That understanding sets in when senior leadership continues to set goals, provide resources, and hold themselves and others accountable for results.

Two library directors who have demonstrated their commitment to succession planning efforts are Charles Brown, director of libraries of the Public Library of Charlotte and Mecklenburg County (N.C.), and Patrick Losinski, executive director of the Columbus (Ohio) Metropolitan Library. They shared insights with us.

When it comes to succession planning, Brown emphasizes three points. One is the importance of providing developmental opportunities so staff are ready to move up when the time is right. The competencies he considers necessary for future leaders not only are technical but must reflect superb communications skills, a good attitude, the ability to deal effectively with change, the skill to get along with others, the vision to

see beyond the four walls of the library, and a strong customer focus. A second imperative is for staff to be trained and groomed to be competitive with the best candidates from outside the library system and with each other. The Public Library of Charlotte and Mecklenburg County seeks a good, strong pool of candidates when a position opens and hopes to be able to say "a selection of one is difficult since we have four or five good candidates."

Brown embraces a big picture of staff development. Although he seeks to retain staff with high potential, he is proud of those who leave for senior positions at other library systems across the country. "Even if we lose some high potentials, it still speaks well of this library. Staff are being trained so well that other libraries want our staff."

Brown's third point provides the foundation of his views on succession planning: the significance of having bench strength when a leader leaves the library system. He believes that there must be some one or preferably several internal candidates in a position to compete with the best and ready to take on any leadership position should someone retire, move on, or get hit by the metaphorical bus. "If a leader doesn't leave a bench, I'm not sure he's been successful as a leader. That is one of the most important jobs of a leader."

Columbus Metropolitan Library's evolving philosophy of succession management focuses on attracting, mentoring, and empowering people so they can compete for senior-level positions in leadership. Like Brown, Losinski wants to develop staff so they can compete for, not be awarded, positions. These library directors are looking for the best, wish to cast a wide net, and would like to see their staff strongly competing against the top people nationwide in and outside the library world. If staff members leave to join other libraries, that too is all right. Many of the directors, deputy directors, and others we spoke with are also comfortable knowing that they may lose some strong incumbents to other library systems.

Losinski brought out an interesting point: "If five positions become vacant and if we fill them with outsiders, that means we don't really have a succession management plan, do we? . . . Clearly," he continued, "we have been inadequately preparing our people for the next level."

Ownership

The HR department may develop succession planning; it may administer it. But it *must* be sponsored and owned by management. The HR unit, as a business partner to library leadership, is vested in the continuity of the organization, but management has the vision, talent, and skills to identify the attributes of future leadership and provide development opportunities and the feedback necessary for high-potential employees to morph into leaders. We spoke with libraries from coast to coast, and each one that considered its succession planning program successful had one thing in common: the library director was an enthusiastic sponsor.

In smaller libraries without HR departments or personnel specialists, the library director probably already takes the lead in thinking about these issues. In such circumstances, do not hesitate to ask your city or county HR staff for support. One of our clients, Patty Wong, director of Yolo County (Calif.) Library, has created such a partnership with the Yolo County HR department, resulting in help and support with workforce and succession planning, organization design, and classification issues—all at no cost to the library.

Vision of What the Library Needs

To achieve strategic alignment of your staffing with your library's needs, you must work from your library's strategic plan. You set important targets, goals, and questions during your strategic planning process. You studied the changing demographics of the library service area, how they will directly affect the library, and over what time period the changes will hit. The question now is, do you have the human capital to support your goals and make them happen? For example, if your strategic plan calls for teaching students and seniors alike how to use social networking tools, you need to ask if you have staff with the technical, training, and interpersonal skills to do this. If not, will you train? Develop? Hire externally? Who are your internal candidates? Why did you select them? What knowledge, skills, abilities, and competencies (characteristics that describe successful performance) have they demonstrated to enable them to undertake this training?

Snapshot of Present Conditions

Do whatever is necessary to get a frank, objective, and accurate understanding of the current workforce. You need a solid sense of which talents currently are found in the organization and which are currently lacking. You need a good understanding of how the skill sets

will change over the planning horizon and ideas of how the library will recruit or develop these skills. Ask the following questions:

- What is your workforce situation? What shortages will you face? Involving which skills? Where? When?
- Where and when will retirements hit you the hardest? What key skills and experience must you retain and pass along?
- What motivates staff at your library? What are their passions? Why do employees join, stay, and leave your library?
- Which skill sets and talent will move your library forward? Which will help fulfill your strategic plan and meet the needs of your customers, patrons, and taxpayers?
- From where do you recruit? What are your feeder programs? Will this continue? Some library schools are closing; fewer people are attending library school and, given the changes in the economy, we are seeing a reluctance to move clear across the country for a job.
- What do the employees who are eligible for retirement want to do? Retire? Work at something else? Come back to the library on a part-time or substitute basis? Mentor?
- Review the "Checklist of Trends to Count On" from chapter 1 (figure 1.1). How will you prepare for them? Record your ideas in a worksheet, as in figure 2.1.

Openness to Nontraditional Sources of Talent

If library leaders continue to look for employees in traditional labor markets, they may fail. More likely, leadership will have to redefine the ideal worker, who may be part-time, multilingual, young, telecommuting, or not a librarian. Alternatives to traditional working hours and locations will facilitate staffing. This is increasingly true as family patterns change and gas prices continue to rise and fall.

Rethink the work as well as the worker. When do you need an MLS-prepared librarian and when are you filling the vacancy with a candidate with an MLS just because you always have? Maybe you could consider a teacher instead of a children's librarian, maybe a library associate with supervisory experience to supervise circulation or a party planner to run your events.

FIGURE 2.1
CHECKLIST OF TRENDS TO COUNT ON: WORKSHEET

Trend	What are its implications for our library? How critical is this trend for us?	What are the local consequences that will stem from this trend?	What action plans should we adopt to prepare for and manage this trend?
Aging workforce with more generations in the workplace			
More ethnic diversity in general population, but not so much in library school graduates			
Increasing lifestyle/life stage variety and differences in how people will integrate work and other pursuits into their lives			
Tightening labor markets mean increasing competition for the best and brightest workers			
Shortages of skills and experience as baby boomers retire			
Shortages of workers once the economy begins to improve			
Shortages of educated candidates for increasingly technical jobs			
Pressure on training and development—employers will need to provide more of it directly			
Tension around HR policies and practices as compensation, benefits, and work arrangements must appeal to the new workforce with differing needs and preferences			
Strain on organizational coherence as the workforce diversifies and disperses			

Culture

Managers and leaders must be, or must learn to be, comfortable identifying and discussing high, medium, and low performers as well as high, medium, and low potential for increased responsibilities and promotional opportunities. It is also helpful if there is an effective performance management system in place and supervisors are able to coach and provide feedback. We cannot say enough about this. So often, employees do not get a clear and specific message about what their performance goals are, and what specifically they are doing that is on- or off-track. It is impossible for someone to learn what to start, stop, or continue doing unless a manager provides feedback that is clear, honest, and direct.

A wonderful example of managers handling staff members' questions and concerns comes from Pat Olafson, the HR director of Sno-Isle Libraries. We asked her if there is any jealousy among staff not given the opportunities afforded to those who have been tapped for additional development in the library's succession planning program.

Olafson did not hesitate in her answer. She did not equivocate, fall into the fairness and equity rap, or indicate any defensive posture or avoidance with employees. She said simply that when that occurs she responds, and encourages managers to respond, as follows:

> I understand that you are concerned that you are not given development opportunities. Let's talk about your performance. Are there any issues with your performance? If so, how can you correct them? If not, have you let your supervisor know that you are interested in these opportunities? What opportunities do think you are ready to tackle? Why? Let's look at your résumé. Let's talk about your talents vis-à-vis the library's leadership competencies. Let's talk about what you can do so that you are someone senior staff seeks out for development.

Your program will be supported even further if managers and leaders are held accountable through their own performance review process for staff development. This will take time and becomes a critical competency for this process. It also takes commitment and honesty—and practice.

Training and Development Programs

Succession planning works best when the library already has a culture of learning and development. If yours does not have one, this is the time to begin to institute it. Whether or not you go forward with a succession planning and development process, the type and pace of change we all live in requires continuous learning, and learning how to learn. "Just in time" learning and development, though important for technical and other skills, is insufficient to cultivate new leadership over a period of years. It takes foresight and patience to get there. Leadership development is a key activity of many libraries across the county. Leadership skills are needed across the library of today and in the library today's leaders will leave behind.

Objectivity

Leaders must be able to put aside their biases about employees and positions and keep an open mind about both. As hard as it is, this is the time to let go of the preconceptions we have about a staff member and focus on her performance and potential and not on poor performance ten years ago that has improved measurably over the years. This is also the time to keep an open mind about hidden talents in employees that to date have not even been considered. You may find yourself being very surprised. Likewise, you may be so accustomed to hiring someone with a particular credential to fill a position that you do not stop to question what the position requires today—and will require in the next few years. "The way we've always done it" might not be the best way to do it now.

/// CASE STUDY: THE BRAVO COUNTY PUBLIC LIBRARY

Succession planning is a trip to the future. We have to plot the course carefully and follow all the route markers to get there; otherwise, we will get lost in space. We examine ten steps to get us there by way of Bravo County Public Library—a fictional library embodying the characteristics and experience of several libraries (see figure 2.2). Bravo County is a medium-sized public library with six branches and about 275 FTE staff. The library has historically enjoyed strong funding support, although its funding has eroded during the recession.

The library system experienced its strongest growth in the late 1980s to early 1990s, when positions were created to staff several new branch libraries. Many employees hired then were in their midthirties and early forties, and the library is now beginning to experience its first wave of retirements from that cohort. In addition, *every member* of the library's senior leadership team is either currently eligible to retire or will be eligible within the next three years, although only one will have reached the traditional retirement age of 65 by then. (Retirement eligibility is based on length of service, age, or a combination of the two.)

Bravo County Public Library sits on the outskirts of a major metropolitan area. It has never paid the highest salaries in its geographic market and in terms of salary is at about the middle of its local cohort of libraries. Although Bravo County is considered a desirable place to live overall, it has no public transportation and the city is more than an hour's drive from some areas of the county. Together, these two factors have sometimes made recruiting staff difficult, despite the library's excellent reputation.

The library system is well used by county residents, who appreciate its ability to keep pace with new technologies and services that meet the needs of the county's increasingly diverse residents. The community was very involved in the library's latest strategic planning process and is asking for more (and more creative) uses of technology, more services for teens (including technology programs and services), continuing emphasis on early literacy, and services and collections that support the needs of the area's small but visible and growing Spanish-speaking population.

Here is the way this public library system worked through the steps of developing its succession planning and development program.

1. Review Your Library's Strategic Direction

Where is your library heading?[1] Are you planning to keep on the same path, holding programs and services to the status quo, or make significant changes? Are changes in your customer base going to force alterations in the way you manage your library? Considering the enormous shifts in the population's age and diversity, tremendous changes in our access to information, social networking, and the role of the library (and librarian) in today's society, you are probably due to make some strategic shifts. How will those changes influence the service to your current customers and new partners as you develop services for the future? From your library's strategic plan and your knowledge of human resource and library trends, you

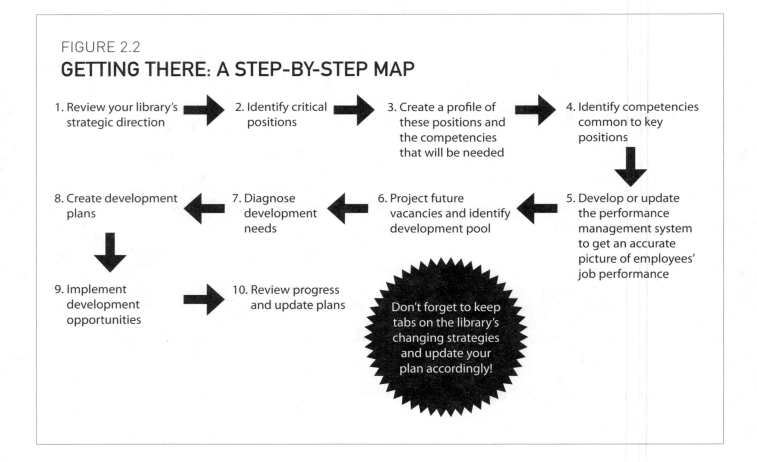

FIGURE 2.2

GETTING THERE: A STEP-BY-STEP MAP

1. Review your library's strategic direction → 2. Identify critical positions → 3. Create a profile of these positions and the competencies that will be needed → 4. Identify competencies common to key positions ↓

8. Create development plans ← 7. Diagnose development needs ← 6. Project future vacancies and identify development pool ← 5. Develop or update the performance management system to get an accurate picture of employees' job performance

9. Implement development opportunities → 10. Review progress and update plans

Don't forget to keep tabs on the library's changing strategies and update your plan accordingly!

know what skills and competencies are needed for the next three to five years. Will the members of your workforce have them? Will they still be there? Will you have the right staff (both technical and leadership), with the right skills, to do the right work? With succession planning and development, your library can better align your human resource requirements with the demands and requirements of your internal needs as well as the external environment. Succession planning and development need to be linked with strategic planning the same way technology, facilities, and budgeting are; they too can support the visionary process.

At Bravo County: The library examined staff development needs as part of its strategic planning and implementation process. Their HR director quickly made the basic assessment recorded in figure 2.3, which was added to the annual system training needs assessment.

2. Identify the Critical Positions in the Library

What are the key positions in the library—senior leaders as well as critical positions and those that are difficult to recruit? Identify them. Once you have a strategic plan and know where the library is heading, you can look at the key work, key positions, and key employees. How? Ask the following questions of key managers and leaders:

- What is the role of your department in implementing our strategic plan? What are the key functions your department must accomplish to make us successful?
- What are the key areas in the library system that require continuity and development of employees? Why?
- Who are the key people we want to develop and nurture for the future? Why was each mentioned?
- Do the high-potential employees in your department believe they have a career path? What do you—and they—see as their future here? Remember that different individuals—with different skills, experiences, and goals—may want their careers to take different paths. It may be typical for a division head in your library to come from the ranks of branch managers, but that does not mean that every

branch manager wants to (or should) become a division head. Nor does it mean that a great division head cannot come from the ranks of the IT or outreach departments—or from somewhere else unexpected. Career paths can, and should, be individualized rather than prescribed.

At Bravo County: It was already evident that the entire senior leadership team was at risk for retirement in the next few years. When the HR director looked at the strategic plan it became clear that there were at least two key positions in the IT department, and the position of marketing and programming coordinator would be key for the strategic plan's emphasis on early literacy and Spanish-speaking programs. Other skills called for in the plan—such as working with teens, developing a facility with social networking technologies, and partnering skills—were present in the system although not the responsibility of any particular positions or individuals. Some skills, such as Spanish-language collection development and cataloging and support for English-language learning, did not appear to be present.

As the HR director began to talk with branch managers and department heads about the abilities of their staffs to implement the strategic plan, the names of some high-potential staff began to emerge. More than one branch manager mentioned staff members who spoke Spanish, were connected to that community, and were willing and able to take on more responsibility, even if it meant transferring to another work location. Names of others who were good at working with teens, had formed great relationships with local schools, or had ideas about using social networking tools to promote library programs also came up. The HR director did not know whether there would be any new positions created—but she was beginning to feel more optimistic that the library's goals could be met by developing the current staff. She took a deep breath and decided to focus first on those current positions the library was most at risk of needing to fill: the senior leadership team.

3. Create a Profile of Positions and Competencies Needed to Meet Leadership Roles and Service Demands

What skills do the next generation of leaders and other critical or hard-to-recruit positions need? Should they

FIGURE 2.3
STAFF DEVELOPMENT NEEDS

STRATEGIC PLAN FOCUS	DEVELOPMENT NEEDS	NOTES
Technology (more, and more creative uses)	Forecasting—what is coming along, and what should we choose? Hands-on in chosen technologies for public service staff. How to manage new technologies for IT staff.	Some needs can be met by course offerings or self-directed learning. Create action learning projects for teams as implementation decisions are made. Forecasting and futuring—may need expert help and some culture change so we are doing more scouting and rewarding staff for it.
Teens (including technology)	Need to know what schools are doing. Public service staff need to know about teen/tween development stages and needs. Social networking technologies are likely targets—which to use, and how? Hands-on.	May be able to develop more partnerships to serve this group. Assumption is that staff have partnership skills but may need to test that. Can do some hands-on, some expert knowledge, some action learning for teams that are developing programs.
Early Literacy	Already have strong program for early literacy. Need to stay on top of emerging research, make sure all staff can incorporate into programs. Coaching and mentoring skills development for experienced staff so they can help new staff?	Have done a lot of training on this topic. Need to make sure that new staff gets it, too. Involve expert partners in early childhood education. Can experienced staff coach and mentor new staff and others as programs need to change?
Spanish (programs, collection, and services)	Spanish language for public service and outreach. Collection development: what does community need and where to get? Cataloging—? Need to know what programs will meet needs and how best to deliver them.	Not many staff are fluent in Spanish, though some have taken basic courses. Look at community colleges, school system ESL trainers, and other sources of instruction for Spanish in the workplace. Collection development staff not experienced with foreign-language collections. We do almost no original cataloging—can purchase cataloging but may not have flexibility we need without more knowledge. Need to draw on community partners—assuming staff have skills to do that but might want to test the assumption. Action learning opportunities for teams as projects are implemented.

be especially adept at understanding and applying technology? Extremely flexible and insightful when dealing with employees of different cultures, backgrounds, and motivations? If you had to write a job description of the library's next-generation leader, what skills, knowledge, abilities, and experiences would you list as critical for sustained organizational performance? Think about what you need these people to *do*. What are the critical performance objectives that must be met for your library?[2] Look even beyond the specific skills you have identified and consider all the characteristics that will be important for competent leaders to exhibit.

At Bravo County: The HR director began to ask herself what the library would be looking for if it had to recruit a new senior leadership team today, or if she had to fill other key positions. She suspected that the library would grow many of its own new leaders, but whether they came up from the ranks or in from the outside, she knew that the library had to articulate what it was looking for—before it had to go looking.

At a senior leadership staff meeting she posed several questions: If you decided to retire tomorrow, what important characteristics would we need to look for in your replacement? In five years, what do you think your position should look like? To implement our strategic plan and meet community needs, what would you be doing? What about those a level or two down from you—what would we be looking for in those people? The group brainstormed quite a list. Not surprisingly, the list included different technical skills needed for each position, such as accounting and budgeting skills for the finance director, knowledge of current and emerging marketing techniques for the marketing director, and experience with proprietary and open-source software for the IT director. The list also included competencies such as the ability to adapt to a rapidly changing environment and the skills needed to influence others. The HR director asked everyone to put notes about their ideas on their current job descriptions and send them to her so that she could create profiles from their ideas.

4. Identify Competencies Common to Key Positions

Review the profiles you have created and look for trends and themes. Which competencies are required for all, or most of, the positions? Building these will bring the most return for your efforts. But don't ignore competencies that apply only to one or two positions,

since these may indicate critical untapped areas for skill development. Ignoring them will leave you without the ability to meet the library's goals.

At Bravo County: At that leadership team meeting, some trends and themes began to emerge. It became clear that the group thought that every leader, regardless of their job title, needed the following competencies:

- Flexibility: the ability to adapt to a rapidly changing environment; be an enthusiastic lifelong learner.
- Model customer-centered service: create services based on what customers want and need, not just on what we think they should have or that we are able to do.
- Be a futurist: know the trends and think about how we could use them to the customer's benefit and in our everyday work.
- Sensitivity to customers and staff from other cultures and backgrounds as well as those with diverse needs.
- Use teamwork to get work done and to grow; hold self and team accountable for results; ensure team learns from both success and failure.

5. Develop or Update the Performance Management System

Does your performance management system link employee performance to the library's strategic goals? Do performance reviews provide an adequate assessment of your employees' ability to do the right work? If not, you need to update the system so that it provides the data you need to get a realistic assessment of employees' skills and abilities.

At Bravo County: The HR director had recently worked with a staff team to update and revise the performance management system. The team was beginning a round of training for supervisors to help them build skill in writing meaningful comments and creating individual development plans.

6. Project Future Vacancies and Identify the Development Pool

You have an existing staff of employees at all stages of their careers. You need an inventory of employees just as you need an inventory of materials in the reference section. This entails looking at who is currently on staff, how much longer you expect them to stay (they may retire, take a break, move to another location, or change careers), and what their capabilities are, given growth and development opportunities. Do you have the employees who, with proper mentoring and assignments, can provide the critical skills, abilities, and knowledge identified in the previous step? Now you can determine your potential leadership and other needs and who might be available to fill them. You may find that you have adequate staff to meet future needs. If not, you will need to look outside your organization.

At Bravo County: Since the entire senior leadership team was at risk for retirement, the HR director concentrated on this group first. There were five positions to be considered, and she developed the assessment shown in figure 2.4.

As she looked at the list, she realized that some of the people in the pool were very close to being ready for promotion while others would need much more development. And for two of the positions there seemed to be only one likely candidate even ready for development. She would look further and talk with the senior leaders about their ideas. In all, she saw that the library might be able to fill some of the positions internally with just a little more development work but

would likely have to search externally to fill one or two of the positions.

7. Diagnose Developmental Needs

With your potential leadership pool identified, the next step is ensuring that they have the skills, knowledge, abilities, competencies, and experience to take on the mantle of leadership. Reviewing your candidates against the job specifications, including competencies, should result in some clearly identified developmental gaps.

At Bravo County: The HR director thought about the profiles and competencies she had developed with the senior leadership team earlier in light of the candidates identified in the development pool for each position. She saw that

- branch manager Adam B needed more experience working with customers and staff from other cultures
- IT manager Jim W was strong in managing the security of the library's IT systems but needed more experience in customer-centered thinking
- training manager Donna F sometimes struggled to put new technology into practice for

---

FIGURE 2.4
DEVELOPMENT POOL

POSITION	DEVELOPMENT POOL
Public Services Director	Adam B, Branch Manager Debbie E, Branch Manager Pat T, Collection Development Manager Steven W, Customer Services Manager
IT Director	Jim W, IT Manager
Finance Director	Sonia B, Grants Manager
HR Director	Cathy C, HR Asst. Director Donna F, Training Manager
Marketing Director	Sara R, Marketing Assistant Anne T, Development Assistant

herself, even though she sometimes provided technology training to staff
- marketing assistant Sara R had been on a system team but had never led one

8. Create Development Plans for Your High-Potential Candidates

Be deliberate in your approach and plan in plenty of lead time. You may believe that leaders are born, not made, but they all need time to gestate. Plan to close the developmental gaps you have identified by carefully selected training programs, special assignments, leadership opportunities, and other means.

At Bravo County: The HR director met with the supervisors of each candidate in the development pool and asked them to be sure they agreed with her assessment and that the identified developmental needs could be addressed. She suggested that each supervisor talk with the candidate to create a workable plan for development. These needs could be addressed by formal training, work projects, team leadership (there would be plenty of new teams coming along as the strategic plan was implemented), or self-study. The senior leaders were also willing to work with and mentor candidates as they went along. In every case, leaders and managers needed to structure opportunities for the candidates to demonstrate what they were able to learn; a project, a product, a proposal for a new program or service, or the development of a relevant new partnership would be good examples. Even though the library had individual development plans in each performance review, the HR director encouraged these supervisors not to wait for the next review process but to develop and implement a plan immediately.

9. Implement Development Opportunities

Your high-potential candidates need care and cultivation to amass the skills still needed. Provide that lead time (two years is a good time frame), and develop several high-potential candidates in parallel to prepare for the alternatives. If you are developing bench strength, you want ideally to prepare several people to become strong candidates for promotion. In addition, it is impossible to know how many future opportunities there may be. And even if you have a "first choice" on your bench, she may abruptly redirect her career or be enticed by another employer. It is always best to be prepared.

At Bravo County: The HR director, along with other members of the senior leadership team, watched as candidates took advantage of the development opportunities in their plans. She also passed along news about new opportunities. And she kept in touch with the supervisors to see how candidates were doing. She worried about those positions for which only one candidate had been identified. Her new mantra became "It's a process," and she kept in touch with the senior leadership team and others, looking for new candidates to develop.

10. Review Progress and Update Plans

Tell your high-potential candidates that you are giving them developmental opportunities for future leadership positions. Tell them what their gaps are and how you see these specific opportunities helping them bridge the gaps. Provide plenty of feedback on how they are progressing. If they are not progressing or meeting expectations, lay the cards on the table. (See chapter 4 for talking points with employees at different levels of potential.) If they are meeting expectations, provide additional assignments to challenge their learning. The more experience they have before they have to take on the leadership role, the greater the likelihood of success.

This is also a time to get a macro view of how your development program is progressing. At this point you have invested a great deal in developing your high-potential employees. Are they progressing in the way you envisioned? Have you actually promoted any of them—and, if so, are they performing in the way you expected?

Evaluate your efforts by asking both senior leaders and high-potential staff what is working well in your program and what should change. Talk one-on-one with leaders and participants if you can. The key questions to ask include these:

- Which developmental activities have been most effective? Why do you say that? (You could give them a list of activities and ask them to react to each one, or leave the question more open ended.)
- Which activities would you change in order to make them more effective? What should we do differently?
- Which activities should be eliminated because they are not providing a significant return to the library?

- What other activities should we consider adding to help fill any knowledge or training gaps?

At Bravo County: The HR director checked in with the senior leadership team early on as the developmental opportunities were put into place, and she kept in touch. Near the end of the first year, she decided to take a closer look. She met with the senior leadership team to ask what changes, if any, they had seen in the candidates who were in development. They felt that, of the ten who had been originally identified, seven were progressing nicely. They had completed their original development plans and were ready for more opportunities. One or two of them had already taken on other, smaller, projects. Two were coming along, but more slowly than anticipated. One was on the verge of deciding not to pursue a promotion.

When asked what they thought was working well, senior leaders agreed that the opportunity to learn by leading teams, while being mentored, had worked well. It met both library and individual needs (in other words, it was a good fit with the library's culture), and leaders could see what the candidates were learning and how they were applying it. They also had the opportunity to model learning from failure as well as from success. What would they change at this point? The senior leaders suggested that some of the candidates might be ready for a brief rotation into some other part of the library, so that they could experience more of the big picture. For example, IT manager Jim could benefit from working in the customer services department for a few months, and branch manager Debbie could learn by working in the IT department. The leadership team agreed to offer the opportunity to candidates who were interested, and the HR director agreed to work with the managers in the affected departments.

The HR director also asked the candidates themselves how things were going. Seven of them said they had learned a lot and were ready for more. Two said they were making progress but struggling a bit to keep up with their development plans and wanted to take things a bit more slowly. One person said that, although she had been interested in promotion, this opportunity had changed her mind. To a person, they expressed their appreciation for the opportunity to develop. One of the top candidates told this story: "Whenever I talk to my friends who work in different library systems I tell them about the team I am leading, the training and mentoring I am getting, and the opportunities here to learn and grow. They usually ask me if we are hiring!" The HR director couldn't wait to share that feedback with the senior leadership team.

On the basis of the group's largely successful experience, the HR director knew that now was the time to offer more systematic development opportunities throughout the library. Senior leaders were on board because they had helped to shape the program and had seen candidates become stronger and more successful. They would be among the program's greatest cheerleaders as others were brought on board, making it more likely that developing staff at all levels would become the new way of doing business at Bravo County Public Library.

One of our urban library clients raised an important question: What is the potential downside of grooming someone to be ready before the position envisioned for her opens up? We do not see this as a problem. With the turnover many libraries are experiencing and the increased need for people to work on or manage special projects (IT, building, planning, E-rate submissions, outreach—the list can go on and on), we think there will be something for people to do in most every situation. Of course, there is a risk that someone who is ready for a promotion that is not available will leave the organization to get one. But we think there is a greater risk in not providing development opportunities. People often leave because they are bored or are not able to grow their skills, whether or not a promotion is available. And your library's reputation suffers as a result, making it difficult to recruit other staff.

Notes

1. We are assuming that your library has a strategic plan or identified goals. If your library does not, see, for example, Sandra Nelson, *Strategic Planning for Results* (Chicago: American Library Association, 2008).

2. An excellent model for thinking this through is provided in Lou Adler, *Hire with Your Head: Using Power Hiring to Build Great Companies*, 2nd ed. (Hoboken, N.J.: John Wiley and Sons, 2002). The concepts presented there work perfectly well for libraries and for hiring, internal promotion, and performance management situations.

HOW DO WE KNOW WHAT WE NEED?
Key Positions, the Right Work, and Library Competencies

THE INFORMATION in this chapter will help you identify the competencies that employees must possess in order to move the library's strategic plan or goals forward; we focus first on those needed for key positions within the library. Identifying competencies is important in both talent development and succession planning. It provides standards against which you assess those identified as having high potential (which we explain in chapter 4).

///// IDENTIFYING KEY POSITIONS

There are a variety of ways to identify key positions, and they differ from library to library. Generally, a key position exerts critical influence on library-wide activities operationally, strategically, or both. Traditionally key positions were limited to those at the top of the library's hierarchy, since that is where most important problem solving and decision making took place. That is no longer the case. Problem solving and decision making have become diffused throughout libraries; they may reside at many points on the organizational chart, where, as often as not, employees are leading from all positions. Criteria to be considered to assist in the identification of key positions include the following:

Critical task: Do you have any positions that would stop a critical task from occurring if the incumbent were to leave, such that the library would suffer in the absence of this function?

Leadership positions (e.g., associate/assistant/deputy library directors and department heads): Depending on the size of the library, consider taking the analysis of leadership positions further. For each leadership/management position, ask what function it uniquely contributes to the library's current mission and to the accomplishment of the strategic plan. If the position were vacant, would the function still operate effectively and efficiently? If the answer is no, then you are looking at a key position.

Future projects: These positions are based on where your library is heading in the future from a strategic standpoint. They may include a director of outreach where one does not exist or a coordinator of innovation or strategic initiatives when such a focus is desired.

Consequences of a vacancy: Are there any other positions which, if vacated, would raise an uproar and bring severe consequences (decisions not made, customer complaints not satisfied, branches not open, computers not started, materials not ordered)?

Other: What other mission-critical positions exist in your library? One could be the archivist, especially if, as in Yolo County Library, there is only one and she serves as both county archivist and records manager for the county. Who oversees government documents, tween services, or your state historical room? Who runs your branch that provides services to the blind and physically handicapped? to Russian immigrants? How difficult would it be to fill these positions? These are possible key positions.

Libraries should follow a consistent format in tracking key positions by answering the following questions for each position:

- What are the requirements (knowledge, skills, abilities, competencies) for this position?
- Who holds this position now?
- Is anyone ready to replace the incumbent if needed? Are there specific positions that could provide needed developmental experience for these key positions?
- What are the career or retirement plans of the incumbent(s)?
- Is this work critical?
- Can the work be split up and accomplished by one or more others? Can it be outsourced? Redistributed?

Sno-Isle (Wash.) Libraries did an excellent job conducting such a review. Pat Olafson, the libraries' HR director, clearly depicted many of these steps in an easy-to-capture spreadsheet. See the story of Sno-Isle Libraries in chapter 7 for an example of her spreadsheet with hypothetical information filled in to provide a picture of the process and for a more detailed explanation of how it was used.

/// OTHER WAYS OF REPLACING KEY POSITIONS

Before a vacancy occurs and certainly before filling a position or planning for successors, a library should consider other options to filling the position, including not filling it at all. Look at the work to see if the position and its responsibilities still add value to the library. Does it still fit into the overall strategy and goals of the library? If not, do not fill the job. If it does fit in, ask if the work can be done differently and more effectively through process improvement or other methods.[1] Assess whether the work is the right work. For example, does the public library need two MLS catalogers? Is ongoing authority work critical to your mission and strategy, or can you let that go? Moving to other options, assess whether the work can be reallocated to others. Without overloading the others, can another department handle it, or can two departments merge and take over the work? Can the work be contracted out at less cost or completed by a temporary employee, part-time employee, or substitute? Being even more creative, how about accomplishing the work via job rotation (developmental assignment) or library school interns? What about reengineering the work or calling in retirees? For example, Queens Borough Public Library offers incentives to retirees who want to stay on in some capacity and assist with the transfer of their knowledge and experience (see chapter 7).

There are many possibilities for filling a position when a vacancy occurs. Keeping open about what needs to be done, what the right work is at this point in the library's history, and who needs to do it leads to a more effective workforce with resources assigned where they best meet the needs of your community.

/// JOB DESCRIPTIONS AND COMPETENCIES

After you identify key positions, it is important to keep job descriptions up to date. Job descriptions and competencies are the source documents for work requirements needed to prepare possible replacements for key positions. The job description should lay out the essential functions of the job along with its duties and responsibilities.[2]

Most libraries require job descriptions. Typically a job description describes the nature of the work to be done as well as its level of complexity, the supervision received or provided, the education and experience required, and the physical requirements of the job. People who work with job descriptions call these requirements "KSAs," short for knowledge, skills, and abilities.

A *competency* is "a cluster of related knowledge, skills and attitudes that affects a major part of one's job that correlates with performance on the job, that can be measured against well-accepted standards, and that can be improved via training and development." In other words, they are the skills, knowledge, and personal attributes that contribute to an individual's success in a particular position. Two examples are "Uses teamwork and project management skills to benefit the library and its users" and "Models self-management."[3]

Competencies and KSAs are related, but competencies go beyond the KSAs required for any individual job. They add, sometimes implicitly, the attitudes and values that are the foundation for behavior and performance. Whether or not it is intentional, many job descriptions contain a mix of KSAs and competencies. Consider these brief examples of statements related to intellectual freedom:

Competency: Models the library's approach to intellectual freedom to ensure the community benefits.

Knowledge: Knows the principles of intellectual freedom as set forth by ALA position papers and library board policy.

Skill: Develops clear and timely written responses to complaints from customers about the library's collection. Consistently applies library board policy in making collection development decisions. Trains staff to respond appropriately and effectively to customer complaints.

Ability: Ability to communicate effectively with a broad range of customers and staff about controversial issues.

Your strategic plan spells out what services the library wants to provide during the next several years. These services were defined by assessing the needs of your community—be it a city, county, or district, your students, the hospital staff, or the corporation you serve. The library's challenge is to respond to these needs with the staff it has now, can develop, or can acquire.[4]

/// COMPETENCIES: JUST A BUZZWORD, OR IS THERE MORE TO IT?

Competencies describe specifically what kinds of skills, behaviors, and personal characteristics all employees are expected to demonstrate. The goal in selecting and defining competencies is to ensure that they are consistent throughout the library regardless of job, level, department, or location. Once you have competencies in place, the job of selecting high-level performers as part of your succession planning and leadership development process becomes more concrete and less subjective. By engaging in this exercise, you reap huge rewards. Indeed, you will have outlined the criteria that define individual as well as organizational success in your library. In the remainder of this chapter, we show you how to take a customized, culture-specific approach as well as some shortcuts to developing competencies.

The beneficial effects of competencies on the library can be seen in many ways:

- Competencies are tied to the values of your library and therefore serve to foster these values.
- Competencies provide clear and specific definitions that support the purpose of the library.
- Competencies provide clear guidelines as to what it takes for your library to be successful.
- Competencies provide practical tools and guidelines for performance management.
- Competencies target training needs required for the development of staff. This process results in the development of a library that has a continuous and dynamic learning environment—a necessity for survival in the twenty-first century.

As Josephine Bryant and Kay Poustie write in the Bertelsmann Foundation's 2001 report *Competencies Needed by Public Library Staff:*

The [competency] system is behaviourally anchored so that both managers and employees can see what is expected of them. The system can also be used to integrate several human resources functions:

The model can be used as the basis for executive development, recruitment, selection, compensation, performance appraisal, career development, job design, and organization design. In its crudest form, it is a yardstick for measuring how someone is performing, comparing current performance to an ideal, and suggesting actions that can be taken to improve that performance. What makes the competency model concept work is its simplicity, the prevailing conditions in the company that provide a fertile bed in which it can grow, managers believing in it, and employees accepting it.[5]

The outcome of the work of developing competencies is that you will have a list and description of what your library values and needs to achieve success at the organizational level and what employees and teams need to achieve success. This model does more than support succession planning and development; competencies can be at the center of many of your human resource policies and programs as they specify performance management criteria, help plan careers, and highlight training and development needs, to name a few.

A common approach to developing competencies is to focus on the people doing the job, that is, the knowledge, skills, and attitudes required to do their job successfully rather than the work itself. This means that cognitive (knowing), behavioral, and affective (feeling) factors are all at work in a competency. Thus a competency includes

knowledge, that is, what is known and understood about a subject in order to ensure successful performance on the job. An example might be knowledge and understanding of the social and intellectual needs of a library's customer group such as seniors or preschool children.

skills necessary to process this knowledge. An example might be effective communication skills.

appropriate *attitudes* and *values,* which are exhibited in behavioral characteristics that impact the way knowledge and skills are brought to bear on the job. These are usually internal evaluations of what might be considered good or important, such as the insistence on giving the best service possible at all times.

If you are a supervisor, you know that attitudes and values are important, but they are not the same as behaviors. We evaluate performance on the basis of observable behaviors, not on attitudes and values, which are often the invisible building blocks of behavior. We know when someone values customer service in the same way we do, because we observe her using negotiation and listening skills to make appropriate exceptions to the rules for customers. But we coach and evaluate on observable behaviors—not on the competencies that build the foundation.

Competencies define what success looks like within the context of a job such as manager, librarian, or supervisor. Each competency developed by a library should consist of (1) a *definition* that contains all the critical elements of the competency, and (2) *levels* of proficiency, which are described as scales for assessment purposes. Again, assessment here does directly translate to performance evaluation. In this context, assessment is most often used to identify and develop needed training across categories of staff. You will probably not find levels of proficiency in published competency sets, since they are usually added as needed by the users. You might consider a scale as simple as 1-2-3:

1. Does not demonstrate.

2. Often demonstrates.

3. Consistently demonstrates.

According to Bryant and Poustie, competencies fall into one of three main categories: core, behavioral, and technical.

Core (or basic) competencies usually reflect the competencies that are essential to the library's success. These competencies reflect what an organization does best and are based on the values of the library. They are considered necessary for *all jobs in the library,* and all employees are expected to demonstrate these competencies. An example of such a competency is customer service.

Behavioral competencies apply to those performance characteristics that influence and drive performance. They are usually relevant to several jobs, job levels, or job families, across the library. Leadership competencies and teamwork could be placed in this category.

Technical or professional competencies relate to technical knowledge or skills that are critical for a specific job/role to be successful. Competencies in negotiating a reference interview, research skills, or learning new databases are prime examples for librarian positions.

In many ways, technical competencies are the least important set of competencies. Most of our staff members have the technical skills to do their jobs, or they pick them up in day-to-day observation and certainly as their performance is managed. In our work and client issues we see that it is the behavioral and interpersonal competencies, as well as those around problem solving and personal mastery, that really make a difference. As work changes, other key competencies staff members need are comfort with ambiguity and change, flexibility, and creativity.

/// WAYS TO BUILD A COMPETENCY MODEL

There are a variety of ways to build a competency model. Bryant and Poustie examine four methods in terms of cost, probability of accuracy, and probability of usage (see figure 3.1).

Although you can look at and even adopt some of the competencies of other libraries, they really need to reflect *your* library's culture, needs, and values. An excellent place to start is the Competency Index for the Library Field published online in 2009 by WebJunction (www.webjunction.org/competencies).

WebJunction has also linked to competencies published by library organizations around the country to make your research even easier.

Competencies should hold true for several years to ensure stability and that development of staff can be focused, and yet they need to be fluid as they are affected by the changing work environment.

Developing a Competency Model through Focus Groups

To increase the probability of usage, ownership, and success, we have seen Bryant and Poustie's third model used successfully with some variation. The variation consists of two additional steps. The first step is to work with a committee that includes a cross section (diagonal slice) of library staff and management to select and validate the model or competencies selected. The

FIGURE 3.1

BUILDING A COMPETENCY MODEL: FOUR METHODS

METHOD	COST	PROBABILITY OF ACCURACY	PROBABILITY OF USAGE
1. Use outside consultant to interview a sample of top performers for each target population group and compare with interview of average performers. Capture what the top performers do more frequently.	High	High	Low
2. Use outside consultants to train insiders to do the tasks in method 1.	Medium	High	Medium
3. Begin with a model from another respected company (with permission); interview a handful of top performers to determine if the borrowed model accurately describes what the top performers do.	Low	High	Low
4. Assemble a group of managers and, using a facilitator, brainstorm about the attributes of top performers today and in the future.	Low	Medium	High

Source: Adapted from Josephine Bryant and Kay Poustie, *Competencies Needed by Public Library Staff* (Gütersloh: Bertelsmann Foundation, 2001), 3–4.

second step is to hold focus groups to test the competencies and levels of proficiency. The cost and time factors increase slightly, but the probability of usage increases from low to high.

For good results, follow these ten tips as you use focus groups:

1. Aim for a group of six to eight people.

2. Invite staff to get the representation you need, whether that be geographic representation, different levels and kinds of jobs represented, length of service, or something else. Make sure you invite people who will speak up.

3. Depending on how many questions you have, allow one to two hours for the session. It often takes a little more time than you expect, and it is better to dismiss people early than to shut down a conversation too soon.

4. Establish a few ground rules at the beginning of the session, such as

   • Everyone is expected to contribute to the discussion.

   • Responses will be aggregated before they are reported, not attributed to specific individuals. (This is standard practice, even if you do not expect to discuss anything sensitive. It does affect people's willingness to be frank.)

5. Determine whether you will take notes directly on a laptop or use chart paper and transcribe the notes later. In either case, consider inviting someone to help you take notes. Be sure to introduce the person (and her role) to the group.

6. Use open-ended questions: What do you like about these competencies? What's missing? What would you change? How would you go about helping someone to develop these competencies? What else should we think about?

7. If no one responds to a question immediately, allow a minute of "soak time" for people to process the question and prepare a response.

8. Spend your time recording what people say, not explaining or defending. You are there to ask and listen, not to lecture. Ask clarifying questions if needed to be sure you record their responses accurately.

9. Decide in advance whether you are willing and able to send the participants your draft notes and allow them to add comments. This is not a standard procedure, and it adds time to your process—so if you want to do it, allow plenty of extra time.

10. Thank people for participating and tell them what your next steps will be.

Developing a Competency Model by Interviewing Top Performers

An alternative to using focus groups is to identify exemplary performers—individuals who are particularly good at demonstrating a competency. Then interview them. This process takes more time than conducting focus groups, but it has the advantage of being more flexible to schedule. In addition, it gives top performers a bit more recognition for being exemplary. And by taking some time one-on-one, the conversation may go deeper than that of a focus group. If you can interview only a few individuals and want broader input, you can also choose to compile interview results and ask a focus group or committee to provide their reactions. Record results in a form such as figure 3.2.

Case Study, Public Library: City of Toronto Core Competencies

These core competencies for the City of Toronto were developed on the basis of the kind of organization and culture desired and the city's values and aspirations. They apply to all municipal employees, including those at the Toronto Public Library. The behavioral characteristics of the core competencies are as follows:[6]

Customer service orientation

   • Clarifies expectations

   • Takes personal responsibility

   • Takes action for the customer

   • Addresses underlying customer needs

   • Uses a long-term approach

Fiscal responsibility

   • Understands key resource issues affecting one's responsibilities and business priorities using resources to increase customer value

FIGURE 3.2

INTERVIEW GUIDE TO COLLECT COMPETENCY DEVELOPMENT STRATEGIES

Use this interview guide to collect information about how to build competencies in the context of your library's unique culture. Select several exemplary performers who have been identified as especially good at demonstrating a given competency. Indicate that competency next to the label "competency" below. Then spend about 15 minutes to interview each exemplary performer using the questions appearing below. When you are finished, analyze the results by identifying common themes and patterns across all the interview results.

Competency: _____

Name: _____ **Title:** _____

Years of Experience in Job: _____ **Date:** _____

Interviewed by: _____

1. Think of a time when you were asked to demonstrate this competency.

    a. What was the situation?

    b. When did this situation occur?

    c. What did you do?

    d. How do you believe the experience helped you demonstrate this competency?

    e. If you had a mentee or trainee, and she participated in an experience like this, would it help to build the competency?

2. Who are some people in this library who are exceptionally good at demonstrating this competency to whom you could refer your mentee or trainee?

3. What are some work experiences in the library that you believe your mentee/trainee should be given to build or demonstrate the competency?

4. How might the pressure to produce by specific deadlines help to build or demonstrate the competency?

5. Where would you send people—to what branch or department—to build and/or demonstrate this competency? (Where are the centers of excellence for this competency in the organization, and why do you think so?)

6. List special and specific work assignments that would be particularly useful in building or demonstrating this competency.

7. If someone asked you for advice on how to build this competency in this library, what advice would you give them?

8. Could you think of some upcoming or pending library projects that might be especially useful to build this competency? What are they, and why do you think they could help to build the competency?

The next step in identifying the competencies is to feed back the results to the exemplary performers to make sure that you heard what was said, to achieve consensus, and to verify that the assignments recommended would actually build the competencies. The competencies could then be linked to training and development needs as well as informing the succession planning and development process.

Source: Adapted from William J. Rothwell, *Effective Succession Planning: Ensuring Leadership Continuity and Building Talent from Within*, 3rd ed. (New York: AMACOM, 2005), 208.

- Demonstrates fiscal prudence
- Models effective utilization
- Advocates benefits for the organization

Innovation

- Seeks new solutions
- Takes action new to the job or function
- Introduces new ideas to the organization
- Introduces new ideas to the public sector
- Encourages innovation in others

Results orientation

- Wants to do job well
- Works to achieve goals
- Sets own standards to improve performance
- Sets and strives to meet higher standards of performance
- Conducts cost-benefit analyses
- Takes calculated entrepreneurial risks

Teamwork

- Cooperates and contributes
- Promotes team cooperation
- Builds a high-performing team

Case Study, Academic Library: Queensland University of Technology

The competencies selected by the Queensland (Australia) University of Technology (QUT) were borrowed from the British Chartered Institute of Library and Information Professionals' research for the summary shown in figure 3.3 of the professional and information and generic skills library professionals need for the twenty-first century in order to best align library services with the university's strategic plan.[7] They were adopted to align with the university's change in approach to learning and teaching, particularly with respect to providing students with more flexible learning. In addition, the university's strategic plan announced its intention to double the number of higher-degree research students and expand significantly its overall research capacity and performance. The implication for the library in providing the range and level of services to support this growth was significant and indicated a changing role for the academic library as well

as the need for librarians to work collaboratively with academics, researchers, learning designers, and IT professionals.

QUT, along with its cohort the Librarians of the Australian Technology Network (LATN), commissioned a consultant to "identify overall issues and concerns related to succession and workforce planning among the libraries and their universities and to make recommendations for the LATN group as a whole and its individual members to address these issues." The recommendations for the QUT library included the following: development of a workforce and succession plan; conduct of an inventory of skills and attitudes needed by the library for both the short and long term; revision of selection criteria (for positions) to focus on learning agility, personal attributes, and leadership qualities; consideration of all vacancies to see if requirements have changed or new priorities need to be addressed; encouragement of staff to take a proactive stance in their own career development; and identification of staff with leadership and management potential and allow them to take on greater challenges. As an outcome of these recommendations, their first task was to investigate the role of the faculty/liaison librarian, which is the position at the development and delivery end of many of the new trends and services, especially in learning and teaching support and the identification and management of access to electronic information sources.

Through focused development of key competencies, not only will employees be better prepared to compete for vacancies, they will also be exhibiting the key attributes needed to drive the library's strategic plan.

/// LEADER COMPETENCIES

Leadership development has been the focus of a great deal of study and work. It is of particular interest to us as we look to grow the next generation of library leaders. Building the leadership capacity of staff at all levels suggests that developing leadership competencies deserves focused attention. Libraries, of course, are not the only organizations interested in developing leaders. In fact, we can learn a great deal from the work of other organizations—particularly those in the public sector. This group of organizations has a lot in common with both public and academic libraries. Libraries are often publicly funded (in whole or in part), making them a part of the public sector. More than that, they are usually part of a local, state, or national political environment and must function well in this milieu in order to survive.

Public Sector Leader Competencies

In her research of public sector succession planning practices, Mary Young found several themes related to the competencies that are most important to help leaders acquire.[8] The three primary development needs are

knowledge and understanding outside the employee's own department or functional area. In many cases, employees' previous career experiences have not exposed them to other areas of government. As a result, they need to understand what other

---

FIGURE 3.3

SUMMARY OF LIBRARY SKILLS (ACADEMIC) FOR THE TWENTY-FIRST CENTURY

PROFESSIONAL INFORMATION SKILLS	GENERIC SKILLS
Knowledge Management	**Project Management**
Information architecture	Planning and evaluation
Information and communication	People management
Technology skills	Research skills
Technical (traditional) professional skills	Bids and proposals
Subject Expertise	**Critical Skills**
Collection management	Thinking
Collection description	Planning and evaluation
Technical (traditional) professional skills	Analysis
	Problem solving
	Research
Information Technology	**Leadership**
Design	General management
Application	Communication skills
Systems	Strategic management
User support (problem solving)	People skills
	Financial skills
Service Development	**Promotion and Marketing**
User information	Design appreciation
Surveys	Presentation skills
Service impact analysis	Multiprofessional appreciation
Planning and evaluation	
Promotion and market	

departments or functions do and how that work is connected to their own. Translating to libraries, this would be about helping the employee learn more about what happens in the branch if they have not worked in one for years, how books get selected and processed, or even how the marketing department's work brings customers of all ages in.

knowledge and understanding at the enterprise level. In part, this content area is an aggregation of learning about other departments and functions; it is about how all the pieces fit together. In addition, it is about work at the executive level—the tasks, functions, and challenges that are important at these levels above departments or agencies, including knowledge and understanding of the organization's relationship to its broader environment. Again in the library world, how does your library determine strategy? Who makes that decision? On what knowledge and with what input?

a broad network of relationships. Knowledge and understanding are important, but they do not assure a leader's effectiveness. The third critical area libraries need to help leaders develop is building a broad network of relationships—across departments and functions, at many levels, and in the library's wider environment. Do employees in your library realize that they are a department in a college or local jurisdiction?

Why are these particular items so important in developing leaders? Not because they are the most critical skills or hardest to develop, but because *these are the competencies that individual employees are least able to develop on their own.* These three competencies are "boundary-spanning: they are about stretching employees' knowledge, understanding, and working relationships and exposing them to people and aspects of the organization outside their current sphere. These objectives have important implications for how libraries go about developing leaders."[9] We discuss how to help people develop these competencies in chapter 5.

Another way of looking at these three development needs is that they help people develop competencies around political awareness and operate effectively in a broader political environment. We have seen some libraries identify these competencies as critical

and begin to help staff develop them. For example, the California Library Association's Competencies for California Librarians in the 21st Century (www .cla-net.org/resources/articles/r_competencies.php) includes political awareness as a core competency for librarians. California libraries such as those in Fresno and Santa Clara counties encourage involvement in local business and community organizations and with local government and nonprofit agencies to help staff identify and enlist the help of strategic partners. More detail about each library's efforts appears in their stories in chapter 7.

Structuring learning opportunities for staff around internal (library) and external (government and community) decision making, as the libraries in Fresno and Santa Clara counties have done, is a way of helping them grasp the bigger picture. As can be seen with recent budget cuts and changes to the political climate, acquiring these skills, and being comfortable using them, might be one of the competencies that separates senior leaders from others.

In addition to these three competencies, Young found the following specific skills that managers and leaders typically need to develop:

- getting things done in this government or in this organization/jurisdiction
- managing change
- managing conflict
- managing the public
- managing the media

To a more limited extent, some respondents reported several more basic supervisory skills that even experienced managers need to develop:

- managing employees, including influencing, motivating, developing, and retaining
- dealing with civil service and personnel policies
- professional skills such as making presentations, managing projects, facilitating meetings, evaluating performance, and leading teams

Sad to say, we have seen that too many managers in library systems are underdeveloped in these areas. The solution is not to penalize them for not having these competencies but to realize that they were not given (or did not take) earlier opportunities to develop them. Fortunately, we are seeing many libraries begin to address these issues by providing supervisory training opportunities for their managers. Some libraries open this training to staff who may want to move into supervisory positions as a way to help them decide whether that is something they really want to do and, if so, to prepare. We offer more detail about some of these programs in chapter 5.

Leadership Competencies and Emotional Intelligence

Leadership competencies run through your entire library, regardless of department, function, or position/classification. Right Management studied emerging leaders, which it defined as those who (usually) manage others, contribute significantly to business results, are perceived as having potential for promotion or additional leadership responsibilities, and would cause pain if they left the organization. The highest rated competencies for these leaders were

1. *Focus on results:* concentrates on the achievement of business results by effectively structuring and carrying out work.

2. *Taking initiative:* takes urgent action to accomplish objectives and achieve business results; is proactive; takes action to achieve goals beyond what is required.

3. *Leadership:* establishes and communicates a vision for the organization. Inspires and empowers others. Leads by example.

4. *Trust/integrity:* trusted by others. Maintains reputation for truthfulness, credibility, confidentiality, and authenticity.

5. *Self-awareness:* understands personal strengths, limitations, needs, and values.

6. *Building bonds/collaboration:* builds positive working relationships with others. Demonstrates the willingness and capacity to collaborate and build partnerships with others.

7. *Creativity/managing innovation:* effectively manages and encourages the creativity of others.

8. *Learning/self-development:* demonstrates commitment to ongoing learning and professional self-improvement. Willing to be coached.

9. *Self-management:* demonstrates self-control. Maintains optimism, energy, and stamina. Manages stress well and models work/life balance.

10. *Decision making:* effectively collects and analyzes data/input from others, considers alternatives, makes sound and timely decisions, collaborates in group decisions, and understands the impact of decisions on others.

11. *Political savvy:* accepts and understands the political dimension of organizational life, anticipates political consequences, and maneuvers effectively through complex situations.

12. *Delegating:* effectively transfers responsibility and authority to others and holds them accountable for achieving results.

The biggest gaps found in the study came under self-awareness, political savvy, delegating, self-management, leadership, and decision making. Our experience affirms these gaps. We are sure they do not surprise you, and you may even find the same in your own library. You may note that some of these competencies relate to the concept of emotional intelligence (EI) as developed by Daniel Goleman.[10] Emotional intelligence "defines how we manage behavior, navigate social complexities, and make personal decisions that achieve positive results."[11] Although it is beyond the scope of this book for us to discuss emotional intelligence and its importance in the workforce, we list the EI components of the Bar-On Emotional Intelligence Inventory (www.eiconsortium.org/measures/eqi.html) as examples:

Intrapersonal scale

- Self-regard
- Emotional self-awareness
- Assertiveness
- Independence
- Self-actualization

Interpersonal scale

- Empathy
- Social responsibility
- Interpersonal relationship

Adaptability scale

- Reality testing
- Flexibility
- Problem solving

Stress management scale

- Stress tolerance
- Impulse control

General mood scale

- Optimism
- Happiness

We believe emotional intelligence to be critical to the success of leaders in any organization and at any level. It has been shown that it is the key to 27–46 percent of workplace success (per Dr. Reuven Bar-On) and that it accounts for 85–95 percent of the difference between a "good leader" and an "excellent leader" (per Goleman). It has also been shown that one can use emotional intelligence to boost job performance. It is so critical to success, write Bradberry and Greaves, that it "accounts for 60 percent of performance in all types of jobs. It's the single biggest predictor of performance in the workplace and the strongest drive of leadership and personal excellence."[12]

Although we mention it in this section on leader competencies, we hope you consider helping employees at all levels in your library to develop and strengthen their emotional intelligence. As we said earlier, these competencies rather than technical competencies are now most likely to be the drivers of potential, performance, or success at any level.

Connection, Contribution, and Collaboration

Today's organization is usually characterized by its networked, flat structure. Change is the expected, not the unusual. Flexibility and adaptability are inherent and required of everyone. The values in such a library system are relationships; sharing information; localized solutions that fit the culture of the branch, department, and *your* library; and a culture that values openness and effectiveness as opposed to (only) efficiency. In *Winning with Library Leadership*, Christi Olson and Paula Singer note that leaders in such complex systems as academic and public libraries find themselves needing to focus around three key competencies: connection, contribution, and collaboration.[13]

Connection: making the right connections between people and organizations, linking people together for a common goal; uses the approach of power "with" rather than power "over."

Contribution: making explicit to each employee how her work or job ties to fulfilling the library's strategic goals; team or group members setting, clarifying, and sharing expectations, leading to commitment and ownership.

Collaboration: creating a shared understanding and interdependency among staff and others who come together to solve a problem; applied in complex, new, unfamiliar, and challenging situations.

Technical, Leadership, and Implementation Skills

Another way to view competencies is in terms of three major categories: library and information system–related skills and knowledge, leadership skills, and implementation skills. Leadership competencies are often personal attributes, and implementation competencies are how one gets things done. Paul Cantor, in "Succession Planning: Often Requested, Rarely Delivered," tells a wonderful and clear story from the Bible that really illustrates the difference:

In the Bible, Noah demonstrated the differences among these three types of competencies. God told Noah that it was going to rain and that he wanted Noah to build an ark and put all kinds of animals on it. Therefore, Noah knew what the industry risks were (it's going to rain) and what should be done about it (build an ark and put the animals on it). However, *knowledge* of what the risks are, and what should be done about them, doesn't get the job done.

But Noah, starting with the limited instruction on ark building provided by God, did get the ark built on time—and today we would say on budget—demonstrating that he had the *implementation skills* needed to take action and manage risk.

Noah's implementation skills can be distinguished from his leadership skills. He demonstrated *leadership skills* by convincing all those animals to board the ark and not eat each other up during the voyage.[14]

/// EXISTING COMPETENCY MODELS

To select for future leadership, identify the competencies that best reflect your strategic direction. In addition to those noted above, there are many competency directories that include competency definitions and assessment options. Library leaders can rely on their HR staff or a consultant to facilitate model development or appoint an individual or team to research and develop a model. A generic model is available through the U.S. Department of Labor as part of an initiative

to assess future workforce needs (http://wdr.doleta
.gov/SCANS/). Johnson County (Kans.) Library, for
example, used this model to select four competencies
it wanted its current and potential leaders to acquire:
leads change, influences people, achieves results, and
fosters communication. Johnson County's detailed
definitions of these competencies, along with the
competencies developed by the City of Toronto, the
New Jersey Library Association, and the Ohio Library
Council, follow.

If the prospect of developing competencies is daunt-
ing, remember that you do not need to start from
scratch, nor do you need an exhaustive set of competencies that covers everything staff need to demonstrate. Start with a few competencies that are most critical to your success. Remember the Johnson County
Library example of looking at other models and pick-
ing four competencies to focus on. Spend your energy
on competencies that will bring your library the greatest return.

Whether you are creating your own competencies
or adapting ones used by others, you must involve staff
and managers and get feedback, buy-in, and ownership. These are the competencies that will drive your
succession planning and development process forward.
You will be recruiting on the basis of these competencies, measuring performance against them, training
and developing to them, and selecting high-potential
performers who meet and exceed them in your succession planning process. You learn how select high-
potential performers in chapter 4.

City of Toronto Competency Definition

Adaptability: the willingness and ability to be flexible and work effectively with various individuals
or groups in a changing environment. Being
open to understanding and appreciating different and opposing perspectives, adjusting one's
approach to changing situations and accepting
changes.

Continuous Learning: taking actions to improve
skills, knowledge and abilities. Applying concepts, strategies and expertise that contribute to
one's marketability and the organization's ongoing success.

Conceptual Thinking: the ability to identify patterns
or connections between situations or ideas that
are not obviously related, and to identify key or
underlying issues and/or principles in complex

situations. Conceptual thinking includes reason-
ing that is creative and imaginative.

Customer Service Orientation: a desire to identify
and meet/exceed the requirements of internal
and external customers. Recognizing the variety
of customers in communities and at all levels
of the organization and accommodating their
diverse needs.

Developing Others: a genuine intent to foster the
long-term success and growth of others by assisting with identification of individual needs and by
providing monitoring and feedback.

Planning and organizing one's work and the work of
others to ensure goals are met. Seeks to develop
others to the extent that tasks and responsibilities can be delegated and minimal supervision
is required.

Fiscal Responsibility: the ability to effectively manage and optimize human, financial and physical
resources, qualitative and quantitative measure-
ment, planning and control of resources to maximize results.

Holding People Accountable: ensuring others meet
objectives and expectations in an appropriate
and effective manner. Ensuring the performance
management process is conducted in the divi-
sion/work unit throughout the year. Provides
clear direction, appropriate tools, resources and
authority to support success.

Impact and Influence: the ability to persuade, con-
vince, influence, motivate or communicate with
others to gain commitment.

Innovation: an effort to enhance performance by
being creative, promoting new ideas and intro-
ducing new solutions or procedures.

Leadership: the ability to create and communicate
a vision and engage others in its achievement. It
is the ability to demonstrate behaviors that model
and support the organization's aspirations and
values and ensure its success.

Leading Change: the ability to initiate, facilitate
or implement a change. Helping staff and the
organization's stakeholders understand what the
change means to them, building a shared vision
and providing the ongoing guidance and support
which will generate and maintain enthusiasm
and commitment to the change process.

Listening and Understanding: the ability to practice active listening, understand and respond appropriately when interacting with individuals and groups. Reflecting on your verbal and nonverbal behavior. The ability to effectively liaise with management, staff, union representatives, elected officials, other governments, community groups and the general public.

Organizational Awareness: the understanding and ability to work within structures and relationships in one's own organization or in other organizations. Knows the formal decision-making processes. The ability to identify the decision-makers and individuals who can influence them, and to predict how new events or situations will affect individuals and groups both within and external to the organization.

Planning, Organizing and Coordinating: proactively planning, establishing priorities, allocating resources, implementing plans, and monitoring and adjusting work to accomplish goals.

Problem Solving: understanding a situation by breaking it apart into smaller pieces, or tracing the implications of a situation in a step-by-step way. The ability to organize information, identify key factors [and] underlying causes, troubleshoot and generate solutions. Setting priorities, determining responsibilities, making decisions and taking appropriate action.

Relationship Building: establishing, building, and maintaining strong and reciprocal relationships and a network of contacts to keep a pulse on public, political and internal issues and to make informed decisions. Identifying who to involve and when and how to involve them in order to accomplish objectives and minimize obstacles.

Responsiveness to the Public: ensuring that the strategic direction and service delivery of the organization are sensitive to public needs through an awareness of how organization programs, policies and decisions impact public interests and concerns.

Results Orientation: the desire or drive to achieve or surpass identified goals. Establishes performance objectives and measures to continuously improve performance and the standard of excellence in the organization. Includes innovative or entrepreneurial behaviors.

Strategic Orientation: the ability to link long-range visions and concepts to daily work. Strategic orientation moves from understanding business fundamentals and strategies to a sophisticated awareness of the impact of the external environment on strategies and how external factors affect choices.

Striving for Clarity and Quality: an effort to increase quality and consistency, and reduce uncertainty through behaviors such as monitoring and checking for accuracy, insisting on clarity of roles and functions, etc.

Teamwork: being part of a team and working cooperatively with others. "Team" is broadly defined as any task or process-oriented group of individuals working towards a common goal.

Source: Josephine Bryant and Kay Poustie, *Competencies Needed by Public Library Staff* (Gütersloh: Bertelsmann Foundation, 2001), 3–4.

New Jersey Library Association Core Competencies for Librarians

PREAMBLE

These competencies pertain to the delivery of services to all ages, to all constituencies, and for all types of libraries. Competencies are the skills, technical knowledge and personal attributes that enable individuals to contribute positively to their organizations and the library profession. These Core Competencies apply to all librarians. Companion documents have been created to focus on the specific skills needed for specialized areas of librarianship. Throughout this document the terms patron, user, and customer are used interchangeably.

This document is intended for several purposes:

- To educate communities, governing bodies and funding agencies about the importance of the knowledge and skills of professional librarians.
- To develop job descriptions and evaluation tools for professional positions.
- To design policies, particularly as these policies relate to the organization and staffing of libraries.
- To guide students attending graduate library school.
- To apprise library school faculty who are involved in the development of curricula of

the continuously changing needs of the profession.

- To assist in planning staff development programs.
- To motivate professionals to take responsibility for managing the development of one's own career.

CORE COMPETENCIES

- Demonstrates a strong commitment to excellent customer service.
- Recognizes and addresses the diverse nature of the library's patrons and community.
- Understands and supports the culture and context of the library and, if applicable, its parent institution.
- Demonstrates knowledge of the library system and the library profession.
- Understands the social, political, and economic context in which the library exists.
- Demonstrates knowledge of library and information science theory, information creation, organization, and delivery.
- Adheres to the Code of Ethics of the American Library Association.
- Exhibits leadership skills including critical thinking, risk taking, and creativity, regardless of position within the management structure.
- Demonstrates commitment to working with others to achieve common goals.
- Acts within the organization to implement the principles of knowledge management.
- Exhibits an understanding of the importance of a multidisciplinary and cross-functional approach to programs and projects within the organization.
- Monitors and implements changes in technology and information systems.
- Shares knowledge and expertise with users and colleagues.
- Displays excellent communication skills and is able to promote the library and advocate for its needs.
- Communicates effectively with publishers and other information providers to advance the interests of the library.
- Recognizes the value of professional networking and actively participates in professional associations.
- Actively pursues personal and professional growth through continuing education.

Source: Adapted from the American Association of Law Libraries' Competencies for Law Librarianship, approved by NJLA Professional Development Committee February 28, 2006, approved by the NJLA Executive Board March 14, 2006, New Jersey Library Association, www.njla.org/resources/competencies.html.

Johnson County Library Tier II Leadership Competencies

LEADS CHANGE

Learns Continually
Creativity/Innovation
External Awareness
Flexibility
Resilience
Service Motivation
Thinks Strategically
Vision

Promotes the library's vision, goals, priorities, and values. Balances change and continuity; continually strives to improve customer service and program performance; creates a work environment that encourages creative thinking; and maintains focus, intensity, and persistence, even under adversity.

Key Characteristics

1. Exercises leadership and motivates team members to incorporate JCL's mission, vision, and values into strategic planning as well as into the full range of the organization's activities; encourages creative thinking and innovation; influences others toward a spirit of service; designs and implements new or cutting-edge programs/processes.

2. Identifies and integrates key issues affecting the organization, including political, economic, social, technological, and administrative factors.

3. Is open to change and new information; tolerates ambiguity; adapts behavior and work methods in response to new information, changing conditions, or unexpected obstacles; adjusts rapidly to new situations warranting attention and resolution.

4. Displays a high level of initiative, effort, and commitment to public service; proactive and achievement-oriented; self-motivated; pursues self-development; seeks feedback from others and opportunities to master new knowledge.

5. Deals effectively with pressure; maintains focus and intensity and remains persistent, even under adversity; recovers quickly with setbacks.

INFLUENCES PEOPLE

Conflict Management
Leverages Diversity
Integrity/Honesty
Builds Teams

Designs and implements strategies that maximize employee potential and fosters high ethical standards in meeting the organization's vision, mission, and goals.

Key Characteristics

1. Provides leadership by inspiring, motivating, and guiding others toward goal accomplishment; empowers people by sharing power and authority.

2. Effectively uses of the organization's performance management system (e.g., accurate performance plans and appraisals, and takes action to reward, counsel, and remove employees, as appropriate).

3. Values cultural diversity and other differences; fosters an environment in which people who are culturally diverse can work together cooperatively and effectively in achieving organizational goals.

4. Assesses employees' unique developmental needs and provides developmental opportunities that maximize employees' capabilities and contributes to the achievement of organizational goals; develops leadership in others through coaching and mentoring.

5. Fosters commitment, team spirit, pride, trust, and group identity.

6. Resolves conflicts in a positive and constructive manner.

7. Recognizes, encourages, and participates in the dynamic nature of leadership and followership.

ACHIEVES RESULTS

Accountability
Customer Service
Decisiveness
Entrepreneurship
Solves Problems
Technical Creativity
Political Savvy

Stresses accountability and continuous improvement. Makes timely and effective decisions based on the library's mission, vision, and values. Identifies the internal and external politics that impact the work of the organization.

Key Characteristics

1. Understands and appropriately applies procedures and policies; keeps current on issues, practices, and procedures.

2. Exercises good judgment in structuring and organizing work and sets priorities; balances the interests of patrons and readily readjusts priorities to respond to customer demands.

3. Anticipates and identifies, diagnoses, and consults on potential or actual problem areas.

4. Holds self and others accountable for decisions and work performance.

5. Identifies opportunities to develop and/or promote new materials, programs, and services within or outside of the organization.

6. Maintains appropriate skill level regarding current and new technologies.

FOSTERS COMMUNICATION

Influences/Negotiates
Interpersonal Skills
Oral Communication
Partners
Written Communication

Creates an environment conducive to an open exchange of ideas. Explains, advocates, and expresses facts and ideas about the library when communicating with individuals and groups internally and externally.

Key Characteristics

1. Represents and speaks for the organization and its work to those within and outside the library; elicits feedback, listens effectively, and clarifies information; facilitates an open exchange of ideas.

2. Establishes and maintains working relationships within the library and throughout the community; approaches each problem situation with a clear perception of organizational goals; gets understanding and support from higher-level management.

3. Collaborates with others; cooperates with others to obtain information and accomplish goals; facilitates win-win situations.

4. Considers and responds appropriately to the needs, feelings, and capabilities of different people in different situations; is tactful and treats others with respect.

5. Communicates effectively in written and oral reports, memoranda, and other documents in a clear, organized, and timely manner.

Source: Johnson County Library.

Ohio Library Council, Core Competencies for Library Staff

COMPETENCY	DEFINITION	SKILLS AND BEHAVIORS	POSSIBLE TRAINING UNITS
Adaptability	The ability to adjust to changing situations.	Interprets and responds quickly to new or changed responsibilities, methods and procedures Learns and applies new skills Remains positive and productive	Current and Future Trends sessions Time Management Keeping Your Balance in the Midst of Change Workshop (NEO-RLS) Change Management: Effectively Dealing with Organizational and Individual Change (SWON)
Communication	The ability, through both verbal and written methods, to provide concise, timely and accurate information, internally and externally, among all organizational levels and with all of the appropriate people.	Listens to others and verifies understanding of the message Uses a variety of communication methods in the most appropriate forms, in the manner that best enables the message to be understood Responds to the comments and questions of others in a timely manner Uses appropriate language Knows how to find and use information on the staff intranet	Interpersonal Communication Intranet/library website tour and orientation Library's e-mail and paperwork orientation

(cont.)

Ohio Library Council, Core Competencies for Library Staff (cont.)

COMPETENCY	DEFINITION	SKILLS AND BEHAVIORS	POSSIBLE TRAINING UNITS
Customer Service	The ability to efficiently, effectively and positively meet the library needs of internal and external customers.	Welcomes interactions Consistently greets patrons and staff with a smile Strives to make library resources accessible to all members of the community Proactively anticipates and addresses patron and staff expectations and needs Knows when it is appropriate to bend the rules and explains positively when denials are required	Intellectual Freedom course Customer Service Diversity Awareness Emotional Intelligence class Library's Policy Manual orientation Conflict Resolution The Customer Is Always Right: Building and Teaching Client Relationship Skills @ www.sirsidynixinstitute.com/archive.php Emotional Customer Service: Turning Customers into Friends Who'll Return Again and Again @ www.sirsidynixinstitute.com/archive.php
Organizational Awareness	The knowledge and ability to support the library's mission, vision, culture and structure.	Understands and identifies with the goals and values of the library and models and actively communicates them effectively Knows and appropriately follows the library's hierarchy Knows, understands, and appropriately applies policies and procedures Keeps current on information sent by administration	Intranet/library website tour and orientation All-department tour of library with possible shadowing sessions Library's Policy Manual orientation OLC's Online Orientation Program: www.olc.org/orientation/index.html
Personal Responsibility	The commitment to take appropriate action to meet patron and library goals and needs, as well as accept responsibility for the results.	Ensures accuracy and completeness of work Accepts responsibility for accomplishments and seeks to correct and learn from mistakes Continually seeks opportunities for learning and training Evaluates own strengths and weaknesses and seeks feedback from others for improvement	Ingredients to Workplace Success (SWON Libraries) Time Management

COMPETENCY	DEFINITION	SKILLS AND BEHAVIORS	POSSIBLE TRAINING UNITS
Problem Solving	The ability to understand the entire perspective of a situation or issue, identifying patterns or connections between situations, assessing problems and troubleshooting in order to identify effective solutions.	Solves problems in a timely manner Acquires new information and applies knowledge to analyze issues and resolve problems Breaks problems down into components to identify required tasks or activities Formulates new and imaginative solutions that reflect careful consideration of patron and library needs and goals Considers risks, benefits, and impact of solution on the present and future library environment Transfers learning from one situation to solve a problem in another Consults with appropriate staff members before implementing solutions	Library's Policy Manual orientation Role-Playing workshop PC and Library Technology Troubleshooting
Team Work	The ability to work collaboratively with others to achieve organizational goals and objectives.	Willingly assists others by sharing expertise and time Prepared to complete assigned tasks Respects the ideas and opinions of others Gives and accepts feedback in a positive manner Proactively involves others to solve problems and achieve results which meet the needs of the library	Interpersonal Communication Conflict Resolution All-department tour of the library with possible shadowing sessions Facilitation and Meeting Techniques Library Conflict Management for Consenting Adults— Turning Enemies into Allies @ www.sirsidynixinstitute.com/archive.php

Source: OLC Core Competencies: www.olc.org/CoreCompetencies.asp; revised January 2008.

Note: SWON: SouthWest and Neighboring Libraries; NEO-RLS: Northeast Ohio Regional Library System.

Notes

1. To help with such questions, see, for example, Sara Laughlin, Denise Shockley, and Ray Wilson, *The Library's Continuous Improvement Fieldbook* (Chicago: American Library Association, 2003).

2. To help with writing job descriptions, see, for example, Paula M. Singer and Laura Francisco, *Developing a Compensation Plan for Your Library*, 2nd ed. (Chicago: American Library Association, 2009).

3. Scott B. Parry, "The Quest for Competencies," *Training* 33, no. 7 (July 1996): 50.

4. To identify the staff KSAs you need to implement your strategic plan, see, for example, Jeanne Goodrich and Paula Singer, *Human Resources for Results: The Right Person for the Right Job* (Chicago: American Library Association, 2007).

5. This passage and the following discussion are drawn from Josephine Bryant and Kay Poustie, *Competencies Needed by Public Library Staff* (Gütersloh: Bertelsmann Foundation, 2001).

6. Ibid., 10–11.

7. The following discussion is taken from Jenny McCarthy, "Planning a Future Workforce: An Australian Perspective," *New Review of Academic Librarianship* 11, no. 1 (April 2005): 41–56.

8. Mary B. Young, *Building the Leadership Pipeline in the Local, State, and Federal Government*, CPS Human Resource Services, 2005, access via www.workforceplanning.state.pa.us/portal/server.pt/community/workforce_and_succession_planning/1442/resources/267538.

9. Ibid., 8.

10. See, for example, Daniel Goleman, Richard Boyatzis, and Annie McKee, *Primal Leadership: Realizing the Power of Emotional Intelligence* (Boston: Harvard Business School Press, 2002).

11. Travis Bradberry and Jean Greaves, *The Emotional Intelligence Quickbook: Everything You Need to Know to Put Your EQ to Work* (New York: Simon and Schuster, 2005).

12. Ibid., 52.

13. Christi Olson and Paula Singer, *Winning with Library Leadership: Enhancing Services through Connection, Contribution, and Collaboration* (Chicago: American Library Association, 2004).

14. Paul Cantor, "Succession Planning: Often Requested, Rarely Delivered," *Ivey Business Journal*, www.iveybusinessjournal.com/article.asp?intArticle_ID=531.

SUCCESSION PLANNING AND DEVELOPMENT PROCESS

ONCE YOUR library has the infrastructure outlined in the previous chapters, you are ready to implement the actual succession planning and development process. This is a three-phase process that consists of (1) identifying and assessing talent, (2) creating succession plans, and (3) creating and implementing individual development plans (figure 4.1). This chapter provides a framework to support the library in making effective and consistent decisions about employees. It includes the tools you need to assess talent; create individual development plans that help retain and advance high-level performers and provide feedback to employees at all levels of performance and potential; and grow a pipeline of talented employees ready to grow, learn, and take on new responsibilities while enabling the library to fill vacancies quickly and easily. In addition, following this process strengthens the library by guaranteeing that the career moves of high-potential and talented staff are planned and designed to develop leadership and fill the key positions needed in the short and long terms.

/// PHASE I: IDENTIFYING AND ASSESSING TALENT

One of the key (and hardest) aspects of any succession management and development process is talent identification. In this phase of the process, you identify employees with the potential (often called "high potentials") for success in filling key roles, including leadership, and develop a talent profile for each. This process is completed by a succession planning committee—the leadership team or a subset of it convened for this purpose—and should always include the library director and HR director.

There are several ways for the library to proceed as it assesses talent:

The first choice point involves scope. Will identification and assessment be made of all library employees? Will talent profiles be created for all? In the alternative, will it be limited to target groups of employees by level (e.g., all first-line managers)? Will the talent review focus only on leadership and star employees brought to the committee by HR, a library manager, or leader? Successful talent reviews have been conducted in all of these ways. Choosing the first or second option helps ensure that no one falls through the cracks because they are not visible or have a personality difference with their boss. Regardless of which method you chose, it is advisable that you begin the talent review process with senior leadership and other key positions, because these positions are usually hardest to fill and are staffed with employees most likely to retire in the shortest time frame.

The second choice point pertains to who completes this first level of talent review; that is, who (specifically) compiles the information to create the individual talent profile. Should it be done by the employee's manager or supervisor and then brought to the succession planning committee for review? In the alternative, should the committee as a whole review staff under consideration and complete the profile together? In large library systems where leadership is not likely to be aware of the abilities and potential of most staff members, it is suggested that managers conduct the first level of review and bring their completed talent profiles to the succession planning committee. If the library is small enough that most members of the succession planning committee have a picture of the staff, even if it is just the top layers of staff, you will benefit from having the input of all. Numerous perspectives are likely to broaden the picture painted of the individual.

The third choice point involves the composition of the committee that performs the second level of review—the succession planning committee. This group should always include the library director, the HR director (if the library is large enough to have one), and a group of senior leaders. They are responsible for the activities in phases 1 and 2 of the succession planning and development process and work from a focused agenda to complete their work. The HR director typically chairs the process and ensures that pre-session work (such as first-level talent reviews, if done by managers) is completed.

Once these choices have been made, leaders complete the following steps for each employee under

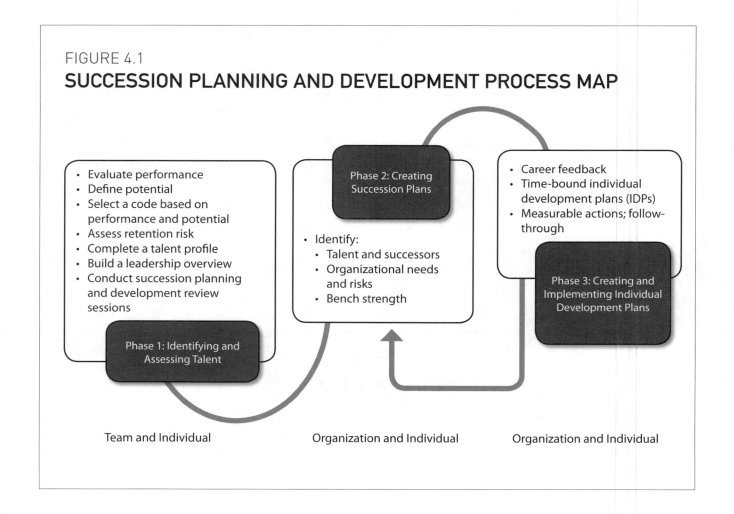

FIGURE 4.1
SUCCESSION PLANNING AND DEVELOPMENT PROCESS MAP

- Evaluate performance
- Define potential
- Select a code based on performance and potential
- Assess retention risk
- Complete a talent profile
- Build a leadership overview
- Conduct succession planning and development review sessions

Phase 1: Identifying and Assessing Talent

Phase 2: Creating Succession Plans

- Identify:
  - Talent and successors
  - Organizational needs and risks
  - Bench strength

- Career feedback
- Time-bound individual development plans (IDPs)
- Measurable actions; follow-through

Phase 3: Creating and Implementing Individual Development Plans

Team and Individual   Organization and Individual   Organization and Individual review, producing a completed talent profile for each employee (figure 4.2).

1. Evaluate Performance

The first step of assessing talent requires an accurate, completed performance appraisal for each employee. It would be shortsighted to build a talent profile on potential alone; performance ratings/profiles must be included as well. You should easily be able to translate the following definitions to your own form and process. If you do not have an appraisal form, you may wish to consider employees as high, medium, and low performers in terms of the following definitions (and then develop a form and a process):

High-performing employees are rated "exceeds expectations." They consistently meet and often exceed goals, consistently meet and often go beyond expectations defined in competencies, and are viewed as outstanding performers.

Medium performers are often rated as "fully meets expectations." Most of the members of your workforce are likely to fall into this category: employees who fully meet expectations, consistently meet most goals, consistently perform at a satisfactory level in most areas, and may exceed expectations in some. These employees perform all aspects of the job with minimal errors and exhibit most of the competency behaviors. Others rely on these employees to perform all aspects of their jobs with a high degree of proficiency. These performers do have some room for performance growth.

Low performers do not meet the expectations of the job. Though these employees may perform some aspects of the job well, they need improvement.

In this process, each employee is identified as a low, medium, or high performer. This rating will be combined with a rating of potential in the next step before it is entered into the individual talent profile.

2. Define Potential

In this next step the library determines the ability and motivation of individual staff members to take on new or more senior roles in the short and long terms. According to many library directors, this is one of the most difficult aspects of the process. But by conducting this review systematically and globally (i.e., throughout the library system), leadership can obtain a picture of its entire workforce and examine employees' potential and possibilities for development, change, lateral transfer, or promotion.

During this step, leadership and HR are able to focus on the individual's key talent and ability for growth and increased contributions within the library system. Leadership should be keyed into looking for high-potential employees. But what is, who is, a "high-potential employee"? Employees with high potential are the library's future leaders and holders of key positions. Broadly, they are the members of your workforce who are able and willing to advance two or more levels in the library, are possible candidates for key positions, or have not yet reached a plateau in their career. High potentials are not the same as stars. Although being rated as a star or as exceeding expectations (or whatever language the library uses to identify those in the top performance category) in the employee's current job is usually a prerequisite to identification as a high potential, not all stars are necessarily high potentials; advancement and leadership potential involve criteria other than current performance, not the least of which are ability, aspiration, and engagement.

Every library identifies its own key positions (see chapter 3), yet experience shows us that many are at a loss about defining "high potential." What follows is a way for library leadership to view the differences between low-, growth-, and high-potential performers based on ability, aspiration, and engagement. Start with these definitions and view them as a draft. Feel free to alter and add, so that you create criteria and a narrative that fit your culture. You may find criteria more applicable than ability, aspiration, and engagement, or your culture may suggest different definitions or language for them. Some possibilities include prior leadership experience, education, learning agility, assessment against competencies (often reviewed in the performance management process), leadership ability based on the library's leadership competencies, risk-taking ability, and project management experience.

The definitions below can help you assess the potential of each employee in terms of ability, employee aspiration, and how engaged each is in her job and with the library. But first, before you review employees, here are some tips:

Be objective.

Be future oriented; do not focus on the past year.

FIGURE 4.2

INDIVIDUAL TALENT PROFILE

Name:					
Title:		Performance		Current	Prior
Location:		Rating: (H/M/L)			
Hire Date:		Potential: (H/G/L)			
Date in Position:		Risk: (H/M/L)			
# of Direct Reports:		IDP in Place: Yes/no			
		Talent Code:			

TALENT CODE

	Potential		
Performance	KC ☐	ET ☐	P ☐
	KC ☐	KC ☐	ET ☐
	AR ☐	IR ☐	IR ☐

COMPETENCY STRENGTHS/DEVELOPMENT OPPORTUNITIES/ACTIONS

Library Core Competencies:	Rating (1–5)	Development Actions	Functional Competencies:	Rating (1–5)	Development Actions
Customer Service					
Teamwork					

SUCCESSION PLAN/CAREER ASPIRATIONS

Recommended Next Position(s):		Timing	Internal Successors	Library/ Function	Timing

Internal Successors		Timing	External Successors	Library

EXPERIENCE AND EDUCATION

Positions w/Library	Years in Job

Positions Prior to Joining the Library	Years in Job

Degree or Certification	School or Association	Date Received:

Completed by:	Date:

Ask: is this employee capable of moving to the next level (e.g., branch manager if presently a librarian, youth coordinator, or subject specialist) or to a leadership or department head role?

Does this employee consistently demonstrate competencies at the next level (high potential), sometimes demonstrate the next level of competencies (growth potential), or not demonstrate competencies at the next level (low potential)? (If you are unaware of what a competency is, please refer to chapter 3.)

Ensure that you hold no biases, like recency (basing an opinion of most recent performance) or halo-or-horns effects stemming from a positive or negative experience potentially from years ago. There are other biases you might have about individual employees as well. Maybe she is not like you in temperament, personality, or

STANDARDS FOR JUDGING POTENTIAL

Here is an alternate list of criteria for judging employee potential. Adapted here for consistency and to fit the library world, they offer a perspective that adds value to any discussion of potential.

High Potential/Promotable

- Exhibits operating, technical, and professional skills that are extremely broad and deep.
- Exhibits managerial skills that are expected at the next highest level.
- Demonstrates leadership skills that are expected at the next highest level.
- Regularly works at building new skills and abilities.
- Aspires to higher-level challenges and opportunities.
- Demonstrates "fire in the belly."
- Has a business perspective beyond current level at the library.
- Is oriented toward total library results, not just focused on the success of own area.

Growth Potential/Emerging Talent

- Exhibits operating, technical, and professional skills that are high for current position and level at the library.
- Exhibits managerial skills that are high for current level.

- Frequently demonstrates leadership skills that are high for current positions.
- Adds new skills when the job calls for it.
- Aspires to greater challenges but primarily at the same level.
- Is motivated to do more than is expected.
- Has a big-picture perspective beyond current position.
- Is focused on the success of own area and the team.

Key Contributor

- On balance, exhibits operating, technical, professional, managerial, and leadership skills that are acceptable for current level.
- Demonstrates little effort to build new skills but keeps current skills sharp.
- Aspires to stay with the library.
- Is motivated to do what is needed in current job.
- Understands the job.
- Is focused primarily on success in the technical/professional aspects of the job.
  Note: This employee may have the desire but has not demonstrated the ability to progress to a larger job.

Source: Adapted from Ram Charan, Stephen Drotter, and James Noel, *The Leadership Pipeline: How to Build the Leadership-Powered Company* (San Francisco: John Wiley and Sons, 2001), 172–74.

style. Maybe she comes from a different culture; reminds you of your mom, dad, or child; is of a different generation, nationality, gender, level of ability, or sexual orientation—or doesn't laugh at your jokes. We tend to want to hire, promote, and work with people who are like us—but such an approach seriously limits the candidate pool (and, of course, can be illegal). Reflect on your thoughts and feelings about the individuals you are reviewing for potential. Separate feelings from facts about performance and potential as a star employee, high potential, or upcoming library leader. Talking with a trusted colleague or HR about employees has helped many reviewers separate potential biases from employees' actual ability and performance.

The leadership team should ask: Does the employee demonstrate competencies, knowledge, skills, and abilities at that next level? How do you know this? Do performance evaluations document it? What about performance as a member of a key team or committee? Do her projects come in on time and within budget? Does she have a role as an informal leader in the library? How does she use that influence? Do other employees ask her to be assigned to their committees or projects? What comments on the performance appraisal, about actual situations, are indicative of the competencies needed to move to additional challenges in your organization?

Finally (and especially where there are gaps), do not rely only on anecdotal evidence. Many off-the-shelf objective and job-related assessments are available for evaluating the potential of individual employees. Results provide the library, as well as the individual, with important feedback as well as input into a development plan.

After reflection, leaders determine each employee's potential for growth or expanded roles within the library as low, growth, or high (L, G, H), using the following definitions (or something like them):

Low-potential employee

- *Ability.* May be a solid performer with consistent execution but has not demonstrated the capacity for growth in terms of a larger volume (e.g., larger branch) or role (e.g., reference librarian to adult services supervisor).
- *Aspiration.* May not have the motivation or interest to advance or transfer laterally into other positions;

does not actively seek and may not be open to development, feedback, and opportunities.

- *Engagement.* May not appear to be happy with the library system or its future plans, or infrequently goes above and beyond.

Growth-potential employee

- *Ability.* Has solid competencies in current job; occasionally exhibits the knowledge, skills, and competencies needed for the next level or another job; is smart; exhibits high emotional intelligence (e.g., self-awareness, self-regulation, empathy) as well as strong social and interpersonal skills.
- *Aspiration.* Conveys the motivation and ability for development and advancement; insightful about own ability and seeks feedback from others.
- *Engagement.* Is committed to the library, excited about challenges and new directions, often goes above and beyond.

High-potential employee

- *Ability.* Has a track record of results and leadership that is clearly superior to peers; demonstrates the knowledge, skills, abilities, and competencies of the next level; is smart, analytical, thinks systemically and critically; possesses a high degree of emotional intelligence and social and interpersonal skills.
- *Aspiration.* Demonstrates the motivation, drive, and ambition to rise in the library; aware of own strengths and limitations, actively seeks development.
- *Engagement.* Values and enjoys being part of the library; is excited to be involved in projects; often goes above and beyond.

Others rate employees on competencies, as shown in figure 4.3.

3. Select Code Based on Employee's Performance and Potential

At this point you have determined a rating for performance (low, medium, or high) and one for potential (low, growth, or high). Now it is time to determine a code that takes both ratings into account. Coding makes it much more likely that staff are evaluated consistently and on the same terms.

Use the matrix shown in figure 4.4 to integrate the employee's performance and potential and to select an appropriate code for succession planning. To complete this matrix, simply identify an employee's performance (low/medium/high) and potential (low/growth/high) and then choose the category where performance meets potential. You can use the code definitions below to confirm alignment with your view of the staff member's talent and potential with the library.

Each box on the matrix has a code that acts as a kind of shorthand to describe the employee's performance and potential:

Promotable (P). Excellent performer; has a history of high performance ratings and consistently exceeds expectations; high-potential employee; has taken on more responsibility; is ready for next level position; seeks a promotion.

Emerging Talent (ET). Excellent performer; typically given high performance ratings by manager or supervisor; shows growth potential; can take on more responsibility; promotable within 12–24 months; lateral transfer within 8–12 months.

Key Contributor (KC). Consistent performer and well placed in current position; management should provide individual with committee or other assignments to see how employee responds. Manager should value the person in this position and support her efforts.

Improvement Required (IR). Inconsistent performer; may lack knowledge, skills, abilities, competencies, or motivation in one or more areas; could become a concern requiring action if performance does not improve; not promotable; performance improvement plan should be in place.

FIGURE 4.3

INDIVIDUAL POTENTIAL ASSESSMENT FORM

Directions: Supervisors rate employees (all, or those felt to be high potential) against various factors leading to success *at your library,* such as skills, values, competencies, and abilities that are felt to be correlated with future success at the next level of responsibility.

SUCCESS FACTORS/ COMPETENCIES	NEEDS IMPROVEMENT			ADEQUATE			EXCEEDS REQUIREMENTS		
	1	2	3	4	5	6	7	8	9
1. Dealing with change									
2. Customer intimacy									
3. Representing the library									
4. Achievement orientation									
5. Strategic/critical thinking									
6. Self-awareness									
7. Relating to others									

Action Required (AR). Poor performer in current role; transfer if appropriate position in library system can be found or ask to leave; time line for action is required.

New Hire (NH). Too new to rate; usually less than six months in current position.

Now you are ready to transfer the code that identifies the employee in terms of performance and potential onto the talent profile form (figure 4.2, upper right corner). There is no box labeled NH for new hires, since they are considered too new for leaders to assess performance and potential accurately.

You might also want to use the figure 4.4 matrix, or some variation of it, to get a picture of all members of a unit or classification of employees at once. For example, you might place all librarians, or all staff from one unit, on the matrix to get a picture of emerging and potential leadership. This approach circumvents the possibility of staff with potential falling through the cracks, since everyone is considered systematically. You will be surprised at how many quiet shining stars emerge through this methodical exercise.

Another way to classify employees by performance and potential is through use of a performance/potential grid (see figure 4.5), using the following definitions:

Stars are the "exceed expectations" performers who are perceived to have high potential for future advancement. They are a key source to replace incumbents in key positions.

Steady Producers also exceed expectations in their performance in the current position, but they are not identified as having strong potential to fill key positions at the library. Since they are still highly productive, the strategy is to capitalize on their skills and knowledge and keep them productive and motivated.

Question Marks are poor performers in their current position, but they might have potential in another position or in the future. The best strategy for working with these employees is to focus on improving their performance, ideally to turn them into stars. Consider coaching, mentoring, or job rotation to help improve performance and productivity.

FIGURE 4.4
CHARTING PERFORMANCE AND POTENTIAL

		POTENTIAL		
		LOW	**GROWTH**	**HIGH**
PERFORMANCE	**HIGH**	Key Contributor—KC	Emerging Talent—ET	Promotable—P
	MEDIUM	Key Contributor—KC	Key Contributor—KC	Emerging Talent—ET
	LOW	New Hire—NH / Action Required—AR	Improvement Required—IR	Improvement Required—IR

Deadwood are poor performers seen as having little potential for growth at the library. Because of retirements, layoffs, limited expansions, and budget cuts, fewer of these performers are left in most libraries. Where they do exist, supervisors should be coached to help them improve productivity or to ease them out.

4. Assess Retention Risk

Now that talent has been identified, there are still a few steps remaining. One is to assess the degree of risk that the staff person might leave the library in the next year. It is suggested that you identify the level of risk as high, medium, or low (H, M, L) and enter it on the individual talent profile. High risk implies that the manager or others believe the person will not be in her current job for the next year, medium that she may not be, and low that she likely will remain in her current position for the next twelve months. Your reason for selecting a high/medium/low risk factor can be based on knowledge you have or on your intuition. (Note: don't minimize the importance of rumors, and don't overestimate their validity either.) Some examples of risk based on knowledge include these: employee might be promoted or given a lateral position or devel-

opmental position; might make known that she is seeking to leave the library, or is interviewing elsewhere; is having performance problems; spouse is relocating. Examples of risk factors based on intuition are the managers' (or employees') perception of readiness for the next level; leaders' perception of risk or fit; perceived satisfaction with direction in which the library is going; and satisfaction with current job, peer group, or supervisor. The risk factor selected, along with the rationale for it, should be discussed at the succession planning committee meeting. Examples of other factors, which may or may not be based on knowledge and yet should be considered, are dissatisfaction with compensation or benefits; recently passed over for a promotion; personal or family issues; dissatisfaction with job rotation assignment (e.g., to branch farther from home); does not feel included by peer group or recognized by manager; dissatisfied with potential for career growth or communications flow; does not agree with the direction in which the library is heading based on its recent planning process; feels lacking in the information or training needed to be successful; does not feel challenged and empowered to make a meaningful contribution to the library; does not feel recognized and appreciated for contribution to the success of work group or the library; does not feel part

---

FIGURE 4.5

CHARTING PERFORMANCE AND POTENTIAL: ALTERNATE GRID

CURRENT PERFORMANCE	**HIGH**	*Steady Producers* Strategy: Keep turnover low. Keep them motivated and productive where they are.	*Stars* Strategy: Keep turnover low. Accelerate development.
	LOW	*Deadwood* Strategy: Convert to Steady Producers. Terminate them if they can't be salvaged.	*Question Marks* Strategy: Convert to Steady Producers. Terminate them if they can't be salvaged.
		LOW	**HIGH**
		FUTURE POTENTIAL	

Source: Adapted from George S. Odiorne, *Strategic Management of Human Resources: A Portfolio Approach* (San Francisco: Jossey-Bass, 1984), 305.

of an effective, diverse, and winning team; and, most important, does not have a good, mutually respectful relationship with supervisor.

5. Complete the Talent Profile

The next step is to complete the talent profile forms to create in-depth, individualized profiles. You have already entered results from the assessments you have completed to date regarding performance, potential, and risk. Now be sure you have collected information from prior performance reviews and the individual's résumé. The completed profile serves as basis for discussion in the succession planning committee meeting. Figure 4.6 is a filled-out example profile.

6. Build Leadership Overview

The next step is to create a talent summary of the library's leadership team or any group under consideration (e.g., all branches, all librarians). You can create the overview from the information listed in the individual talent profiles. The resulting overview provides a comprehensive, high-level view of top talent and the multiple leadership opportunities available. Figure 4.7 is a sample version of a leadership overview.

7. Conduct Succession Planning and Development Review Sessions

The succession planning committee meets to review employees with an eye toward growing leaders and providing development opportunities to maximize their potential at the library. At the review sessions, the committee uses the completed individual talent profiles and leadership overviews to move into phase 2 of the process—creating succession pans.

/// PHASE II: CREATING SUCCESSION PLANS

Leaders create succession plans on the basis of organizational needs, goals, and priorities as well as individuals' performance, potential, ability, and motivation. To accomplish this, they utilize the documents completed in phase 1 to prioritize needs and potential candidates to fulfill these needs. Leadership evaluates library needs in the future through the risk assessments and anticipated retirements to identify bench strength and internal candidates for positions.

At this point, leadership has already identified key positions, including those in leadership. From their risk and retirement analysis, they know which positions may become vacant. High-potential employees are identified, and developmental needs are at least identified. Now is the time to identify successor candidates.

When considering successor candidates, start by asking the following questions: How would this position further develop the employee being considered? Would the employee be interested in this opportunity?

Figure 4.8 is a sample of a succession planning report summary for leadership positions. As you can see, it builds on the leadership overview prepared for the review sessions.

One easy way to assess bench strength, to see if the library can fill vacancies from within with relative ease, is through replacement charting or planning. Replacement charting was the original goal of succession planning before it broadened out to include, as in the case of this book, talent development and building a pipeline of employees ready to fill vacancies.

Replacement charting indicates one or more successors for key positions and also helps to create a management inventory for the library. Smaller libraries may not need this at all, but larger libraries will find it useful. Figure 4.9 is one format for a replacement chart. It lists the positions in the hierarchy. Successors are identified under each position with a notation as to readiness to take on the higher-level job. The number "1" identifies those ready for the promotion immediately, number "2" those ready in six months, and so on. Those identified as successors should be both stars and high potentials, or those with a talent profile coded Promotable and Emerging Talent. If they are not, review why the selected code was assigned; is the identified successor truly a successor or just a fill-in in the event of vacancy? In either event, plan to create a robust individual development plan for those identified as replacements (unless there is indication of interest being limited to filling the position only until a replacement is located internally or externally).

/// PHASE III: CREATING AND IMPLEMENTING INDIVIDUAL DEVELOPMENT PLANS

Talent Development

A good understanding of where employees fall in the matrix is not where developing talent stops—it is

FIGURE 4.6

INDIVIDUAL TALENT PROFILE: COMPLETED SAMPLE

Name:	Jane Smith			
Title:	Branch Mgr	Performance	Current	Prior
Location:	West Regional	Rating: (H/M/L)	H	H
Hire Date:	10/1/00	Potential: (H/G/L)	H	G
Date in Position:	6/30/05	Risk: (H/M/L)	M	M
# of Direct Reports:	6	IDP in Place: Yes/no	Y	
		Talent Code:	P	

TALENT CODE

	Potential		
	KC ☐	ET ☐	P ☒
Performance	KC ☐	KC ☐	ET ☐
	AR ☐	IR ☐	IR ☐

COMPETENCY STRENGTHS/DEVELOPMENT OPPORTUNITIES/ACTIONS

Library Core Competencies:	Rating (1–5)	Development Actions	Functional Competencies:	Rating (1–5)	Development Actions
Customer Service	5		Reference	5	
Teamwork	4	Lead new outreach team	Technology	5	
Adaptability	5		Facilities Mgmt	4	Serve on planning team for South Branch renovation

SUCCESSION PLAN/CAREER ASPIRATIONS

Recommended Next Position(s):		Timing	Internal Successors	Library/ Function	Timing
Public Services Director		1 yr			

Internal Successors		Timing	External Successors	Library	
Sam Jones—Br. Mgr. @ smaller branch		12-18 mo.	None known		
Sally Green—Adult Department Mgr. @ West		12-18 mo.			

EXPERIENCE AND EDUCATION

Positions w/Library	Years in Job
Branch Manager—West Regional	4
Branch Manager—South Branch	5

Positions Prior to Joining the Library	Years in Job
Outreach Manager—Green County Library	4
Children's Librarian—Anytown Library	3

Degree or Certification	School or Association	Date Received:
MLS	State University	1993
Online Trainer	Online University	2000
Results Boot Camp	PLA	2008

Completed by: SBB	Date: 7/1/09

FIGURE 4.7

SAMPLE LEADERSHIP OVERVIEW

EMPLOYEE	POSITION/ TITLE	LOCATION	TALENT CODE	DEVELOPMENTAL NEEDS	RECOMMENDED NEXT POSITION	TIMING	NOTES
Jenny Fir	Deputy Director	Central	KC	Current position: managing four generations			
Jane Tree	Director, Public Services	Central	P	Executive coaching to improve understanding of impact of behavior on individuals and groups			
John Oak	Manager, Central and Outreach	Central	ET	Experience with building projects and facilities management			
Harry Maple	Director, Research and Strategy	Central	KC	Excellent in current role; does not seek promotion; does not hold an MLS			
Annie Pea	Manager, Community Branches	Central	ET	Leadership development; presentation skills			

actually where it begins. The critical work comes from providing feedback and developing staff. Although each employee is different, each more or less fits into one of the nine matrix categories according to performance and potential. Still, it is not sufficient merely to identify an employee by category; providing useful and insightful feedback is key to talent development. How managers and leaders approach each employee and their individual situations requires thought. It calls for honest feedback of potential along with a meaningful conversation about the individual's career growth and development. Below are some things to think about, tips for development, and talking points for managers and leaders to reflect upon when giving feedback to (1) promotable/high-potential employees, (2) emerging talent, (3) fully successful key contributors, and (4) employees requiring performance improvement. Do not forget that every employee, regardless of category, is different; it is the manager's role to consider the needs and motivations of each employee, how they receive and internalize feedback, and to act accordingly.

PROMOTABLE/HIGH-POTENTIAL EMPLOYEES
Key Considerations

The primary challenge in working with high-potential employees is to communicate that they are valued without prematurely raising expectations about promotions. These employees often want to see that they are making measurable progress toward their career goals. As a result, they actively seek additional responsibilities that broaden skills or offer new challenges. They may need help from you to modify their sense of urgency for promotion. Here are several ideas for working with them:

- Give frequent reassurance that you and the library regard them highly.
- Do not make promises about promotions or next assignments unless the situation is very clear.
- Most libraries are unable to provide compensation increases that align with this level of performance. But, to the extent you can, provide salary increases, incentives, and awards commensurate with performance. In addition to or in lieu of monetary recognition, provide recognition to such employees in the manner they want to receive it.
- Make sure the employee understands the competitive nature of promotion decisions

when there are others equally or better skilled. In other words, there are no assurances; no employee is anointed to fill the position of another.
- Assess retention risks and develop a specific plan if appropriate and allowable within civil service or other rules.

Tips for Development

- Help the employee create and implement a vigorous individual development plan (IDP; see below).
- Establish frequent one-on-one sessions to discuss career goals and progress in meeting IDP goals. Openly discuss concerns the employee may have about the future. This is particularly important to members of generations X and Y.
- Develop "stretch assignments" by delegating projects or responsibilities you are currently doing (in the important, not mundane, areas).
- Look for opportunities for the employee to get broader visibility and "showcase" her talents (e.g., task force assignments, presentations to library leadership or the board of trustees).
- Allow the employee to stand in for you at meetings or provide backup when you are out of the office or on vacation.
- Encourage the employee to present at state and national library conferences and to get involved in these (and other) organizations to develop talents, learn new skills, get exposed to other ideas, and take on leadership roles in a nonwork environment. Encourage volunteer work with local nonprofit groups of any type as well as participation in Rotary, chamber of commerce, or other business associations.
- Identify cross-functional developmental (lateral) moves or rotational assignments.
- Arrange a mentoring relationship with a well-regarded, successful internal or external leader who can assist in targeted developmental needs.
- Ask the employee to participate in 360-degree feedback or other developmental assessments to gain more insight into career strengths and developmental needs.
- Partner with a coach for targeted developmental needs or prepare for the role in a promotional assignment.

FIGURE 4.8

SAMPLE SUCCESSION PLANNING REPORT SUMMARY

EMPLOYEE	POSITION/ TITLE	LOCATION	TALENT CODE	DEVELOPMENTAL NEEDS	RECOMMENDED NEXT POSITION	TIMING	NOTES
Jenny Fir	Deputy Director	Central	KC	Current position: managing four generations			
Jane Tree	Director, Public Services	Central	P	Executive coaching to improve understanding of impact of behavior on individuals and groups	Deputy Director	12 months	
John Oak	Manager, Central and Outreach	Central	ET	Experience with building projects and facilities management	Director, Public Services	9–12 months	
Harry Maple	Director, Research and Strategy	Central	KC	Excellent in current role; does not seek promotion; does not hold an MLS		Not at this time	
Annie Pea	Manager, Community Branches	Central	ET	Leadership development; presentation skills	Manager, Central and Outreach	18+ months	

FIGURE 4.9
REPLACEMENT CHARTING USING A DEMAND FORECAST

TABLE 1

Key Leadership Position or Knowledge Base	Primary Skills and Knowledge Required	Approx. Months until Needed
Central Library Director	• Knowledge of librarianship • Well-developed leadership/coaching skills • Networking within community	60

TABLE 2

Three Potential Successors, in Order of Readiness	Rate Successors' Readiness Level[a]	Strengths	Developmental Experiences Needed
Central Director • Knowledge of librarianship • Well-developed leadership/ coaching skills • Networking within community			
Anni Reference	1	Strong leadership skills Strong reference skills	Community networking
John Smith	3	Good reference skills	Community networking Leadership/coaching skills
Jerri Frank	4	Good communicator, networker	Leadership/coaching skills

Source: Adapted from Paula Singer and Jeanne Goodrich, "Workforce Planning in Your Library," PLA Spring Symposium, 2007, San Jose, Calif.

[a] 1 = ready now; 2 = ready within 6 months; 3 = ready within 12 months; 4 = ready within 24 months

- It is important to spend some time with you specifically to have a conversation about your career goals and aspirations.
- You are highly regarded by me and other leaders throughout the library. You continue to be an excellent performer—always delivering results in a manner that is congruent with our library's goals, mission, and values. For example (insert appropriate examples). You continue to expand the scope of your responsibilities, and your work is consistently high quality (again, insert examples—be they the quality of responses to reference questions, helping a page team leader work out schedules, forming a partnership with the local day care center, etc.). These are exactly the types of characteristics we look for in our future professionals/leaders (as appropriate). (It is critical to use specific examples of the employee's observed behavior so that she understands exactly what you value.)
- Based on your performance, it is appropriate to begin considering other opportunities for you to enhance your career within our library. Just to check, is that something you want? If so, let's talk about what those possibilities might look like (and really listen to what is being said).
- Now let's discuss how to align your IDP properly with where you would like to see your career heading.
- Please keep in mind that your performance (both results and behaviors as articulated in the competencies—the what and the how) in your current position is one of the most important factors in determining future advancement. We encourage you to continue providing the exceptional performance you have been demonstrating.
- It is also important for us to ensure that we have a qualified individual who is ready to move into your position. Let's talk about who may be a potential successor for you and what we need to do to get her ready (if appropriate).
- What other questions do you have for me? How can I support you in your development? What else could I be doing to help make your work more satisfying and for you to feel that you are learning and growing?

- We will continue to have this type of dialogue on a (insert frequency) basis as a part of our regular meetings. I look forward to our future discussions.

What is it like to be identified and developed as key talent? Succession planning has been a key initiative at OCLC for more than ten years. George Needham is vice president of Global and Regional Councils at OCLC. He went through the first and more recent talent management and succession planning programs at OCLC and is also someone who identifies and manages others. We asked him to remember being identified as someone with high potential and being invited to participate in the first program. He paused for a few seconds to reflect, and I could hear the feeling in his voice: "It was an honor to learn that my boss feels that way [about my potential]. It was a heady feeling." Very appreciative of the opportunities, he said that it made him feel valued and very loyal. He worked harder, stayed longer, and now gives back by developing others.

EMERGING TALENT
Key Considerations

The primary challenge in working with emerging talent is to convey that they are valued without prematurely raising expectations about growth opportunities. Development plans for these staff members should include activities that help clarify their growth or performance potential.

- Give frequent reassurance that you and the library hold them in high regard.
- Avoid absolute promises about promotions or next assignments unless the situation is very clear.
- Most libraries are unable to provide compensation increases that align with this level of performance. But, to the extent you can, provide salary increases, incentives, and awards commensurate with the performance. In addition to or in lieu of monetary recognition, provide recognition to this employee in the manner she wants to receive it.
- Make sure the employee understands the competitive nature of promotion decisions when there are others equally or better skilled. Create teams of highly talented peers to accelerate growth and elevate the level of performance.
- Consistently assess retention risks and develop specific plans, if appropriate.

Tips for Development

- Ensure that a vigorous IDP exists and is being implemented.
- Establish frequent one-on-one meetings to discuss career goals and progress in meeting those goals. Openly discuss concerns the employee may have about her future.
- Develop "stretch assignments" by delegating projects or responsibilities you are currently doing (in important, not mundane, areas).
- Look for opportunities for the staff member to get broader visibility and "showcase" her talents (e.g., task force assignments, presentations to library leadership or the board of trustees).
- Allow the employee to stand in for you at meetings or provide backup when you are out of the office or on vacation.
- Identify cross-functional and other developmental assignments.
- Arrange a mentoring relationship with a highly regarded, successful internal or external leader who can assist in targeted developmental needs.
- Ask the employee to participate in 360-degree feedback or other developmental assessments to gain more insight into career strengths and developmental needs.

Suggested Talking Points

- It is important to spend some time to have a discussion with you regarding your career.
- You know that you are well regarded by library leadership and me. You continue to be a very strong performer—consistently delivering results in a manner that is consistent with library values (insert appropriate examples of observable behavior). You demonstrate the desire and capacity for further development and growth. Just to check, is that something you want?
- Let's talk for a moment about your career interests.
- Now let's discuss how to align your IDP properly with where you would like to see your career go.
- Please keep in mind that your performance (both results and behaviors) in your current position is one of the most important factors in determining future advancement. We encourage you to continue providing the high

level of performance you have been demonstrating.
- What other questions do you have for me? How can I support you in your development? What else could I be doing to help make your work more satisfying and for you to feel that you are learning and growing?
- We will continue to have this type of dialogue on a (insert frequency) basis as a part of our regular communication. I look forward to our future discussions.

KEY CONTRIBUTOR

Everyone eventually reaches a level beyond which promotion would be ill advised (for both the individual and the library). This limitation does not imply poor performance in the current position. Typical types of key contributor:

- Strong individual contributor who may be well placed in her current assignment, whether cataloger, circulation clerk, or department head.
- Employee who prefers to remain in her current role. Not everyone wants to rise in the library hierarchy; sometimes overachiever leaders forget that.
- Staff member with limited experience in broader, more strategic, or big-picture roles or tasks and little or no desire to gain more.
- Staff member with limited ability, or desire, to supervise or manage others.
- Employee who is simply not as qualified as others in the position in the library.

Key Considerations

Regardless of the scenario, your conclusion is that for the time being the present position is the one for which the individual is best suited. Your role is to manage the employee's career expectations constructively. Here are several ideas on how to provide feedback to these members of the workforce (most employees are likely to fall into this category):

- Regularly recognize contributions the employee is making (especially directly following the initial career discussion).
- Gain a clear understanding of the real reasons behind the employee's desire (if any) for career advancement. Is the motivation income growth, a position or title of "importance," professional recognition, the need for

continued challenge and growth, or something else? Acknowledge these needs and develop an understanding that they may not be met immediately or that an alternative way of meeting them may need to be determined. This is critical because these are good, solid employees who are contributing a great deal to the library and are successful in their roles. There are likely many opportunities to meet all but the desire for increased income. Point out opportunities for expansion of current responsibilities and the room for growth in compensation without a promotion.

Tips for Development

- Ensure that an appropriate IDP exists and is being implemented.
- Establish regular time to discuss career goals and progress in meeting those goals.
- Openly discuss concerns the employee may have about her future.
- Identify what the employee is "best at" and leverage that skill in other parts of the library.
- Provide opportunities for the staff member to "showcase" her skills.
- Assign special projects or "stretch assignments" that provide challenge and visibility both functionally and cross-functionally.
- Use the employee to help train new staff in her classification or below.
- Allow the employee to stand in for you at meetings or provide backup when you are out of the office or on vacation.
- Consider a job rotation to provide appropriate technical skill or leadership experiences.

Suggested Talking Points

- I want to have a discussion regarding your performance and career growth.
- As you know from our past performance discussions, you have made numerous important and significant contributions in your position as (insert job title). You are a solid, highly successful performer with consistent execution (or insert applicable comments and applicable examples of observed behavior).
- We believe it is in your best interest—and the library's—to continue to challenge you to develop your skills and competencies in your current position.

- I am committed to helping you continue to grow and develop in the direction that best suits you and the library. I look forward to working through the details with you as part of your IDP.

EMPLOYEES WHO REQUIRE IMPROVEMENT
Key Considerations

Employees who require improvement may fall into this area for several different reasons. In general, this employee is either not meeting expectations from a performance standpoint or is exhibiting low growth potential in terms of ability or motivation to succeed. The main point of focus is to discuss the sustained improvements required to remain in the position and with the library. In some cases, a lateral move into another position may be the appropriate solution. If so, keep in mind that at some point this employee was likely seen as having potential and good job performance. She may even have been promoted at some point. You need to reassure her of your commitment to work with her to improve performance. You should also assess factors that could cause this individual to lose motivation and leave the library rather than improve performance and stay.

Tips for Development

- Develop and implement a healthy performance improvement plan. The plan should be time bound with specific measurable actions.
- Establish check-in meetings to discuss career goals and performance progress.
- Openly discuss concerns the employee may have about her future.
- Identify what the employee is "best at" and leverage that skill.
- Provide structured on-the-job training with a trainer, peer, or supervisor.
- Engage the employee in appropriate education-based programs.

Suggested Talking Points

- I want to respond to your questions about your potential for career growth here at the library.
- As you know from our past discussions, I have several concerns regarding your performance. Specifically, you are not demonstrating (insert appropriate skills, observable behavior, etc).

- Your most concentrated effort right now needs to be focused on improving and sustaining your performance in the areas I just mentioned.
- I sincerely want to see you turn this situation around. Therefore, I will work with you to create a targeted plan that incorporates (insert appropriate tactics).
- We will meet on a biweekly basis to discuss your performance plan objectives and progress. As your performance improves, we can talk more specifically about your career growth.
- Aside from the steps that I have mentioned, how else can I support you in your development? What do you specifically need from me? Please don't hesitate to discuss with me any future ideas you may have.

Feedback Styles

In the context of career development discussions and feedback, it is important to know the person to whom feedback is being given and to account for personal style, needs, and motivations when planning these conversations. The literature and anecdotal evidence point to the ways members of different generations view and seek feedback, summarized in figure 4.10. Consider these ideas for volunteers as well as staff.

Individual Development Plans

Development plans are based on thoughtful feedback, the individual's career interests, and organizational needs. A time-bound development plan assists in closing the skill and competency gaps between an employee's current role and her next position, be it a lateral or promotional opportunity. By creating an IDP, managers are able to identify specific activities and opportunities for each individual on their staff.

Once you have assessed the employee's potential and performance, consider what key experiences would most benefit them in reaching their career goals. These experiences serve as the framework for the IDP and must include the what, how, and when of activities to ensure that the employee is making progress toward her next position. An IDP is essentially a learning contract that conveys what learning gap is being filled (e.g., what competency or skills are acquired), what the employee will learn, how she will learn it, and how this learning is to be demonstrated. Figure 4.11 is a sample IDP.

A few tips:

It is critical that managers understand staff members' needs and desires, as well as the needs of the library, when identifying activities for

---

FIGURE 4.10

FEEDBACK PREFERENCE BY GENERATION

TRADITIONALISTS (BORN 1922–1943)	BABY BOOMERS (1943–1960)
• No news is good news • Do not seek applause • Seek a subtle acknowledgment that what they have done makes a difference	• Like and expect feedback once a year and appreciate a lot of documentation • Good at giving feedback to others, but not necessarily receiving or needing it
GENERATION X (1960–1980)	MILLENNIALS/GENERATION Y (1980–2000)
• Seek a lot of feedback and on a regular basis. "Sorry to interrupt," I've heard members in this age group say in the middle of a conversation or meeting, "how am I doing?" • Need positive feedback to know that they are on the right track	• Seek and value instantaneous feedback, at the push of the button • Accustomed to frequent praise, so may mistake silence for disapproval • Need to know that they are doing a good job

FIGURE 4.11

SAMPLE INDIVIDUAL DEVELOPMENT PLAN

NAME: __JANE SMITH__ DEPARTMENT: __BRANCH MANAGER—WEST REGIONAL__

DATE PREPARED: __7/15/09__

DEVELOPMENT GOAL	DEVELOPMENT ACTIVITIES	DEVELOPMENT SUCCESS	INVOLVEMENT OF OTHERS	TARGET DATE
What competencies for knowledge, skills, or abilities are you going to learn or develop?	How are you going to do this?	How will you know you have learned it? How will you demonstrate it?	Did you get their agreement? Are additional resources needed?	Start? Completion?
Models team leadership by building consensus and helping a diverse group develop to meet a system goal	Lead new outreach team to develop programs for English-language learners (Spanish-speaking families) new to our community	• Team members learn what community wants and agree on a way to provide it • Team produces 3–5 programs that can be used as models for the system • Community members attend programs and say they are on target	• Identify community partners—schools, nonprofits, churches • Programming and marketing coordinator • Training manager—for team development needs	9/1/09 through 6/30/10
Designs and manages facilities so they are customer-centered and easy to use	Serve on renovation design team for South Branch	• Research best practices of other libraries and contribute ideas • Use some of the ideas at West Regional	• West Regional staff, to implement ideas • Facilities director, for resources needed at West	1/1/10 through 12/30/10

Supervisor's Signature: _____ Staff Member's Signature: _____

the development plan. Employees own their development plan, so you should work with them on a regular basis to foster their development and prepare them for career growth.

To create IDPs, managers and employees must conduct the following two activities: First, determine a lateral career move or the next-level position on the basis of career goals. Then, jointly identify the gaps in the employee's current role to the skills, knowledge, abilities, and competencies needed in the next-level position or to enhance performance in the current position. It is possible that the employee's next career move will not be within your organization, perhaps because you do not have an opportunity for her when she is ready. Yet IDPs are for everyone, whether they are "growing in place" or preparing to move up or move on.

We suggest that, once the areas of development to focus on have been determined, development activities should be structured to include a variety of approaches, including on-the-job experiences (70 percent), relationships (20 percent), and education (10 percent) (see figure 4.12).

Identify and schedule specific time-bound (i.e., six to eighteen months) activities that provide the employee with an opportunity to demonstrate competence or to work to close the gap between her current position and the next (lateral or promotional) position.

Activities and time line should be captured in the employee's development plan.

Do not just assume that, once it is completed, you and the employee can check off the IDP box. Rather, managers and employees should schedule regular conversations to check progress, reevaluate activities, and provide feedback, support, and recognition. Progress toward completing the IDP should be a regular component of each performance review.

IDPs are useful for staff at all levels, independent of whether they have been identified as candidates for a succession planning program. OCLC is a good example of an organization with both a strong succession planning program and a strong focus on individual career development for *all* employees (see chapter 7).

At the County of Los Angeles Public Library, every librarian (levels 1–5) is interviewed by her boss in July of each year. They discuss the librarian's career goals and how the library, and the manager, can help the librarian reach them. These discussions are separate from and in addition to the performance management process and conversations surrounding it. The assistant director of public services reads all plans.

Margaret Donnellan Todd, the county librarian, reports several additional outcomes to this method of development planning. First, managers get to know the librarians, even all new level 1s. They are able to discuss how realistic or inconsistent with performance an employee's goals are, then use this occasion to reinforce any changes in performance needed for the librarian to

FIGURE 4.12
DEVELOPMENT ACTION SUGGESTIONS

EXPERIENCES (70%)	RELATIONSHIPS (20%)	EDUCATION (10%)
The most effective developmental opportunities are on-the-job experiences. Examples: • Stretch assignment • Job shadowing • Job rotation • Job swap	Forming formal or informal relationships with peers and leaders provide a variety of perspectives not otherwise considered. Examples: • Mentoring • Executive coaching • Feedback	Education includes both formal training and self-directed learning opportunities. Examples: • Classroom training • E-learning • Self-directed learning, including reading

proceed with her career goals. This is not always a matter of poor performance or attitude. Todd shared a story about a manager who told a librarian that she could not be promoted or developed unless some changes were made. However, this librarian is creative with an artistic (rather than managerial) temperament. She decided to alter her career goals rather than change.

Note

Special thanks to Paula's brother, Ezra D. Singer, senior vice president of Limited Brands, for some ideas used in this chapter.

STRATEGIES FOR DEVELOPING STAFF
Talent Pools and Beyond

OUR "LEGACY" staff members (and that may include us) entered the workforce at a time when there was an implied lifelong contract between employer and employees: both expected an employee to spend her whole career in one or maybe two places, so if the employee met performance standards, she essentially had a job for life. In today's world, that contract no longer exists. The new contract is about mutuality of purpose. Employers cannot promise to "take care of" an employee for life, and employees stay only as long as their needs are met.

The new employment relationship is about mutual benefit, and developing talent benefits both the library and the staff member. In such a scenario, we ask, are we ready for these employer and employee realities?

Employer perspective:

- Your education is not a qualifier for this job.
- We are not offering you a job for life, and we do not expect you to spend your lifetime here.
- You may not work with the same workmates while employed here.
- You will be part of many self-managed teams responsible for a full range of tasks.
- Your assignments will provide learning experiences that enhance your employability.
- We expect you to support our vision and values passionately while employed here.

Employee perspective:

- I know my stability will be based on my reputation for performance.
- I will be responsible for managing my own benefits.
- I will continue to hone my skills and grow.
- I will embrace entrepreneurship.
- I will always be open to new jobs and new employment opportunities inside the library and elsewhere.

If the library provides top-notch training and tools for employees, in return it will have ready, competent employees who are continually growing to meet the library's changing needs.

Developing talent throughout the library is key to having an effective succession planning program. Many traditional succession planning programs focus on identifying and developing one to three successors to key positions, especially at the leadership level. This is certainly an important aspect of a succession planning and development program, but we think it is even more effective to develop talent pools. In this model, the library helps to create as many backups as possible among talented staff members at all levels who are willing and motivated to develop themselves. All staff in the talent pool are developed in accordance with both the library's and the individual's short- and longer-term needs.

To be effective, a talent pool should be paired with competency models (chapter 3), suitable performance management practices to encourage individual development and performance, the right strategies to assess employees' potential (chapter 4), and appropriate developmental efforts that align individual goals with organizational needs. When a vacancy occurs, individuals compete. Instead of offering the job to those with the most tenure or to the personal favorites of immediate supervisors, individuals are prepared to compete on the basis of demonstrated track records in performing their work and developing themselves.

In the library world, several examples of potential talent pools come to mind—for example, branch manager, regional manager, department head (based on specialty as well as management and leadership competencies), circulation and technical processing supervisors, subject specialist. But why use talent pools only for specific positions? Why not develop all employees (who are willing and able) to the level of "exceeds expectations." Can you imagine a library system where all employees are adding that kind of value?

Whether your library is large or small, there are several things you might consider to help your staff grow and develop. In this chapter we provide a variety of examples, and there are several more in chapter 7. In addition, you should capitalize on programs offered by your jurisdiction/academic institution, and be mindful of requirements or limitations in your civil service rules or union contract.

/// GROW YOUR OWN WORKFORCE

There are many ways to provide support for employees seeking a bachelor's degree or MLS. Give employees who are working full-time while attending college or library school tuition assistance (any little bit helps) as well as some time off to study every week. Just an hour or two makes a huge difference to a working student. If you cannot afford tuition assistance or paid time to study—or even if you can—support students in developing practical projects for their course work, and use those projects to benefit customers. A student who can point to her project being used by the library can see the value of her education *and* see how the library values her contribution. Support may also be more formal. For example, the Fresno County (Calif.) Public Library has a librarian trainee program in which an MLS student may be selected to work under the direction of a librarian and receive mentoring along with preprofessional training and work experience. (See this story in chapter 7 for more detail.)

/// PROMOTE MLS STUDENTS TO AN INTERIM GRADE LEVEL

After a student has successfully completed one-half of the degree, reclassify her job from library associate to librarian trainee or another title. Award a grade increase as well as a salary increase. The employee will value your appreciation and show it in her work as well as in her loyalty and decision to remain after graduation.

Taking this approach can also have a downside. It is one thing to encourage someone with great potential to go to school; it is another thing entirely to promote anyone who completes a degree, whether or not she is someone you would hire to fill an MLS position. The disadvantage of paying for education rather than for job responsibilities is that you may find yourself paying for an MLS when the incumbent is not doing MLS-level work, or eventually paying someone an MLS salary when she is not someone you would have promoted into an MLS position.

Another option is to encourage staff with demonstrated potential to apply for available MLS jobs even before they finish their coursework. Promote them and hire them at a provisional rate, giving them salary increases at milestones to degree completion. This is a useful practice when it is hard to recruit qualified

MLS librarians and results in loyalty, too. Encouraging people to apply even if they have not completed the qualification helps them demonstrate their interest in advancement and gain skill in interviewing. You may discover previously hidden potential and then provide coaching or mentoring to help your students become stronger candidates for promotion.

The Carroll County (Md.) Public Library has used this model to promote several MLS students into MLS jobs, with great success. Over the years they found that they were not seeing the quality of external candidates they wanted to fill entry-level MLS positions, yet they had several experienced bachelor's-prepared staff who demonstrated the library's core competencies (e.g., customer service and teamwork) and were interested in developing themselves. The library supported some staff in pursuit of MLS degrees in order to "grow their own" librarians, but there were not enough students graduating quickly enough to compete for vacancies coming available. So the library began to advertise to staff that students enrolled in an MLS program would be considered for some (clearly identified) MLS jobs. Students began to apply for these jobs, and one or two staff members even enrolled in MLS programs after seeing such job postings. Though it is never a given that an MLS student will be promoted, internal candidates who have demonstrated their interest have the advantage of having their work seen over time. Successful candidates have had several things in common:

- relevant experience (such as supervisory experience) acquired from previous jobs
- demonstrated competencies in the library's core areas, such as customer service or teamwork, and good progress in learning the technical competencies of their jobs (and sometimes of the jobs a level above theirs)
- enough employment history with the library to have been identified (even informally) as Promotable or Emerging Talent

These librarians would be the first to admit that taking on a new and higher-level position while completing graduate school is not easy. Several of them have talked about "running to keep up" with all the competing demands on their time. Despite this, they have brought to the system a new energy level as their new ideas and new skills are put to use. It is important to note that not every MLS student gets a promotion, even after completing the degree. They must com-

pete for vacant positions, sometimes against external candidates who already have an MLS. But even when a student is not promoted, the library gets a return on its investment, because it finds that students are engaged in learning and in applying what they learn to their work.

/// DEVELOP A PROGRAM OF JOB ROTATION AND CROSS-TRAINING

Have staff swap jobs for three to six months. All will return with increased job knowledge, vitality, perspective, and appreciation of the library, its work, and the workforce. Do this as part of a structured program in which staff members keep a journal or record questions they encounter and discuss their key learnings with their peers, a coach, or both.

Alternately, job rotation can be less extensive. You can rotate library associates assigned to the central facility into a branch for a week or rotate employees among branches, if you have more than one building. Cross-train public service, technical services, and business office employees. Not only do such assignments develop the individuals involved, they provide the library with a more flexible and capable workforce, reducing work stoppages or backlogs when vacation is taken or someone is out on extended sick leave. The Santa Clara County (Calif.) Library story in chapter 7 provides examples of several approaches to job rotation, including an example of how one manager's medical leave resulted in developmental opportunities for three staff members.

Don't just send these staff off without learning objectives. Employees undertaking a job rotation should develop an IDP that clarifies developmental goals for taking or seeking the assignment (see chapter 4). The person is expected acquire new knowledge, skills, and abilities as an outcome of the job rotation.

"It's like springtime renewal when a person takes over a new area," says Patrick Losinski, executive director of Columbus (Ohio) Metropolitan Library. Columbus Metro also "switches deck chairs" around (as Losinski calls it), rotating or combining jobs. In one recent example, collection development staff and technical services staff were supervised by the marketing department. This is one way to help someone see the bigger picture, in this case to support centralized collections. Losinski was able to report seeing new ways of thinking within three weeks. Switching deck chairs was also mandatory for five branch managers in order to provide lateral transfers, new challenges, and new ways of thinking.

Many of the branch managers in Cuyahoga County (Ohio) Public Library were reassigned when this twenty-eight-branch library system reorganized. The reorganization resulted in a rotational move for all branch managers with less than three years of tenure in their branch. Yes, there were some tears and some opposition; a few branch managers even retired a little sooner than planned. Despite some short-term pain, library director (and current PLA president) Sari Feldman and her mover-and-shaker deputy Tracey Strobel report that the move was energizing overall. They see branch managers as pivotal to making the library's mission a reality, and according to Strobel this move "ramped everything up" across the system. The "jolt" reenergized the whole system, with staff rising to work with (and impress) their new bosses, managers looking at their new location and staff with fresh eyes, and all facing and growing from new challenges. New branch teams initiated many changes; more than a few of these resulted in higher efficiencies, improvement to effectiveness, increased circulation, higher door counts, and more.

/// TAKE ADVANTAGE OF TASK FORCES AND INTERIM JOB ASSIGNMENTS

Do not repeatedly ask the same people to serve on task forces or committees. For each new task force or job assignment, seek out a promising person who has not been given an opportunity to participate. Ask her to serve. If she agrees, provide support and watch her blossom.

Fast teams are frequently used for problem solving and employee development at Santa Clara County (Calif.) Library. A fast team provides an intensive focus to an issue or problem facing the library. There are few people on fast teams, three to five, from targeted organizational units. Teams usually meet for no more than four weeks. The team decides who will chair it, how many meetings are needed, and how communications up, down, and sideways will take place. One fast team rolled out chat reference. Another was tasked to provide the community with help getting connected with the library. Charters for fast teams have a reasonable scope, and staff members provide their best thinking and research. The library has seen people rise to the

challenge, and Melinda Cervantes, the library's executive director and county librarian, celebrates their success along with them.

Shared leadership models such as task groups and committees are frequently used to develop employees at Fresno County (Calif.) Public Library. A combination of employees having subject knowledge, those new to librarianship, and long-term staff participate on the same committee. For example, a task force was created to plan the events around the library's hundred-year anniversary as a county library.

Fresno County Public Library also capitalizes on staff development under civil service regulations, even though they are often seen as limiting options. For example, a special salary upgrade for up to nine months can be offered to an employee filling a temporary vacancy. In this manner, a Librarian II who might have the years of experience to qualify as a Librarian III (supervisor) could work in a higher classification during a vacancy or leave. This not only helps the library provide continuous services but provides the librarian with the range of experiences needed to compete for promotion opportunities. County librarian Karen Bosch Cobb and training librarian Camille Turner have used this approach to create opportunities for all, resulting in staff with more competencies, trained and available for promotion.

/// ACTION LEARNING

Learning through action serves to help employees develop critical competencies by completing important library work. An action learning team tackles a strategic issue and makes recommendations to library leadership. Action learning has also been used to select, assess, and develop stars and high-potential employees to new levels of knowledge, skills, experience, and competencies. The characteristics of action learning are as follows:

- It is a team-based approach to learning.
- The team works on real-world problems or business challenges that are often for high stakes.
- There is often a training component such as team functioning or problem solving built in.
- The real-world challenge is a stretch assignment that extends beyond members' experi-

ence. Thus, teams are challenged and put into a stressful situation while knowing their work will be reviewed and supported by leadership.

Action learning is a prime source of development at the County of Los Angeles (Calif.) Public Library, reports county librarian Margaret Donnellan Todd. When Todd took on the director's role in 2001, she found a gap in candidates for potential leadership positions and few employees between the ages of 40 and 50. She was not too surprised; the library, like many in California, had faced several waves of financial problems, resulting in hiring freezes and talented employees moving on. She realized that she had to promote sooner than she might have wanted in order to fill vacancies, from employees who had the tools but not the experience; she likened it to skipping a grade in school. Action learning became her way to fill the gap. The library began this strategy after one of its librarians attended an Urban Libraries Council Executive Leadership Institute (ELI) program.

The library's action learning teams do not include senior managers and are limited to librarians early in their career. A chair is appointed and a charter provided. Management helps shape the scope of work and then steps out of the picture. Action learning teams engage in real work, often advancing strategic initiatives of the library. Teams have engaged in practical as well as theoretical (policy) work, including providing services to seniors, studying the future of electronic services, and creating a model for warehousing lesser-used books. Todd reports that the system has seen many librarians rise to the occasion, acquire new skills and confidence, and flourish as leaders.

/// IMPLEMENT A 360-DEGREE FEEDBACK PROGRAM

In a 360-degree feedback program, performance data are obtained from peers, subordinates, and the supervisor in order to provide an assessment of an employee's performance up, down, and sideways in the organization. It provides full circle, or 360-degree, feedback. This type of evaluation process offers employees a learning tool and feedback mechanism to promote growth and development. There are a variety of ways to conduct a 360-degree feedback program, and not all are expensive. As with other approaches to employee performance evaluation, it is essential that everyone involved understand the purposes of the evaluation and receive thorough training in applying the process.

/// CREATE A DUAL CAREER LADDER SYSTEM FOR LIBRARIANS

Career ladders allow employees to focus on their expertise as, for example, an individual contributor (e.g., children's librarian) without having to take on a management role to earn more. In this scenario, an employee might advance from Librarian I to II by taking on more responsibility in collection development, conducting research, or designing new programs in early childhood learning. Other options might include the Librarian I moving up by becoming a specialist in literacy, readers' advisory, information technology, or training. Some libraries, such as Queens Borough (N.Y.) Public Library, have career ladders that extend through supervisory and management levels in order to prepare even senior managers to fill anticipated vacancies due to upcoming retirements (see chapter 7 for more detail).

There are many ways to acknowledge and reward your staff for increasing their responsibility and value to the library outside advancement to a management position. Though the library may ultimately place the employee in a higher grade level and pay a higher salary, that amount will be far less than the cost of replacing her if she goes elsewhere or the cost of low morale and mistakes if she takes a management job she does not really desire, just to earn more.

/// OFFER COACHING TO MANAGERS AND LEADERS

Most employees are not ready to take on management/leadership roles when first promoted to them. And why would they be? It is an entirely new role they were not taught in library school or as individual contributors. There are job content and process coaches. As the name implies, a job content coach helps the leader learn what the job entails. A process coach, on the other hand, focuses attention on how the leader affects others, creates roles and boundaries, creates an agenda, and works with a group to achieve results. The coach especially works with the leader to gain an awareness of the special competencies needed at the new organizational level.

Where do you find a coach? A staff member who is already experienced in that job, especially if her experience includes supervisory coaching for staff, can do most job content coaching. Process coaching requires some different skills, including the ability to maintain objectivity. Some HR departments provide process coaching. For some top leadership positions, the library may be willing to pay for an experienced process coach from outside the organization. There may be someone in your library who already has the right skills or is interested in developing them to fill a unique and valuable role; providing training for a "designated coach"—or a coaching team—may be a worthwhile investment. An excellent resource on coaching is Ruth Metz's *Coaching in the Library.*[1]

The County of Los Angeles Public Library provides an external coach to its action learning teams, team leaders, and management. The coach helps members through sticky situations and covers team effectiveness, presentation skills, and problem solving. Observing the teams allows the coach to see people in action, showing her who the high achievers are and who needs to develop which strengths; who talks a good game but has little substance; who is quiet but very capable. The process brings valuable input to management to augment the talent assessment process. The library's action learning teams typically work on their own once they are chartered; the executive team does not get involved unless asked. The coach, however, may suggest that a team or team member call the county librarian, for example, to ascertain direction or understand the politics of a course of action. Often teams members say they "do not want to bother her," but of course they are missing a valuable resource and opportunity. An important learning experience results in either case.

/// ASSIGN MENTORS TO NEW AND LONGER-TERM EMPLOYEES

Mentoring can be a powerful tool in employee development, especially when an employee is promoted or assumes a new role. An effective mentoring process takes some thought and planning. It is important to match the mentor and the mentee carefully. Their personal styles and interests should be compatible. Allow a trial period for the relationship to settle in, and if there are problems make needed adjustments.

Expectations for the mentoring relationship should be identified clearly. Define the results you expect and discuss responsibilities, roles, and expectations with both mentor and mentee. Provide training for mentors. Monitor and evaluate progress, and reset expectations as the relationship grows and changes. The formal mentor/mentee relationship is not intended to be permanent. The final phase of the formal relationship should encourage independence at the appropriate time. Lois Zachary's *Mentor's Guide* is a wonderful resource for developing a mentoring program or relationship.[2] An example of a successful internal, informal mentoring program is included in the OCLC story in chapter 7. In this program, a vice president of one division may mentor a young employee in another division. Both mentor and mentee learn from each other and build relationships that allow both to understand what happens in other parts of the organization as well.

The "Build the Bench" program at the Public Library of Charlotte and Mecklenburg County (N.C.) created an "intimate type of learning environment" for high-potential managers. Rick Ricker, HR deputy director, told us that six high-potential managers (defined as potential to be promoted into a senior management position) were identified and paired with six senior managers, who were tasked to provide mentoring and one-on-one development as well as exposure to different management styles. All twelve were provided with mentor/mentee training to help set goals and expectations. The program offered collaborative project work and development over an eight-week period. Feedback was provided to the mentee managers and the executive leadership team about the potential for success and development needs of each participant. Participants also worked on an action learning project: small groups were responsible for creating a section of a disaster recovery plan for the library and then cohesively working (intergroup or across teams) to develop an effective plan. One manager from this group has since been promoted. All have created IDPs that will help them acquire the necessary knowledge, skills, and experiences to move toward their career goals.

Mentoring is an ongoing activity at Santa Clara County Library. There is no formal program, but mentoring is institutionalized and has helped many employees. Sarah Flowers is one:

> I was hired as a program librarian at the Morgan Hill Library. I had a very good mentor in Catharine Fouts, who was the community librarian then. She spent a lot of time with me, talking about her own under-

standing of the system and her own philosophy of management. She was tremendously influential in my own development as a leader. Beyond that, though, probably the best thing she did for me was to take at least one four- to six-week vacation every year, leaving me in charge. After three years, she transferred to Los Altos and I was promoted to community librarian. I continued to call on her as a resource on how to do my new job, until she retired a couple of years later. Probably one of the biggest opportunities I was given during the time I was a community librarian was to be on the negotiating team for the SEIU contract negotiations. It was very helpful to have that background when I applied for the deputy county librarian job. [During a vacancy] I was asked to work out-of-class as deputy county librarian for six or eight weeks. That was a big help in preparing me too [for the job I currently have]. I realized later that of course Julie knew she was leaving and wanted to start training someone for her job.

Nancy Howe is currently the deputy county librarian and has spent most of her library career with Santa Clara County. She has moved to a new position or been promoted six times during her fourteen-year tenure. Howe says that she has found ample opportunities for new challenges within the Santa Clara County Library.

I spent most of my career working in the not-for-profit sector, and only came to the library when I was staying home raising my family. I started working as a substitute librarian, almost as a hobby, but quickly decided that my personal ambition was to bring my community and managerial experiences from my previous career to the library. Santa Clara County Library is large enough to have lots of movement and I always have been quick to raise my hand to take on a project, often that no one else wanted to do. I told my supervisors that I wanted to advance and I received lots of encouragement. In taking the deputy position, I really am stretching myself by managing the technology side of the library. I am grateful to Melinda as well as other people who have sensed my passion and believed in my abilities. From working as a substitute librarian in every one of our libraries, to a supervising librarian, adult services manager, staff development librarian, community librarian and now as deputy, I have a breadth and depth of experience that I can apply to future positions, either inside this system or elsewhere. I love the Santa Clara County Library for its values and am proud to be a part of it throughout my library career. It's my turn now to mentor many of our new hires, and one of my proudest accomplishments was having a hand in creating our intern program that

provides library school students with practical experience, often ending up with them working for us as librarians.

/// OFFER ON-THE-JOB TRAINING

Both formal and informal on-the-job training can be offered. The informal situation is like shadowing. It requires matching a high-potential employee with a star performer and permitting observation and dialogue about the work, situations encountered, how they were handled in the manner they were, and why. Formal on-the-job training is more akin to reference or the training offered on databases or a new integrated library system. In this approach a training plan is developed, usually following a tell/show/do/follow-up format of instruction. Formal on-the-job training is a popular approach to staff development. All of the following programs have a leadership or management curriculum as their cornerstone, but most use more than one strategy—not only classroom learning or on-the-job training—to help staff grow.

Baltimore County Public Library

Did you know that twenty percent of our top management team (Branch Managers, AO Department Heads, and Executive Leadership) are eligible to retire today? We are in the midst of the "graying of the profession" and must position ourselves to be ready for inevitable staff retirements in the near future. That is where you enter the picture. This memo describes three different succession management initiatives for FY-2009 designed for staff members that a) wish to improve upon management and leadership skills to be more effective in their current role; or b) aspire to move into higher-level supervisory and management positions within BCPL. Please note that while these programs serve to strengthen your skills in leadership, supervision, and management, participation does not guarantee promotion into future management vacancies.

This is how Jean Mantegna, HR manager of Baltimore County Public Library (BCPL), opens the invitation sent to all staff to participate in the library's succession management initiatives.[3] She then goes on to describe the three succession management initiatives: Leadership Development Program, Supervisory Skills for New Supervisors, and the Effective Managing Series.

BCPL's philosophy is one of creating a pipeline—a pool of viable candidates ready to fill management vacancies when, as Mantegna puts it, "the baby boomers bust out to retirement." Individual staff members are not selected for grooming into targeted positions, and it is acknowledged that leadership competencies are desired at every level in the organization.

LEADERSHIP DEVELOPMENT PROGRAM

In its third year, the Leadership Development Program is intended "to provide learning opportunities around qualities of leadership for staff members that aspire to future management roles." The program is both theoretical and practical (mostly the later) and very experiential. Increasing competencies around self-awareness and learning by doing are critical components.

Mantegna and Jim Fish, the library's director, partnered with the Community Colleges of Baltimore County to design the program. Sessions take place in half- to full-day sessions on a college campus covering the following topics: communications, team building, project management, problem solving, conflict resolution, and managing change. Participants learn how to work as a member of a cross-functional team with other leaders at varying levels of the organization. They are also developing their leadership competencies from the list of twenty selected by the system.[4]

Phase two of the program begins six months into the program, after participants learn how to function as a team. They begin to work on a team project—a project of key importance to the library, one that drives its work plan forward. The most recent project is to develop virtual new staff orientation. Prior projects include service to new populations; self-check evaluation and recommendations for improvement; service to teens; and improving the telephone system. Each project has a sponsor (a seasoned manager within the library system), and seasoned managers provide developmental coaching throughout the experience as an aid to the learning process. Continuing education units are provided for the full-day programs with the college.

Peer feedback is provided to and by all (a skill also practiced in the program). At project completion, presentations are made to the administrative council. Feedback is unfailingly followed by a well-deserved celebration.

BCPL, always a learning organization, has made some recent changes to the program. The current class is limited to seven participants, and the length of the program has increased from nine to sixteen months. Feedback from the first year demonstrated that the class size of twenty-one was too large and the nine-month time line too short.

To date, thirty-four employees have completed the program with excellent results. Seven participants have been promoted into managerial positions, and several learned that management is not for them. A few left BCPL, taking their newly acquired leadership skills to another library system. Regardless of whether anyone is actually promoted, there are many positive outcomes. According to Jean, program graduates are more self-aware, have a better sense of what they want their career to look like, have acquired project management skills, have learned new skills and competencies, and, most important, are leaders in their position.

SUPERVISORY SKILLS FOR NEW MANAGERS

BCPL offers Supervisory Skills for New Managers in a blended learning environment (face-to-face, independent, and group) as a way to introduce supervisory skills to employees new to their role or aspiring to supervisory positions. The curriculum is broadly shaped around the topics of communications, leadership, management, personal development, and team building.

The Division of Library Development and Services of the Maryland State Department of Education purchased the license to online business skills courses provided by Skillsoft, a provider of on-demand e-learning training programs of both business and technical topics. Participants complete three courses selected by BCPL. The schedule alternates, with participants completing a self-paced course individually one month and meeting as a group to debrief it the following month. During the debriefing, in a highly interactive way, supervisors share their learning and discuss how it applies to supervising staff at BCPL.

The first three topics of independent learning taken over a six-month period are "Becoming a Manager—Responsibilities and Fears," "Communicating as a Leader," and "Leading through Change." Starting in month seven of this ten-month class and twice in alternating months, teams of two are formed to review the course catalog, select a topic that addresses a specific area of skill development, and present their learning to the group. They share key points, along with a review of the course, noting what they liked and disliked about it.

Individual learning is not limited to the classes or topics. All learners have access to the full catalog of programs until the site license expires.

EFFECTIVE MANAGING SERIES

The third BCPL succession management initiative is the Effective Managing Series. As outlined in the course description, the purpose of this series "is to provide an opportunity for less-seasoned supervisors and managers to come together as a learning community to explore and develop their unique management styles in the context of BCPL's culture and philosophy of effective management." This program runs for ten months. With a little bit of theory but mostly lively discussion and practical application, it covers the following topics:

- Managing oneself
- Planning and evaluation
- Organizing oneself/time management
- Delegating
- Managing change
- Managing challenges, conflicts, and crises
- Managing one's boss/managing others
- Communication
- Decision making
- To be determined (as selected by the group)

These classes are facilitated by Mantegna, Fish, and experienced managers, who view it as an opportunity to give back, to model different managerial styles to participants, and to transfer their institutional knowledge to the next generation of BCPL leaders.

Columbus Metropolitan Library

Though it is known for creating and even selling strong training and development programs, Columbus Metropolitan Library did not have a standard curriculum to support managers and leaders or those aspiring to move up. Patrick Losinski, the library's executive director, and his staff went on a search for a program of study and selected Business of People leadership training (www.businessofpeople.net), based in Columbus. The program focuses on how one uses oneself to develop the core foundational skills of leadership, acknowledging that each person is the most powerful force for change in her organization. The curriculum includes

- Great people skills: contact skills (two sessions)
- Commitment to the ongoing enhancement of the managed group

- Wearing two hats effectively: representing your people to leadership and leadership to your people
- Working with accountability as a personal development process; reviews, monitoring employee growth over the year
- Understanding the managed group
- The skills of raising and maintaining high morale
- Commitment to your own training beyond the training
- Getting good buy-in, giving direction, dealing with spot problems, expecting response, and having a framework for dealing with lack of follow-through
- Integration of Business of People skills

In the first year, one hundred of the library's managers, in ten groups of ten, went through ten five-hour sessions each month. In the second year, fifty more managers will go through the program—this time run by library staff who completed a train-the-trainer program in partnership with trainers from Business of People. Outcomes, from Losinski's perspective, have been very positive: "It's the best thing we've ever done." In addition, all managers now have a common language and shared experiences. "Staff," Losinski notes, "are dealing with resistance and change far more effectively; they are also more empathetic and results-oriented as managers; their listening skills have been fine-tuned; they understand how to get buy-in from staff, give and accept feedback; and hold staff accountable. Trust has gone up and managers are feeling good about systemwide decisions that are made. Staff are using the training, and using the language." According to Losinski, "It is sticking!"

Cuyahoga County Public Library

Sometimes events or circumstances signal that it is time to do something differently. Cuyahoga County Public Library (CCPL) was at just such a point when the system lost five branch managers over a short period of time. The jobs were posted, but leadership did not see the caliber of candidates they expected. Applicants simply did not have the knowledge, experience, or understanding of the job. CCPL recruited branch managers externally, but library director Sari Feldman and deputy director Tracey Strobel thought the library system had not adequately developed internal candidates. They then put their heads together and, working with a consultant, designed the two-day Branch Leadership Academy to expose staff to the roles and expectations of a branch manager. They expected ten to fifteen staff to apply; forty-eight librarians volunteered to attend the learning event. Feldman and Strobel structured it as an opportunity for interested staff to learn the expectations, including competencies, of a branch manager in their system.

CONTEXT

Per its strategic plan, CCPL focuses on six priorities: connect with reading; ensure every child enters school ready to learn; help youth to reach maximum potential; put Cuyahoga County back to work; keep seniors healthy, happy, and independent; and connect with new Americans. One way to fulfill these priorities is through community partnerships. Therefore, it is no surprise that CCPL branch managers are expected to know their communities and local players well. Indeed, branch managers are expected to be proactively involved in the community and to be seen as important players at the community level. For example, library staff and branch managers are expected to have an impact in and on workforce development, serve as a gateway for new immigrants, and take a leadership role in early childhood education. Strobel offered an example of difference in expectations for different levels of library staff: while it is anticipated that the adult librarian will serve as liaison with the senior center twice a month and have a connection with the senior center director, the branch manager is expected to be visible in the community, liaise with mayor and city council members, serve on a chamber of commerce board, and attend Rotary lunches, press briefings, and Kiwanis breakfasts, to name a few. The expectations and competencies flow directly from the library's mission statement.

LEADERSHIP ACADEMY APPLICATION PROCESS

All public service librarians and subject specialists with more than one year of experience were invited to apply (see figure 5.1). To be accepted into the Branch Leadership Academy, candidates were required to link their desire to attend with a commitment to, and experience with, CCPL's branch manager competencies (taken directly from the job description of branch manager).

The agenda for the Leadership Academy included welcomes by Feldman and Strobel and discussions about the library's new customer service model, trends in libraries, and best practices for bosses. How-to sessions on analyzing library metrics and problem solving and risk taking were followed by exercises in which the potential branch managers could put into practice what they had just learned.

A panel of senior branch managers shared experiences of connecting with their community, and all engaged in an exercise called "community opportunity scenario." Later, after sharing information on circulation, holds, and other library data, Strobel described initiatives the library was planning over the next one to three years to create efficiencies and improve customer service. Participants learned about them here first. A few of the initiatives included changes in delivery models, online booking of meeting rooms managed centrally, online program registration, systemwide centralized selection of materials, floating collections, programming with experts, and a rethinking of materials security measures. It was truly added value that forty-eight system leaders were in on the new customer service model and other initiatives and, as a critical mass, could help move these initiatives forward.

Evaluations showed that one of the most highly valued discussions took place at the end of the session when Feldman and Strobel, along with two regional managers, shared their expectations of branch managers, took questions, and provided sincere answers about leadership.

Of the forty-eight attendees, five have become branch managers and eleven have received other promotions (nine at CCPL and two elsewhere). Eight or so participants decided either to slow down on the track to management or not to pursue a management position. Strobel speaks of the Branch Leadership Academy as a huge success, one that CCPL plans to offer again in the near future.

Harford County Public Library

Harford County Public Library (HCPL) used the changing economic climate to analyze its staff development program. Library director Audra Caplan and HR director Terri Schell realized that limited funds would compel the library to hire and retain the right people in the right job with the right skills. The components of the library's program are staff development, competencies, supervisory training, mentoring, and leadership development.

Succession planning is one part of HCPL's staff development program, which is designed "for cultivating knowledgeable and skilled staff, developing strong supervisors, managers, and administrators, and preparing emergent leaders for the libraries of tomorrow." As portrayed in figure 5.2, HCPL begins its focus on staff development from an employee's first day on the job, indeed during the recruitment process. Retention starts at orientation, and development is about continuous learning. HCPL builds staff knowledge and skills through both in-house and external efforts, using a variety of learning modalities. Mentoring is an opportunity provided to new supervisors, managers, administrators, and other professional staff.

In 2000, HCPL developed a competency-based performance management system. Working with a committee and consultant, the system identified and defined seven core and four managerial competencies. The core competencies, on which all employees are assessed, are sensitivity to internal and external customer service; communications skills; team player; dependability; efficient management of job responsibilities; knowledgeable of policies, procedures, and technology; and problem solver. Successful managers are expected to mentor and cross-train employees, recognize and reward employee performance, demonstrate leadership, and serve as an employee/system liaison. Staff are recruited and promoted on the basis of these competencies, and training is offered regularly. An HCPL-specific refresher course, "Concepts and Culture," is offered to incumbents twice per year. Also offered regularly are classes on innovation, a key organizational value articulated in the library's strategic plan.

Caplan and Schell know that, for HCPL to remain a thriving twenty-first-century library, staff need to be developed into successful leaders—and that leadership occurs not just at the top but throughout the

---

FIGURE 5.1
ANNOUNCEMENT AND APPLICATION OF BRANCH LEADERSHIP ACADEMY

ANNOUNCEMENT AND APPLICATION OF BRANCH LEADERSHIP ACADEMY

We are pleased to announce the first Branch Leadership Academy scheduled to take place on September 26 & 27, 2006 at the Cleveland Metroparks Zoo. Our goal is to identify and begin developing individuals with strong leadership capabilities, enthusiasm, flexibility, and collaborative skills who are interested in applying for a Branch Manager position in the next 1–3 years. Staff members who have worked as a PSL I, II, III or Subject Specialist for at least one year are eligible to apply. Topics will include the new customer service model and current trends in library service. Instructors will include Sari Feldman, Jeanne Goodrich and Jodi Berg.

To apply, please select three of the competencies for branch managers below. Write a paragraph for each of the three illustrating how you have demonstrated your ability to meet that competency. Your application should include your name and location, and be no longer than one page.

Required competencies for Branch Managers:

- Excellent verbal and written communication skills in interpersonal and group situations including the ability to actively listen, consider diverse perspectives, and resolve conflict.
- Demonstrated commitment to embracing change and ability to initiate and facilitate change.
- Possesses the ability to analyze data, recommend action as a result of that analysis and execute suggested improvements.
- Proven ability to develop and effectively administer a budget.
- Proven ability to hire, coach and mentor the best possible workforce and a capacity to encourage and nurture individual initiative.
- Skilled at creating strategic alliances and community partnerships by developing and maintaining effective relationships with community leaders and change agents.
- Committed to providing direct service to the public and actively modeling best practices to employees.
- Demonstrated skill in using technology appropriate to the job and the proclivity to embrace and adapt quickly to changes in technologies introduced to meet customer needs or improve organizational efficiencies.

FIGURE 5.2
HARFORD COUNTY PUBLIC LIBRARY STAFF DEVELOPMENT PROGRAM

A framework for cultivating knowledgeable and skilled staff, developing strong supervisors, managers, and administrators, and preparing emergent leaders for the libraries of tomorrow.

RECRUITING AND HIRING	ORIENTATION OF STAFF (ONBOARDING)	BUILDING STAFF KNOWLEDGE AND SKILLS	MENTORING STAFF (GUIDANCE OUTSIDE OF SUPERVISOR)	SUCCESSION PLANNING AND TRANSITIONAL LEADERSHIP

Recruiting
• Expand recruiting efforts to increase candidate pool
• Seek new sources based on changing technology and interests of applicants
• Analyze candidates in additional ways to identify broad potential
 	
Hiring
• Use appropriate, trained interview panel members
• Use updated position description
• Incorporate "hard" skills and "soft" skills into the interview assessment process
• Set the tone for the organization and employee
• Adapt practices to maximize number of candidates likely to be successful in promotional situations
	New Employee
	• New hire—first day introduction to HR, payroll, technology training, and branch visit
	• Orientation manual completed within 90 days of hire
	• Assign orientation peer (buddy)
	• Attend NEO program under the direction of HR
	• 2-day program every other month
	• 3rd day conducted three times a year on shared vision (concepts and culture)
	
	Employees changing position or location
	• Review of benefit changes
	• Department overview
	• Building/location overview
		In-House Efforts
		• Ongoing technology training
		• Job-specific skills
		• Basic supervision (introduction)
		• Advanced supervision
		• Leadership development program
		• Management development
		• Identified organizational training needs
		• Develop in-branch professional collection of training materials
		
		Outside Efforts
		• Tuition reimbursement for higher education
		• Support participation in local, state, and national professional organizations
		• Leadership development
		• Local and state-sponsored offerings
		• Identified individual training needs
			Mentoring Program
			Establish mentor relationship for
			• new supervisors, managers, administrators, and other professional staff, whether hired from outside or promoted from within; coordinated by HR
			• a defined purpose or skill
			• leadership role and responsibilities; coordinated through senior staff
				• Focus on proactive means to prepare staff for promotional opportunities
				• Provide organizational education:
				  Establish formal work rotation assignments
				  Offer cross-training at peer level within and outside of department/branch
				  Develop broader understanding of department responsibilities and relationships, including the library board
				• Manage anticipated personnel shortages in key positions
				• Identify through a variety of methods those staff who have potential to become successful supervisors, managers, administrators, and leaders
				• Develop individualized development plan to strengthen necessary skills

organization. Accordingly, the library system created and HR offers a basic supervision course for all supervisors and those considering a supervisory position. This course is offered as self-study and in the classroom. Learners are provided with a video and new supervisor toolbox consisting of eight DVDs and a workbook. They are expected to review this material in advance and be prepared for classroom study by the time training begins. One advantage of this program is that all supervisors go through it, thus enhancing consistency in practice, application, and language. An unanticipated outcome has been that some employees, peeking through the window of what is really involved in supervision, choose to opt out before making what might be a poor career choice. Many participants express a new appreciation of what a supervisor—their supervisor—actually does. This look into the backroom work of supervision, if nothing else, shows the library as a system leaving participants with a bigger picture of the library world.

To support the transition into supervision and leadership, the library created a mentoring program. The program received very positive feedback from its first group of thirteen mentoring pairs and helped acculturate leaders into their new roles.

Succession planning is HCPL's most recent addition to staff development. The succession planning program was purposefully developed as a proactive means to "prepare staff for promotional opportunities, allow for organizational education, manage anticipated personnel shortages in key positions, identify staff who have potential to become successful supervisors, managers, administrators and leadership, and develop individualized development plans to strengthen necessary skills."

In thinking holistically about succession planning, HCPL realized that it did not really know how many employees were interested in staying in their current positions and how many aspired to a leadership role. To learn more about staff wishes, they conducted a needs assessment and asked. To their surprise, findings indicated that many employees sought new responsibilities, including leadership roles. The next step for HR was to take supervisory training to the leadership and executive level.

A leadership program offering advanced information for senior staff to gain more experience was custom-designed to meet HCPL's culture and strategic needs. It is a blended program offered through print, online, and face-to-face meetings. It is designed for participants to L.E.A.D.: learn, experience, apply, and develop. As seen in figure 5.3, skills to be acquired include project management, facilitator training, and advanced leadership skills. Still in development, the program offers nineteen topics to choose from, including public speaking, the Public Information Act, intellectual freedom, strategic planning, seeing the big picture, and

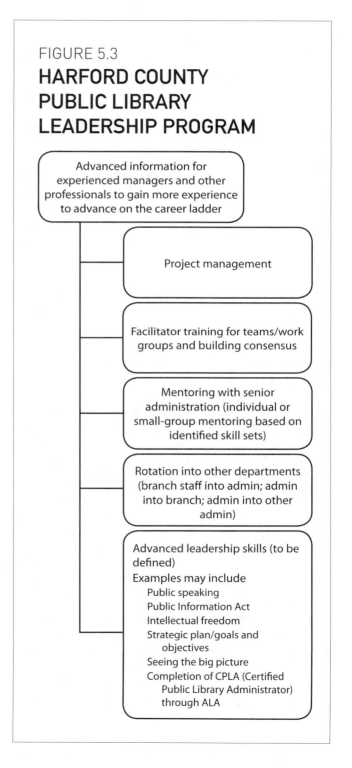

FIGURE 5.3

HARFORD COUNTY PUBLIC LIBRARY LEADERSHIP PROGRAM

Advanced information for experienced managers and other professionals to gain more experience to advance on the career ladder

Project management

Facilitator training for teams/work groups and building consensus

Mentoring with senior administration (individual or small-group mentoring based on identified skill sets)

Rotation into other departments (branch staff into admin; admin into branch; admin into other admin)

Advanced leadership skills (to be defined)
Examples may include
  Public speaking
  Public Information Act
  Intellectual freedom
  Strategic plan/goals and
    objectives
  Seeing the big picture
  Completion of CPLA (Certified
    Public Library Administrator)
    through ALA

completing ALA's Certified Public Library Administrator course.

Mentoring by a senior library administrator is a key component of leadership development at HCPL, where leaders are expected to take a global approach, engaging in big-picture and systems thinking. To help them acquire this perspective, HCPL plans to structure rotational assignments for leaders to spend a month or more in other departments to learn what really happens throughout the system at the senior level.

HCPL's philosophy and approach are to develop all people and provide everyone the same opportunity to move to the next level. Until budget costs became prohibitive, HCPL provided tuition reimbursement for employees attending library school. At one time, graduates were automatically promoted to librarians; now, graduates compete for professional-level positions in order to ensure that the library is promoting those with the most leadership potential. Figure 5.4 shows the development tracks that will be offered during FY 2010 and 2011. Caplan and Schell realize that there will not be enough leadership positions for all employees ready, willing, and able to take the mantle, but they too are thinking globally—globally for all public libraries, knowing that talented employees might leave for another system. If they do, Caplan and Schell are proud of their contribution to leadership at other libraries.

Public Library of Charlotte and Mecklenburg County

The Public Library of Charlotte and Mecklenburg County (PLCMC) has engaged in three efforts to date that involve leadership development and succession planning: manager training, a leadership learning initiative for new supervisors and managers, and the "Build the Bench" mentoring program described earlier.

The manager curriculum was designed internally for all managers, is mandatory, and must be completed within eighteen months. The curriculum consists of nine courses designed to build the competencies of integrity, customer service, communication, individual leadership/influencing, teamwork and collaboration, planning, organizing and work management, visionary leadership, analysis/problem assessment, and maximizing performance. Most courses are taught by internal staff—senior members of the HR department. Managers can register easily on a PeopleSoft module at their desk. Each course is scheduled for between two hours and one day. The curriculum includes these courses: New Employee Orientation; Communicating and Listening; Sexual Harassment: A Manager's Responsibility; Salary Administration; Ethics for Supervisors and Managers; Library Practices and Policies; Essentials of Leadership; Working through Conflict; and Behavioral Interviewing Techniques.

The plan going forward for this program is the creation of virtual classrooms, to save both time and money. The goal of the manager training program is to improve individual as well as organizational success and to develop future leaders for the organization.

The Leadership Learning Initiative was created for newly hired managers and supervisors throughout the system. Seeking a diversity of candidates, the library invited employees of all levels and with different types of experience to participate.

The initial iteration was a six-month program built around Rachel Singer Gordon's *The Accidental Library Manager: Who Am I?*[5] The core curriculum also focuses on developing managers in the areas of conflict resolution, building successful teams, and communications—competencies PLCMC finds to be the building blocks all supervisors and managers need to be successful. Multifaceted and multimedia, the curriculum consists of a combination of face-to-face meetings, virtual meetings, in-house speakers, and external community speakers (see figure 5.5).

The pilot program received rave reviews, and PLCMC plans to implement it again, and on an ongoing basis. The change they will make is to shorten it, keep the class size to twelve participants, offer classes more frequently, and eliminate redundancies that may occur with the manager training program. New action learning projects pertaining to the system's mission, values, or strategic plan will be identified as the program continues.

Notes

1. Ruth Metz, *Coaching in the Library: A Management Strategy for Achieving Excellence* (Chicago: American Library Association, 2002).

2. Lois J. Zachary, *The Mentor's Guide: Facilitating Effective Learning Relationships* (San Francisco: Jossey-Bass, 2000).

3. As of 2009, BCPL has seventeen branches and four bookmobiles. The population of its service area is 788,994. It has 482,361 cardholders. One of the book authors (Paula) and her husband are two of those cardholders.

4. A resource suggested by Jean Mantegna is Marshall Goldsmith et al., *Global Leadership: The Next Generation* (Upper Saddle River, N.J.: Financial Times Prentice Hall Books, 2003).

5. Rachel Singer Gordon, *The Accidental Library Manager: Who Am I?* (Medford, N.J.: Information Today, 2004).

FIGURE 5.4

FY10–FY11 HARFORD COUNTY PUBLIC LIBRARY LEARNING AND DEVELOPMENT TRACKS

GENERAL SKILLS	CULTIVATING RELATIONSHIPS (CUSTOMER SERVICE MODULES)	SUPERVISORY TRAINING PROGRAMS	L.E.A.D. PROGRAM (LEARN, EXPERIENCE, APPLY, DEVELOP)
<ul><li>Better Organization</li><li>Book Group Moderators Training</li><li>Communicating the Right Message; Mastering the Written Word</li><li>Continuing the Quest for Innovation</li><li>Disability Training—Communication, Sign Language, Homebound</li><li>Facilitation Skills</li><li>Fun Is Allowed! FISH Concepts and Other Avenues for Fun and Recognition in the Workplace</li><li>Handling Stress and Maintaining a Positive Attitude</li><li>Healthier Living</li><li>HCPL Culture and Concepts</li><li>Intellectual Freedom and Material Changes</li><li>Leading from Any Position: Positively Impacting My Department/Team</li><li>Project Management: Department/ Team Activities</li><li>Public/Personal Safety: Work Environment (Blackbelt Librarian, etc.) and Personal Safety</li><li>Readers' Advisory</li><li>Taking on Change in Difficult and Good Times</li><li>Time Management</li></ul>*NOTE:* Admin Department Info Sessions to be scheduled	<ul><li>Civility and Internal Citizenship</li><li>Behaviors/ Professionalism</li><li>Coping during Difficult Times and Staffing Shortages</li><li>Creating a Positive Work Environment</li><li>Customer Service Recovery Techniques</li><li>Direct and Indirect Customer Service Skills, tailored to job specifics (e.g., reference interview skills, etc.) where appropriate</li><li>Emotionally Speaking (compassion, etc.)</li><li>Handling Difficult Customers, External and Internal</li><li>Managing Conflict</li><li>Personality Conflicts</li><li>Supporting Each Other</li></ul>	**Basic Supervisory Training Program** Continue to offer same core topics *NOTE:* Look at modifications:<ul><li>Design to include fewer face-to-face meetings but longer sessions when done to cover multiple topics</li><li>Design to include yearly drop-in at any time for (1) new supervisors so s/he does not have to wait until another class is formed; (2) experienced supervisors to attend certain segments as desired</li></ul>**Advanced Supervisory/ Management Training Program—NEW**<ul><li>Influencing your staff through sharing information appropriately</li><li>More effective/creative scheduling, including budget analysis</li><li>Recognizing potential conflicts and using as opportunities for proactive/positive action</li><li>Understanding the work of others through rotation</li><li>Others to be determined</li></ul>	**Core Classes**<ul><li>Defining Leadership from the Systems Thinking/Big-Picture Perspective I</li><li>Big Picture—Project Management</li><li>Fiscal Awareness—Systems Budget (state, local, and fees or service vs. expenditures—capital and operating)</li><li>Organizational Education: Understanding Your Value to the Organization (strategic planning)</li><li>Understanding the Work of Others through Rotation</li><li>Influencing Others: Political Advocacy/Savvy Working with a Library Board, Friends' Groups, Elected Officials Public Speaking</li><li>Library Environment (national, state, and local)</li><li>Using Your Passion to Inspire/Lead Others (HOPE—Helping Other People Excel)</li></ul>**Add-On Development Program**<ul><li>Formal Mentoring for Transitional Leaders</li></ul>

FIGURE 5.5
LEADERSHIP LEARNING INITIATIVE: CALENDAR

This calendar outlines the learning experiences that the Leadership Academy participants can expect to be involved in over the next six months. The dates and times given are accurate at the time of publication but may be subject to adjustment based on the availability of the participants and associated resources. Every effort will be made to minimize any changes, participants will be notified in such instances and attempts will be made to accommodate schedules.

DATE AND TIME COMMITMENT	INVOLVEMENT	EVENT EXPERIENCE	EXPERIENCE DESCRIPTION
March 2 hours	In-person	Program description	A description of the Leadership Experience program and time commitment requirements.
		Kick-off—1-hour workshop, "The Accidental Library Manager—Who Am I?"	"The Accidental Library Manager—Who Am I?" This workshop will engage participants in identifying their unique instinctual style that impacts what they do and how they do it.
April 1 hour	Self-paced online workshop	"The Accidental Library Manager," a prerecorded Dynix-Sirsi workshop	"The Accidental Library Manager" takes a practical look at the skills and background new and potential library managers need to succeed in their positions. It reassures those with little preparation for their management roles, who never realized they would be going into management (or never intended to do so), or whose library school coursework failed to prepare them for the challenges of management. In an era where younger and potential managers are told what their elders think they "need to lead," find out what library staff really want from their managers, how to use your current background to succeed, and how to reduce the fear inherent in common concerns.
April 1–1.5 hours	Online group discussion— Live Meeting or Talking Communities	Debrief and discuss "The Accidental Library Manager"	Participants will meet virtually to discuss their observations from the prerecorded workshop "The Accidental Library Manager."
May 1–1.5 hours	Self-paced online workshop	"Building a Successful Team" (A pre-coursework assignment will be given to participants for completion prior to starting the online workshop.)	Many people think of team development as providing a pep talk to a group when spirits are low or challenges are fierce. Or they think of assembling a group of people who have the right mix of technical skills to get the job done and then just letting them do it. But team development is much more than this. Leaders who effectively develop teams know how to fully utilize available resources. They help the team efficiently and enthusiastically accomplish its mission.
May 2 hours	In-person Team Building Activity	Low-ropes course or other similar highly interactive activity	This in-person activity will seek to involve participants in an interactive team-building exercise to problem solve.

DATE AND TIME COMMITMENT	INVOLVEMENT	EVENT EXPERIENCE	EXPERIENCE DESCRIPTION
June 1 hour	Self-paced online workshop	"Communication" (A pre-coursework assignment will be given to participants for completion prior to starting the online workshop.)	Effective communicators think clearly and speak and write succinctly in order to accomplish their goal—to inform, instruct, or influence others.
June 1–1.5 hours	Online group discussion— Live Meeting or Talking Communities	Debrief and Discussion— "Communication"	Participants will meet virtually to discuss their observation and assignments resulting from online workshop "Communication."
July 3 hours	In-person workshop	Guest presenter from Mecklenburg County Training and Consultation Team—Leadership Academy participants will decide on relevant topic.	TBA
August 1–1.5 hours	Self-paced online workshop	"Managing Conflict" (A pre-coursework assignment will be given to participants for completion prior to starting the online workshop.)	Disagreement among people is inevitable. When differences cause people to become angry and close-minded, the resulting conflict disrupts working relationships and has a negative effect on quality, productivity, communication, and cooperation. Managing conflict means dealing with differing ideas, interests, or perceptions in a way that addresses both the personal and the practical needs of those involved. Properly managed conflict can help people understand others, encourage creativity and innovation, improve the ability to accomplish tasks, and maintain ongoing functional relationships between the people involved.
August 1–1.5 hours	Online group discussion— Live Meeting or Talking Communities	Debrief and Discussion— "Managing Conflict"	Participants will meet virtually to discuss their observations and assignments resulting from online workshop "Managing Conflict."
September half-day	In-person wrap-up and Graduation	Program Perspectives Graduation	Participants will have the opportunity to provide perspectives as a result of involvement. A leadership presentation will be required.

SUCCESSION PLANNING FOR THE LIBRARY DIRECTOR

Dear Paula,

Here is what I've been thinking about this evening. I'm looking down the road, trying to figure out what to do as I plan to retire, and find a process that will work for me and the institution I've devoted so much of my life to. What I'm after is not the "normal" routine, and I don't want to consult or work full-time—instead I want to be an example of how things can work better (and incidentally perhaps encourage baby boomer directors to stay on board longer?).

So often you see this happen: director leaves, then there's a big recruitment show, looking for the perfect candidate who can do this, that, and the other. Often we go through the process twice if we don't find the perfect somebody the first time. There are always a limited number of seasoned choices, and so they end up hiring an inside person that you have to assume wasn't quite ready (or why go through the big recruitment?). In the end, the board and VPs end up compromising in some way to take a "known" person and "develop them."

My idea is: when you look at research and what baby boomers say they want in their future, you hear:
—more free time
—less money is ok
—creativity, doing new things, learning new things
and so on.

So what should boards, VPs, even directors do/look for/plan for when your director approaches age 60? Can the board look for ways to move the director to a more senior role (i.e., fund-raising, marketing, capital project planning) and "grow" the bench strength?

Does it have to be all or nothing? You work full bore . . . until you stop. And the cycle begins again. Or is there a way that boards and executives can look ahead and see if a transition to start this process means they can tap into a known resource longer? Maybe 4 or 5 years before the "normal retirement" date, the board should make a point to find out what the director is planning.

Right now, directors retire and then go consult. Well, they could have done some of this for their own organization! This would not work if the "transitioning director" butts into all the library business. But if they put their consultant hat on, work fewer hours, move office to another place in building, have a set work plan . . . then it can work. The individual and the institution can both benefit.

Your retiring friend,

Director, Smithville University Library

MANY LIBRARY boards and local governments across the country will be going through a search process for a library director over the next five to ten years—some more than once. Some boards and local government officials will be putting their heads in the sand to avoid thinking about this issue; others will peek up slowly, until they willingly engage in the process. It is, after all, their most important function. Why is it so difficult? It is not hard to answer this question. It is about change, it is about real work, it is about risk, challenge, and uncertainly. It is also about evaluation and assessment. There will be more meetings, more dialogue, and a need to talk honestly and look at yourselves—as leaders—and at your organization—as an important entity in your community or educational institution. It is hard: change is hard, and costly, and frightening—and it the most important activity the members of a board will undertake. While fraught with challenge, this period is also filled with opportunity if you take the time to pause and reflect before rushing to fill the vacancy. This chapter helps you navigate the white water of both.

Unlike the other chapters in this book, this one is written and directed first to those library boards of trustees that hire library directors, second to library directors, and third to everyone else—staff, consultants, students, and faculty. Our values are reflected in our belief that the board's role is to set policy and that the library director, with staff, is responsible for implementing policy. Further, research and our experience have taught us that trustees should steer far away from micromanaging the library; the most important task of the board is to recruit, retain, evaluate, provide feedback to, engage in dialogue with, and support the library director—as well as to terminate the library director if warranted. There is no more important function. We direct this chapter to you, the library board, to support your efforts in director succession planning. If your library does not have a governing board—if, for example, a university search committee or city or county hires the director—many of the principles that follow still hold true.

We hope you are reading this before you have to hire a new library director, because the most effective boards are thinking and planning ahead in order to stay ahead. They are looking at ways to capitalize on the inevitable opportunity they will have to shape the library and search for the new. They may even be working with retiring directors to create new models for succession, like those envisioned in the e-mail that opens this chapter, that could bring the library new benefits and create a win for everyone. There *will* be many retirements in the next five to ten years as baby boomers leave our libraries. It will be a very competitive time. We are not seeing a plethora of members of the Generation X community ready and waiting in the wings—and that is why we are writing this chapter to help libraries, their boards, or other governing bodies plan for the inevitable, be proactive, rise to their fiduciary responsibility, and continue to meet community needs. But if you find yourselves with a hiring emergency, this chapter can still help you. It offers a step-by-step emergency plan for succession that you, your departing director, HR department, and city or county leadership should become very familiar with.

ASSESSING THE RISK

Ask yourself: is our library director over the age of 50? Is she eligible to retire? Do you know what her plans are? If she resigned tomorrow, what would you do? What would the library do? If you do not have answers to these questions, read on. Succession planning is not something that should take place at the last minute, at the time the director resigns; rather, it should begin well before—even several years before—the need arises. It is about planning; indeed, it is a form of risk management and an important part of governance. Think about it this way: it is like writing a will or signing up for homeowner's insurance. You are trying, in these cases, to minimize risks. Just like succession planning.

Figure 6.1 is a quick survey to help you assess your level of risk should your library director depart. Take a few minutes to answer these questions by checking off yes or no. If you checked off no to four or more questions, you may be risking a difficult transition to a new director; this is a good time to begin placing succession issues on your agenda, building a case for leadership development throughout the organization (see especially chapter 1), and creating an emergency succession plan.

WHY PLAN?

The primary purpose of an effective succession plan for a library director is to facilitate a seamless transition to the new director. A commitment from the board of trustees or other governing body to a timely planning process ensures that the library makes this transition most effectively and successfully, so that the transition appears seamless to the library's community stakeholders. There are many decisions to make, prompted by many questions, outlined below. These questions are about time lines, responsibilities, and desired outcomes—all of which guide the planning process. To be most effective, the process must be systematic and suited to your library's specific needs.

In other words, what follows is *not* in and of itself a succession plan for your library director. There is no one single cookie-cutter plan. Rather, to be effective, the board of trustees, with staff support, must engage in a dialogue that responds to key questions. There is no one right answer to these very delicate questions. What is important to note is that the *process* is a critical aspect and can make or break a succession. The other crucial and often neglected aspect of a leadership change is that it is a *transition* and needs to be considered holistically, not as a one-day or one-time event. The questions and issues we build into the

FIGURE 6.1
RISK SELF-ASSESSMENT

QUESTION	YES	NO
1. Our library has a strategic plan in place with goals and objectives for three years.	☐	☐
2. Our strategic plan includes goals for leadership and/or people development.	☐	☐
3. Our library has a written emergency succession plan.	☐	☐
4. Our library director has been in her position for less than ten years.	☐	☐
5. Our library director has said either formally or informally that she plans to remain with the library for four or more years.	☐	☐
6. Library leadership (staff) performs as a high-performing team, such that: a. there is a solid culture in place in which leadership team members support one another and can reach decisions as a group efficiently and harmoniously;	☐	☐
b. staff leaders share leadership of the library with the library director in having significant input into all major library-wide decisions;	☐	☐
c. staff leaders can lead the library in the absence of the library director; and	☐	☐
d. staff leaders have the authority to make and carry out decisions within their respective areas of responsibility.	☐	☐
7. (For libraries where the director has fund-raising responsibility) Our library director shares responsibility for fund-raising and/or the relationships we need for fund-raising (including grantors) with other staff and board members.	☐	☐
8. Our board of trustees evaluates the library director at least annually based on performance and achievement of strategic goals.	☐	☐
9. The members of our board of trustees engage in an annual evaluation of the board's performance.	☐	☐
10. Based on its self-evaluation, our board of trustees performs its major governance roles in a satisfactory manner. These include financial and executive support as well as policy development and strategic planning.	☐	☐
11. The board of trustees has a plan for developing its own officers so that they are comfortable and knowledgeable when assuming office.	☐	☐
12. (To the extent allowed by state law) Our board of trustees has a committee or task force responsible for identifying and supporting new board members who have skills needed to support the library.	☐	☐
13. Financial systems meet government and industry standards; financial reports are up to date and provide accurate data needed for those board and staff members responsible for maintaining the library's viability.	☐	☐

(cont.)

FIGURE 6.1 (cont.)

QUESTION	YES	NO
14. Operational manuals are in place for key systems; they are both useful and accessible.	☐	☐
15. Our senior staff have documented their major responsibilities and each has developed a staff person who can take over if needed.	☐	☐
16. The board of trustees has clearly defined term limits.	☐	☐
17. Our board represents a level of economic, cultural, and racial diversity approximate to our library's community.	☐	☐

Source: Adapted from Tom Adams, *Succession Planning and Executive Transition Management for Nonprofit Boards of Directors* (Baltimore: Annie E. Casey Foundation, 2006), 3.

following outline for succession planning address both of these aspects of recruiting a library director, helping to make the transition a smooth and successful one. Our outlined plan is broken into three major phases: preparation, recruitment, and transition.

/// PHASE I: PREPARATION (WHEN YOU HAVE TIME TO PLAN)

During this first phase the library has an opportunity to take stock, reflect on the past, anticipate and plan for the future, and identify the competencies needed by the incoming library director. Keep in mind that each library needs different competencies of its director at different points in its life cycle as well as in accordance with changing community, staff, governance, or other needs. Libraries facing a union drive, major fund-raising or bond challenge, building projects or construction difficulties, technology overhaul, political upheaval or contentious board relations, low staff morale, or other challenges require unique skills sets of their director. Be very honest, first to yourselves and then to your candidates, about your needs and the knowledge, skills, abilities, and competencies required of the director entering your system.

Do not skip over the preparation aspects of this process. When a library hears that its director is leaving, it is too easy to just rush into the hiring phase. Do that at your own peril. Remember: sometimes you have to go slow to go fast. The work you do in the preparation phase provides a foundation that enhances the success of the library and its incoming director. If you are

open, you will see many opportunities in this time of transition. Not rushing, and taking the time to look forward, will help you hire the right leader, one who has the competencies to bring the library to new phases of growth in line with its strategy.

Getting Started: Should You Use a Consultant?

In recent times many libraries, large and small, have been engaging search consultants or transition consultants. Some consultants generally focus their attention on helping the library recruit a new director. Some assist the board of trustees to ascertain the needs and expectations of the library or to prepare for the arrival of the new director. Some help the library build internal and board capacity so that it is in stronger shape before welcoming the new director. Others recommend working through the roles of the board and director so there is an easier transition and both can hit the ground running in an effective and healthy manner (yes, this includes eliminating practices of micromanagement, promoting open communications, creating a performance plan, and other forms of open feedback and dialogue). In a few cases, "houses are cleaned," with ineffective or inattentive staff and board members being retired early or otherwise asked to leave prior to the new director coming on board. There are pros and cons to retaining the services of a consultant.

Why retain a consultant?

- Unlike library staff, the consultant is an expert experienced in the search or transition process.

She can also provide an unbiased perspective, and the library is the beneficiary of best practices learned from her research and experience with other organizations.

- A consultant who specializes in libraries (academic or public) knows, and has connections with, many of the most effective leaders in the country—some of whom may never consider applying for a position advertised in a journal but would respond to a phone call from a respected colleague.

- A consultant can help provide an objective assessment of a library's situation and help identify issues library leadership may not have been able to articulate effectively.

- The board of trustees may desire a fresh look at the library's strategy, its structure, and the nature and scope of the position of library director.

- You may recognize the need for external help with the transition, because you do not have the time to devote to a search or for other reasons.

Why conduct the search in-house?

- Members of the board of trustees and staff have the expertise and time to conduct the search and design a transition process.

- Consultants are an extra expense.

- Board members may see every candidate fresh by not having relationships with potential candidates.

- Your staff or board members have been active in the state and national library associations and personally know or are aware of potential candidates.

- An external consultant cannot know the details of your situation as well as you do.

If you are considering engaging a consultant to help with a search and transition but do not know where to start, appendix 6.1 is a list of tasks from a request for proposal sent by a library client. It provides a clear picture of the work that must be done—whether by trustees, staff, or consultant.

Primary Tasks of the Preparation Phase

In this phase, you begin looking at yourself and your library. Taking the time to assess the library's strategy, culture, and governance honestly supports and guides the succession planning process. It also helps your library board's capacity building and development process.

IDENTIFY LIBRARY VULNERABILITIES

This is an excellent time to take a realistic look at the state of the library and to design and implement strategies where they are needed. For example, this might be the time to create a position of deputy or assistant director—perhaps a step the director had been avoiding. Or it might be a good time to create an advisory board for marketing, or fund-raising—if the assessment identifies these as areas of weakness. Ensure that the library's financial and HR systems are in order, so that the library's daily operations can run smoothly during any period of interim leadership.

SOLIDIFY THE MANAGEMENT TEAM

This is also a time to think about staffing in light of what is required to achieve the strategic direction. For example, suppose there is a gap in marketing competencies at the staff and leadership levels, and strategies to move the library forward indicate a need for marketing expertise. In that case it would be appropriate to establish a plan to develop these competencies in the senior staff, agree to hire a senior staff person with these competencies, or retain the services of a marketing consultant. You may realize some salary savings in the turnover of the director position, and now is the time to use whatever financial flexibility is associated with her departure. But whether the changes you need cost money or not, consider what changes should be made in leadership, systems, staffing, or structure to ease the director's transition into your library and her ability to hit the ground running.

Also at this time, the board should ensure that there is staff or board backup for key director functions. It is also critical that administrative systems (especially financial and human resources) are in order, so that the library can operate effectively during the transition to a new director, which often involves a period when the library must function with interim leadership.

ASSESS STAFF FOR LEADERSHIP POTENTIAL

Whether or not you have a succession plan in place, you should ask:

- Are there current employees who have the potential to fill any given position? Now? After a formal training and development process?

- Are these employees interested and motivated to pursue this growth opportunity?
- Will the succession planning process in which your library is engaging put in place a formal training and development process to cultivate these new leaders?

IDENTIFY THE LIBRARY'S BROAD STRATEGIC DIRECTIONS

Where are you in implementing the strategic plan? How are your customers and partners responding? Is the annual performance evaluation for the director tied to progress measured against your strategic initiatives? Is there a process for the new director to provide input to the plan?

BUILD THE BOARD'S LEADERSHIP ABILITIES

Is your board operating at an optimal level? Is there a job description for the trustees? Does the board have trouble making decisions or working through conflict? Is there agreement about the kind of authority you are prepared to give the next director and what kind of accountability mechanisms you should consider to ensure responsible board oversight? Assess board governance practices and organizational health, looking at mission, vision, and strategic and operational planning processes. This is an ideal time to build the leadership capacity of the board and its members. A board member with organizational or board development skills can do this, although you might prefer to use an objective outsider to help you address these often complex, difficult, and very human issues.

Using a consultant to interview the departing director as well as individual board members in confidence can really assist the process of moving ahead quickly. The consultant can use this information to help move the board forward in its thinking about roles, relationships, and how board members can individually and collectively support the library and its director.

BACK UP THE LIBRARY DIRECTOR'S KEY RELATIONSHIPS

Too often we find that the library director is the only person who knows key elected and appointed government officials, important community leaders, grantors, and executive directors of other partners. This is the time to make sure that staff and board members also know and have connections with these leaders.

PREPARE A COMMUNICATIONS PLAN

This is one of the most important steps. Communications to all key stakeholders (city/county officials, higher education leadership, board of trustees, Friends of the Library, library foundation, community leaders, and staff) should be ongoing, sincere, and transparent. Updates at each step in the process are critical. Connect with stakeholders (internal and in the community); talk to them about their needs and expectations for a new director in your community. Determine by whom and how communication will be handled. Board members may develop the plan or assign communication responsibilities to a board committee or staff member to be coordinated.

The communications plan you prepare now will be used regularly and often with staff, board members, and all stakeholders is to keep them up to date on the status of the search and transition. It should utilize all of your library's communication channels, such as your website and intranet, newsletter, and news releases. Ultimately, it will

- Announce why the director is leaving and highlight her many accomplishments.
- Announce the formation of a search committee.
- Invite community input regarding possible attributes for success, candidates, and organizational priorities.
- Circulate the profile and encourage applicants to apply.
- Provide status reports.
- Announce selection of the new director and let the community know how they can meet her.

At every milestone in the process, your communications plan should answer these questions: who needs to know what is happening, and how do we tell them?

SET FINANCIAL PARAMETERS

Discuss possible financial and budgetary issues for the succession (hiring costs, severance package costs for the exiting director, training and development and compensation package for the new director, fee for a search or transition consultant if used).

DEAL WITH THE PERSONAL AND PROFESSIONAL BARRIERS FOR THE DEPARTING DIRECTOR

Issues might be the degree to which the director is emotionally and financially prepared for retirement or the best exit strategy to make all parties feel good about the ending. You will want to help make the departing director's transition as easy as possible, especially if she is appreciated throughout the community and has served for a long time.

Set a fixed departure date. Everyone needs to be able to move forward, and there is much work to do. Or, you may even decide to continue some new kind of working arrangement with the departing director, redefining what retirement means. In that case, all parties want and need clarity about what the new arrangements and roles are—and are not.

Make plans now for when and how you will say good-bye, publicly and graciously, to the departing director. Celebrate her successes and contributions.

//

EXAMPLE: ABC COUNTY PUBLIC LIBRARY

Whether you are working with a consultant or doing the work yourselves, the first thing to look at is context. We use ABC County Public Library's recruitment process as an example. ABC County Public Library is a medium-sized, top-flight library with whom we worked on succession planning. The library was in stable condition; no factors at the time led the board or staff to think they needed a succession plan for their staff or library director. The director was motivated to develop a succession plan by an aging senior staff, the board of trustees by a desire for good governance. Interviews with senior staff and members of the board, data analysis of staff demographics (age, eligibility for retirement, replacement for key tasks/positions, leadership development programs in place, etc.), the library's strategic plan, and a sense that community needs were changing led to an understanding of the context of the system as summarized below.

STAFF CONTEXT

- The library director is an effective, nationally respected, long-term employee with a good relationship with the community, board, and staff.
- Many members of ABC's senior staff are nearing retirement age or eligibility for retirement. Although the director is not planning to leave her position in the short term, the board, as part of its governance responsibility, wishes to ensure that a plan is in place "in the event something happens."
- The director has major fund-raising responsibilities, which she handles with little staff involvement or support.
- Most senior staff members are long term as well as strong. Several are cross-trained and have a big-picture perspective of the library, but most understand and care about only their own department. None currently has the skills or relationships to work with current or prospective funders or grantees, elected officials, or the county administrator, and only the director of marketing has ever engaged in legislative activity at the local or state level.
- There is no identified heir apparent to the position of library director from among the library's senior staff.
- ABC is currently updating its strategic plan, and systemwide succession planning has begun.

BOARD OF TRUSTEES CONTEXT

- The library board of trustees wishes to collect community data in order to evaluate perceived shifts in changing community demographics, wants, and needs.
- The board has limited capacity to support the library in the (limited) number of members (five), skills, time, and professional support that would ordinarily be available to augment the talents and experience of senior staff.[1]
- Although there is little evidence of micromanagement, roles, responsibilities, and expectations of board members are not clear. There are no explicit job descriptions for board members or officers, and committee responsibilities are vague.
- One member of the board has quite a bit of experience with transitions.
- The library director and board chair communicate regularly and effectively.

(cont.)

EXAMPLE: ABC COUNTY PUBLIC LIBRARY (cont.)

We suggested questions and steps to prepare ABC County Public Library for a library director succession. We reminded the leadership that a side benefit of engaging in this process is that it helps build capacity by taking stock, opening up to new strategic directions, and making changes based on current and anticipated challenges and opportunities. The steps we recommended included the following:

1. Complete the library's strategic plan; obtain board approval and support.
2. Engage in board capacity building and development work. Look at effectiveness, leadership, and skills needed in support of library operations. Ask the hard questions pertaining to governance, library culture, strategic direction, and others (such as those outlined above). To this end, we suggested that ABC Library do the following:

   - Hold a board retreat with senior staff to engage in this assessment.
   - Given that the board had only five members, we suggested the creation of an advisory task force with skills in marketing and finance, areas identified for strengthening in the board assessment process, to augment the skills of the board. Although not an explicitly stated outcome, we also saw this as an opportunity for the board to audition potential members and at minimum to think about the kinds of skills needed to fill upcoming board vacancies.

3. Continue its succession planning process (library-wide) as well as incorporate a leadership development component to tap and develop staff at all levels of the library as soon as feasible. Not only does this action increase staff retention, but also a leadership pipeline emerges and staff members assume higher levels of responsibility with increased performance. Through this process, capacity is built, and the library is strengthened.
4. Learn if any members of the library's senior staff aspire to the position of library director or other leadership role. Depending on relationships, this could be done by the HR department or by the departing director. We have seen it done by both, as well as by an external consultant in the process of creating a succession plan or leadership development program.
5. Integrate succession planning into the strategic plan and training and development plans.
6. We also suggested that ABC Public Library's director (and senior staff) take some actions:

   - Prepare an organizational overview and an executive profile, defining critical competencies, knowledge, skills, and abilities as well as desired management style and outcomes for the position.
   - Align position descriptions with the library's human resource and strategic plans.
   - Consider any changes to the organizational structure. In this case we asked if it was time to consider a model that included a deputy director/COO so that the director could devote more time to external relations. We also suggested that the library consider centralized collection development and programming in order to free up staff time to devote to customer service, outreach, and specialized services to a new immigrant population as well as homeschoolers.

/// PHASE II: RECRUITMENT AND SELECTION

Primary Tasks of the Recruitment and Selection Phase

As soon as the library director announces her intention to leave the system and sets a date for so doing, the recruitment and selection process begins. Figure 6.2 presents a basic outline of this process, and you may also be able to use it to record the progress of your own recruitment. We elaborate on some elements of the process below.

You may find it useful to adapt your process outline into a meeting schedule for the search committee, such as in figure 6.3. This makes a nice overview to use in your communications plan with internal stakeholders as well.

DEVELOP AN UP-TO-DATE JOB DESCRIPTION

Although your inclination may be to reach for the departing director's job description, resist the temptation. Instead of looking to the past and what was, focus on the future. Look forward toward the library's aspirations and then shape the job, and job description, around your current and future leadership needs. What are the core values, beliefs, and assumptions about how the library operates that are important for the new director to understand? What are the "non-negotiable" behaviors that the director should uphold and nurture? What current processes and activities create the most frustration, confusion, or dysfunctional behavior within the library that the board wants the director to change? Does the new director need to fit the current culture, or is she expected to change it? How? (See "Questions to Help You Find a New Library Director" below.)

Completing a profile of the ideal candidate helps you update the library director's job description as well

---

FIGURE 6.2

LIBRARY DIRECTOR RECRUITMENT PROCESS OUTLINE

1. Position Description
   a. Develop ideal candidate characteristics.
   b. Revise and finalize position description.
   c. If desired, develop web-based survey tool to solicit input on library director knowledge, skills, abilities, and competencies.

   Time line Finalize position description by _____

   Finalize survey tool by _____

2. Decisions Regarding Recruitment Responsibilities
   a. Determine whether to hire search or transition consultants.
   b. Determine whether assistance is available from local government/university officials.
   c. Which tasks will board members perform? Who will handle each?
   d. Will HR or others staff the process? Who, and which tasks?

   Time line Decisions made by _____

3. Identification of Potential Candidates
   a. Share position description and candidate characteristics with key constituents to garner input and names of potential candidates, including

   library board of trustees

   past board members

   funders

   ALA, PLA, ACRL, state library associations, etc.

   state library

   other local or regional libraries

   other key constituents as appropriate
   b. Advertise according to any institutional or government/civil service rules and channels.

   Time line Begin position description distribution week of _____

   Résumés will be accepted through _____

4. Screening of Candidates
   a. Develop consistent screening criteria and methodology based on position description and candidate characteristics to evaluate remaining candidates.

   (cont.)

FIGURE 6.2 (cont.)

    b. Establish interview guidelines and the key questions you plan to ask.

       Time line Review and finalize criteria, methodology, and questions by _____

    c. Perform an initial "paper screening" of potential candidates to match past experience to position description of ideal candidate characteristics.

       Time line Perform "paper screening" by _____

    d. Decide if you will conduct screening interviews by phone or in person.

    e. Determine individual(s) to conduct screening interviews—search committee members or outside consultant (please note that staff is not suggested as an option).

    f. Establish process for selecting no more than three lead candidates for the library director position.

       Time line Screen, review, and select lead candidates by _____

    g. Conduct reference and general background checks on lead candidates.

       Time line Have background results by _____

5. Search committee/full board interviews of lead candidates

    a. Conduct interviews of lead candidates by search committee or full board of trustees.

       Time line Conduct interviews on _____

6. Staff and Community Review of Final Candidates

    a. Finalists (separately) hold open forums to which staff members are invited to listen and ask questions. Staff is asked for their written feedback to be sent to the chair of the search committee.

    b. In an open or by-invitation forum, members of the community also have an opportunity to hear from candidates and ask questions from their perspective. Library systems might also consider hosting a cocktail party or other event where community members and staff can get to know the finalists on a less formal basis.

       Time line Public events scheduled on _____

7. Final Decision/Offer

    a. Executive committee makes final decision and offer to candidate.

       Time line Offer made by _____

8. Formal and informal meet and greets of new library director for staff, board, and key constituents

       Time line Meet and greets scheduled on _____

as recruitment materials such as job postings. Craft a profile by answering these questions.

- What are the desired experiences and qualifications of the director?
- How are your library's values and needs matched to the director?
- What is exceptional about your library and why is *this job* a wonderful opportunity?
- What leadership skills and competencies are unique to the library's needs and challenges?
- What are the key attributes needed (e.g., visionary, seasoned manager who provides stability and structure, turnaround expert, transformational change agent, entrepreneur, community builder, strategic thinker/actor)?
- Does the new director have to be a librarian?
- Does she need to be politically astute?
- Does she need to have skills in fund development?
- Does she need to be skilled in working with a union?
- How does the director attend to the board's feelings and needs?
- How does the director envision changes in organizational functioning?
- How does the director communicate and interact with the board?

Appendix 6.2 is a public library director job description and is used with the permission of that director. It is tailored to one library's specific situation and goes so far as to indicate by weighted values how the board of trustees wants the new director to spend her time. Your board might ask the library's HR director to gather some examples from other libraries that should be suitable models.

APPOINT A SELECTION COMMITTEE

Such a task force, appointed by the board, might be composed of members of the board as well as key constituents such as county elected or appointed officials, the school system superintendent, the director of the county's literacy group, the head of the United Way, a teenager, and a representative from the chamber of commerce. The library's HR director staffs the

---

FIGURE 6.3

SEARCH COMMITTEE, OVERVIEW OF MEETING SCHEDULE

1. Kick-off session: 1½-hour phone session, week of September 3

Agenda

    Introductions

    Review of process

    Review and finalize candidate selection rubric

    Review and finalize candidate screening process

2. Initial candidate review: 1-hour phone session, week of September 24

Agenda

    Check in on résumés received

    Review of web survey results

    Determine if enough qualified candidates to move to next steps

3. Candidate review and selection of interviewees: 2-hour in-person meeting, week of October 15

Agenda

    Review of initial candidate screening interviews relative to selection rubric

    Select no more than six final candidates to be interviewed by committee

    Outline final candidate interview process/questions

4. Final candidate interviews: two half-day sessions, Thursday, November 1, and Tuesday, November 6

Agenda

    Conduct interviews with each candidate

    Complete post-interview debriefings based on selection rubric

    Recommend no more than two final candidates to continue process

5. Final candidate recommendation to board of trustees: 1½-hour phone or in-person, week of November 17

Agenda

    Review feedback from staff and key constituent meetings with two final candidates

    Recommend final candidate to board of trustees

committee process. The charge for this group is very specific: identify and prioritize the key competencies, knowledge, skills, and abilities that the next library director should possess *before* advertising the position. Input from the library's key constituencies is important to this process. Ultimately, the full board will interview the final two or three candidates. When finalists are brought in for interviews, the selection committee members will attend public presentations or meet-and-greet sessions and provide feedback to the board, to help them make a better decision.

Should you use staff in the recruitment process? There are differences of opinion about how and to what extent staff should be involved in the leadership selection and transition process. We believe, again,

that staff should be kept informed and that ongoing communication is important to staff at all levels, but that they should not play a deciding role in selection. We strongly support Tom Gilmore's thoughtful perspective: "The only universally wrong step a board can take (and many do) is not to have thought through how the staff will be involved and be kept informed at all stages of the process."[2] Gilmore suggests that staff should be very involved in assessing the library's strategic challenges and identifying the characteristics needed of the director as well as in recommending candidates and resources for recruitment. Staff should also be invited to meet the final candidates, often as part of an interview process, and provide their advice and input. However, the final selection should not

QUESTIONS TO HELP YOU FIND A NEW LIBRARY DIRECTOR

Tom Gilmore suggests ten questions that should be asked that will help specify the desired characteristics of a new leader and place the job in a strategic context. Adapted for the library world, they are as follows:

1. What are the strategic challenges facing this library leader in the coming six months? Year? Two to three years?
2. How would you know or suspect within the first three months whether your choice was going to be successful? What would the early indications be?
3. What people and roles does this person need to interact with? What specific behaviors does each of them want from this leader? Where might conflicts arise?
4. What behaviors, attitudes, and skills are required to be effective in relating to the major stakeholder group? They will not be the same for each. Consider staff, board members, county officials, funders, and others.
5. What are the leaders' day-to-day tasks and responsibilities? How does the overall flow of work occur? What particular skills would add value? Which ones are essential?
6. What are the magnitudes of the major internal tasks, such as budget size and complexity, numbers of employees supervised, total employees, and other important measures? What is the size of your service area

(community, population, or faculty and student base)? Your circulation? Note that these activities may very well be different if there is, or will be, a deputy director or COO in place.
7. Given your forward-looking perspective and strategy, what will be the typical daily, weekly, monthly, and annual activities of the job?
8. What are five to seven key adjectives that describe the ideal candidate?
9. What skills and past experience must the new director possess? Which of them are the nonnegotiables? Which are the "nice to haves"?
10. Sometimes we like to start with this question: where do you want the library to be in five years, and what skills will be important to have to get there? (Consider viewing the responses to the second part of this question when it is time to bring new trustees on board. Letting the appointing authority know what skills would be helpful to support the library may lead to selection of board members who can augment the library's skills base with some helpful and timely expertise.)

Source: Adapted from Thomas N. Gilmore, *Finding and Retaining Your Next Chief Executive: Making the Training Work* (Washington, D.C.: BoardSource, 1992), 18.

be made by staff; that is a decision to be made by the board of trustees.

In general, we agree that staff should not serve on the search committee. If your library has an HR director, it would be appropriate to ask her to staff the process and work directly with the members of the search committee. If not working with a search or transition consultant the HR director should, at a minimum, support the search committee by engaging in the following tasks:

- Work closely with the committee chair throughout the process in a support capacity.
- Issue invitations to serve on the search committee, prepare agendas (with committee chair), and arrange for meeting room space, refreshments, and so forth.
- Take notes at meetings; send to committee members.

- After search committee conversations, draft the job description and other collateral public relations materials.
- Help prepare the communications plan for staff and community.
- Advertise the job opening as appropriate, for example, in *Library Journal, Library Hotline*.
- Determine how and when candidates will receive communications throughout the process, and who will communicate with candidates.
- Screen résumés against established criteria.
- Prepare summaries of highly qualified candidates for the search committee.
- Provide sample interview questions and any other preparation needed by interviewers.
- Schedule telephone screening interviews on behalf of the search committee.

THE TOP JOB

The Columbus Metropolitan Library board of trustees is (rightly) now concerned about succession planning for Patrick Losinski, the library's executive director. They have asked him to submit a plan that includes three different scenarios: replacement in ten years, replacement in five years, and an unexpected, immediate emergency. This is an important process for all directors and their boards to go through.

It started with a frank discussion with the board of trustees to clarify their philosophy of succession management at the most senior level. Did they wish to identify a few potential candidates among the leadership team and groom them for this position? Or did they want to continue the philosophy endorsed for the organization as a whole: invest in the growth and development of all people, but without an implied promise of elevation? The board reaffirmed its philosophy of open competition to fill this position, believing that it is in the best interest of the library to open this (and all) positions to both external and internal candidates. "We have a business to run," Losinski noted. "Individual interests should not supersede the needs of the enterprise."

Once the philosophy was clear, Losinski talked with the members of his leadership team. He identified some who could engage as coleaders in case of an

emergency. Several members of his leadership team expressed interest in development toward the executive director slot should it become vacant in the next five years. Going out ten years, the recommendation for replacement was to look beyond the current leadership team.

Step three was to prepare profiles of the identified staff members, including their role, tenure with Columbus Metropolitan Library, work history, educational background, strengths, accomplishments at the library, budget managed, direct reports and number of indirect reports, developmental opportunities, and current salary.

Finally, Losinski provided the members of the board with a list of recruitment firms and other resources.

"I feel great," said Losinski when asked how he felt about going through this process. On one hand, of course, it is a crucial exercise for the library's board and chief executive to accept. On the other hand, I wondered, was it a little like planning for one's demise? Losinski clearly focused on the former, proud to be part of a team capable of handling something that is sensitive *and* an important part of his, and the board's, responsibility. He did not find the exercise at all threatening, seeing instead the greater good of sustainability and growth of leadership.

- Schedule and arrange interviews for finalists.
- Check references.
- Suggest, based on data, a fair and equitable compensation and benefits package for the person selected. Determine who will handle the offer and salary negotiations.

The HR director must act with the highest integrity and utmost confidentiality throughout this process. You may wonder if another staff member could take on this role. The answer is possibly, and probably not. In our experience, general staff are accustomed to and respect the barrier of silence from HR staff about all personnel issues. They do not have the same expectations of other staff, nor are other staff members accustomed to this level of confidentiality. Keep in mind that the confidentiality extends beyond your library. Many applying for the position will not make their interest known at their present workplace. Recruiting at this level must be handled delicately and with the utmost confidence. Many high-potential and highly visible candidates working in other libraries will not apply unless confidentially can be guaranteed unless and until they are named as a finalist.

There are other considerations as well. Consider the plight of one system that did not have a full-time HR manager. With the resignation of the library director, the library's four senior managers were asked to function as a team in an "interim director" role. We worked with this team to help them clarify roles, responsibilities, and expectations. The group worked together rather effectively—until a shift in roles occurred. One of the team members was assigned by the board to work with the search consultant and staff the search committee. Although this individual was capable, other team members became jealous and insecure because they were not privy to the same information as their colleague. This made for a less than effective process and also affected the team's longer-term working relationships.

PLAN THE SEARCH, AND SEARCH

Plan a national, or at least regional, search. To assist with this, the board asks the library director and senior staff for a list of five to ten key library leaders to talk with who either might be interested in the job or could recommend other viable candidates. Through conference attendance and journal reading, staff and board members also keep an eye out for current and emerging leaders. The library announces the position vacancy formally, using a variety of communications channels including its website, statewide and national electronic discussion lists, and professional journals. The library's public relations staff helps by developing a piece that sells the position, the library, and the community to potential applicants. (See appendix 6.3 for an example developed by consultant June Garcia for the Santa Cruz Public Libraries.)

WHAT TO DO IN AN UNPLANNED TRANSITION: THE FIRST 72 HOURS

1. Convene the executive committee or board of trustees to decide/affirm who the acting library director is.
2. Clarify the responsibilities of the acting director and who on the board will provide supervision and support.
3. Clearly communicate to the board and staff (and, if appropriate, city, county, or other officials) about a short-term plan and a time line for developing a longer-term plan to find the next permanent library director.
4. Review and make changes to check-signing authority and related security issues.
5. Communicate with external stakeholders about the circumstances of the departure and the interim plans.
6. Appoint a transition/search committee chair and committee and begin the broader work of assessing the library and commencing an effective succession planning and transition process.

Source: Adapted from Thomas N. Gilmore, *Finding and Retaining Your Next Chief Executive: Making the Training Work* (Washington, D.C.: BoardSource, 1992), 10.

Note the individual responsible for each recruitment step (as in figure 6.2). Add more time, because a search always takes longer than one thinks it will. The board can take advantage of any additional time to plan and prepare adequately.

IDENTIFY AN INTERIM LIBRARY DIRECTOR

This should not be a candidate for the permanent position. Establish a separate job description for the interim position that articulates scope, boundaries, duties, and responsibilities. If the interim director is a member of the library's senior staff, the library should provide a salary supplement in the form of a separate check or temporary pay increase (rather than part of base pay).

COMMUNICATE

It is critical to begin implementing the communications plan you began to develop in the preparation phase so that all of the library's key stakeholders—both internal and external—are kept informed throughout the process. Figure 6.4 is one example.

/// PHASE III: TRANSITION

Trustees need to be aware that a leadership transition is a time of stress and anxiety for staff, especially senior staff. They will have many questions that are rarely articulated: What is my role? Will she like me? Will she bring in her own leadership team? Will I have a job here? Will I like and be a part of any changes in direction or strategy? Where will I fit in? Is it time for me to get off the bus? Rumors fly and water cooler chatting increases substantially. Having a schedule, sticking to it, and communicating regularly help to allay the anxiety.

Another thing that reduces staff anxiety is helping the leader get off to a good start—ensuring that she too has a smooth transition. Board members set the tone for that transition and for how they will work with the incoming director. From the time they offer the job and begin negotiating a salary and employment agreement, they are beginning to orient the new director to the culture of the organization. Thus, they must give some thought to structuring the kind of orientation that serves their board, the library, and the new director well. Considering these questions can help:

- Who on the board will serve as the director's primary contact for management and coaching? How—and how often—will the board expect to hear from or meet with the director?
- Who on the board can help introduce the director to community partners, university or local government department heads, and other valuable people outside the library? How

---

FIGURE 6.4

EXAMPLE OF A SUCCINCT UPDATE

MEMO TO LIBRARY STAFF SENT ON BEHALF OF MARY SMITH, BOARD CHAIR

I wanted to quickly update all of you on our Library Director recruitment process. The Search Committee met earlier this week and reviewed the résumés and initial screening interview results on the seven most qualified candidates. From that meeting, we selected three individuals for the Search Committee to interview next week. After those interviews are completed, the Search Committee will determine whether one or all of these candidates will become finalists.

We have sent the candidates copies of our new strategic and facilities plan as well as a variety of additional background information. We've asked the three candidates, based on their review of this material, to outline for us what their 90-day entry strategy would be; how they would help the Library realize our new vision and mission; and what steps they would take to move the organization's key priorities forward.

I will be back in touch after those interviews are completed and the Committee has had an opportunity to determine next steps.

As always, if you have any questions, please do not hesitate to contact me at marysmith@xyz.net or 999-1234.

can the board pave the way for the director to establish her new network of connections?

- What role should senior (or other) staff take in orienting the director?
- What are the performance goals and expectations for and with the newly hired director at three, six, and twelve months? What mechanisms will be used to review performance and share feedback?
- How quickly can the new library director be scheduled to go through the same orientation process that all staff attend?

Remember that your new director will have a list of tasks to undertake shortly after coming on board that will be a part of her orientation to the job, the staff, the community, and the board of trustees. These important activities include (if a public library director) meeting local elected and appointed officials, community leaders, partners, funders, media representatives, and local and statewide library directors. She will also want to meet all staff quickly, especially those who report directly to her, and visit all branches; spend time reviewing the budget, policies, HR policies, strategic, facilities, marketing, technology, and other important library documents; meet with all board members one-to-one and as a group; and review bylaws, the trustee manual, and other relevant documents. Be prepared to help your new director into each of these tasks.

Finally, don't forget that there is another element to being new in a community. If you have ever moved to take a new job, whether across town or across the country, you know that your orientation to the community is not complete until you find a trustworthy auto mechanic, the best bakery, a good handyman, a great hairdresser, the physicians who take your new health insurance plan, and so on. Your new director will not really feel at home until she knows the territory, so be sure to let her know that, when she needs a local recommendation, you stand ready to help.

/// EMERGENCY SUCCESSION PLAN

Sometimes a surprise happens: the director lets you know, with little or no warning, that she is leaving the job for another opportunity, family issues, health, or other reasons. In the worst case, she has been struck by a bus or challenged by a major illness, and there is little time to prepare. That is why it is important to have in place, at a minimum, an emergency plan.

The trustees of one of our academic library clients made the mistake of not worrying about succession planning since the library director, who was 60 years old, said that he was planning to stay for another five years, at least until age 65. They did not want to upset the director, whom they valued highly, by raising the issue of succession planning before he was ready for it. And what happened? They were surprised—and so was he! His daughter had triplets, and he and his wife decided to move cross-country to help her. The moral is clear: every library should have at least an emergency plan for library director succession at all times.

An emergency succession plan ensures the continuous coverage of executive and administrative duties critical to the ongoing operations of the library and its services to its customers or patrons and funders, political officials, and others by outlining policies and procedures for the temporary appointment of an acting executive director.

There are several key components to such a plan. It should identify the priority functions of the library director, both the general functions of a library (or any) leader as well as tasks that are exclusive to your library. Second, the plan should specify what happens in the event of a short- or long-term absence of the library director. This includes notification of trustees, the process that the board or board president begins once notified, the compensation and authority of an acting director (as specified in a previously developed job description), and provisions for recruiting a new director.

Another component of the emergency succession plan should be the identification of one or two senior staff members capable of appointment to the position of acting or interim director. If the board decides to divide the functions of the director, these should be clearly delineated in writing. If necessary, any provisions for cross-training staff to help them fulfill priority director functions should be made. Such cross-training should begin with the adoption of the plan.

Finally, a communications plan and protocol should be outlined, including categories of constituents (e.g., public officials, customers) who should be personally notified, how (in writing, personally, by phone) and by whom (the board, interim director, other), and in what time frame.

If the succession plan has to be implemented in an emergency, the board should ensure that the following are in place:

- Board members who have experience in search/transition

- Senior staff member(s) or others who can serve as interim director
- An up-to-date job description for the position of interim or acting library director
- A key contact list to notify individuals and communicate plans/status
- Written procedures for conducting a search (with and without a search firm) and for the selection process
- Identification of a key spokesperson for the library board

/// SUMMARY

There is work to be done to plan and implement a succession planning process for any library. With guidance and following the tasks outlined in this chapter, the board of trustees, library director and leadership staff should engage in important conversations that answer many of the questions posed in this chapter. Answers to those questions will shape the process and the outcome for the new library director and the community served by the library. The time invested at the outset will yield greater dividends than anything you can produce while addressing an unexpected emergency vacancy.

APPENDIX 6.1

Minimum Consultant Requirements for a Library Director Search and Transition Process

THE CONSULTANT WILL:

Assist the Board of Trustees in determining Library needs.

1. Review the Library's current strategic plan, Facilities Study, and other information about the Library and its community.
2. Facilitate a meeting of the Library Board to identify characteristics wanted in a new Director and an application process likely to identify and attract such a person.
3. Solicit the opinions of library staff and others as appropriate, as to characteristics needed and wanted in a new director.

Assist the Board of Trustees in the recruitment of candidates.

4. Develop recruitment materials such as advertisements for professional journals and websites.
5. Place advertisements and distribute other recruitment materials.
6. Develop and send letters to prospective candidates.
7. Prepare list of individuals who should be encouraged to apply for the position and distribute recruitment information to them.
8. Develop and implement a process to acknowledge receipt of applications and to help ensure candidate confidentiality.

Assist the Board of Trustees in the applicant assessment process.

9. Facilitate Board's screening of applicants by developing appropriate quantitative and qualitative candidate assessment tools (e.g., rubrics, checklists) to determine which candidates will be invited to participate in the interview process.

Assist the Board of Trustees in screening applications.

10. Facilitate by telephone conference call the Board's screening of applicants to determine which candidates will be invited to participate in the interview process.
11. Recommend to the Board the names of the candidates who should be interviewed.
12. Check references of each finalist before any interviews are scheduled and convey results to the Board.
13. Notify candidates being invited to final interviews.
14. Notify candidates who are not being invited to final interviews.

Assist the Board of Trustees in conducting the interview process.

15. Propose interview process and time line to the Board and revise based on Board's comments and suggestions.

16. Coordinate with library staff the preparation of a persuasive orientation packet of library and local information that will be distributed to finalists prior to the interviews.

17. Contact finalists to be interviewed and review interview process with them.

18. Make all travel and hotel arrangements for all interviewees.

19. Develop documents to be used during final interviews, including interview questions, scoring sheets, and response forms to be used by open-forum participants. (See "Assist Board in the applicant assessment process," above.)

20. Develop schedule for final interviews including specific times for

    a. Orientation tours

    b. Interviews with the Library Board

    c. Open forums to allow staff and invited guests to hear presentations by and interact with each finalist

    d. Coordinate the interview process, attending events and participating in interviews and other related activities

Facilitate the Board of Trustees' selection of the new Director.

21. Facilitate the Board's selection of the best candidate from among the finalists.

22. Provide assistance to the Library Board, as requested, in negotiation of employment terms with the finalist selected to be the new director.

23. Conduct a pre-hire background check of the preferred candidate, including [credit check], academic credentials, driving records, and county and federal records for past or current criminal or civil cases.

24. Notify other finalists of appointment of new director.

25. Assist the Board with the development of a transition plan, which also provides an orientation for the new director.

Clerical and administrative tasks

26. Perform all clerical and administrative tasks associated with the search (writing and sending letters, placing ads, making travel arrangements, preparing packets for Board review, tracking and summarizing responses, etc.) with the exception of the compiling and sending of persuasive packets about the library system and the local area and the provision of information to the consultant (as stated in the Library responsibilities, below).

THE LIBRARY WILL:

1. Develop, provide, and arrange for the consultant to receive in a timely and expeditious manner and suitable format for use and review by the consultant, at no expense to consultant, copies of all documents, materials, policies, and other data and information necessary to consultant's performance of the above tasks.

Source: Adapted from an RFP issued by the Somerset County (Md.) Library board; used with permission.

APPENDIX 6.2
Omaha Library Director Job Description

I. Basic Purpose: The Library Director leads community and library staff efforts to meet present and future library needs of the metropolitan community by optimizing use of available resources while striving for increased resources in order to reach or exceed the median level of services within Omaha's peer-group libraries.

II. Dimensions of the Job:

A. Serving library needs of a 450,000-citizen metropolitan community.

B. Lead a staff of approximately 110 full-time and 140 part-time (65 FTE) employees.

C. Oversee a library collection of approx. 2.5 million items.

D. Manage a ten-library system, with an annual budget of approximately $10 million.

III. Job Qualifications: To be fully qualified, the Library Director should have:

A. *Education:* A Master's Degree in Library Science from an American Library Association–accredited institution, or an equivalent degree, so as to understand library operations as well as the needs of organizational leadership.

B. *Experience:* At least five years of library-related experience that includes the demonstrated ability to successfully plan, organize, motivate, control, and lead within a library environment.

C. *Personal qualities:* Demonstrated personal qualities that include the following:

1. Understanding of library needs and interests.

2. Knowledge of how outstanding libraries are operated.

3. Ability to understand and deal well with diverse peoples, including community and political leaders, volunteers, employees, and current or potential library users.

4. Communications skills that are down to earth, honest, open, clear, and persuasive.

5. Technologically literate and able to direct technology use productively.

6. Problem solver through use of motivated team effort.

7. Able to plan creatively for future trends and needs.

8. Optimistic and "can-do" by nature. Gets things done!

9. Self-starter who likes to keep people well informed and lead by personal example—of highest ethical character.

10. Likes to work hard. Realizes that this is an FLSA exempt leadership position. Willing to invest the time to do it well.

11. Without physical (as set forth in Exhibit A), personal, or legal difficulties that could negatively impact job performance in any way.

IV. Specific Job Circumstances: This position encounters the following realities that are specific to leading Omaha Public Library system:

A. The Omaha Library Director reports directly to the OPL Board of Trustees, which by law is authorized to "take charge of, manage, and control the Omaha Public Library." Members of this nine-person board are appointed by Omaha's mayor, confirmed by its City Council, and serve a three-year term that can be extended for only three additional years (maximum time on board of six years). Appointees generally have skills and experience in areas not directly related to library operations. Thus educating and clearly informing Trustees is an important responsibility of the Library Director.

B. The vast majority of library funding comes from Omaha's General Fund and requires approval of the Mayor and City Council. This political process has historically resulted in annual per capita library funding below the median of comparable peer-city libraries. The Library Director is thus challenged to achieve improved funding while managing available resources to best achieve Board approved library objectives.

C. Omaha's library staff is represented by two city government bargaining unions and is subject to City personnel policies. The Library Director must manage these interests while striving to develop a motivated, well-organized, cohesive, and productive library staff.

V. Job Evaluation: The dimensions and requirements of this position are set forth below:

A. *Know-how:*

1. Technical—acceptable job performance requires a solid understanding of library principles, methods, practices, materials, and trends.

2. Managerial—acceptable performance requires internal and external integration and coordination of functions affecting the success of Omaha's library system.

3. Human Relations—acceptable performance requires a high degree of understanding of interpersonal relationships and motivation of stakeholders.

4. Scope—job accountabilities involve responsibilities that have long-term impact on library service to the community. The Director should provide continuity of leadership.

B. *Problem solving:*

1. Thinking Environment—approximately 60% of this job involves clearly defined thinking environments, 30% is only broadly defined by Board policy and objectives, while the remaining 10% is thinking "outside the box."

2. Thinking challenge—answers to problems that must be solved by the Director generally have known choices, although expansion of choices is also important. The challenge is more in selection of the right alternative and implementing it well.

C. *Scope:*

1. Freedom to Act—approximately 40% of this job is subject to City practice and procedure, and 60% to library policies and goals that are subject to Board approval. The Director must feel free to "stretch" for new ideas and solutions but understand where City and/or Board approval or coordination is either appropriate or required.

2. Magnitude and Impact—actions affect the entire Omaha library system, often for many years to come. No other position within the Omaha Public Library has more impact upon library services in the community than does its Director.

VI. Accountabilities: Set forth below are accountabilities that are specific to successful job performance by the Director. These should guide the day-to-day activity of the Director and will be used by the Board when evaluating the Director's performance and determining compensation.

The Board may change these accountabilities, or the required time input factors, in order to rebalance Board priorities or reflect changes to strategic or tactical plans. The Director must be very sensitive to these changes and understand their implications. This document is the Board's primary vehicle for communicating job expectations to its chief executive officer/Director and will be evaluated annually.

The Director has personal authority and responsibility for some accountabilities. These are designated below with a (P).

On others the Director's involvement is primarily through the management of others, even though final responsibility lies with the Director. These are noted with an (M).

Some require the Director to secure Board approval before implementation. An (A) is used to designate these accountabilities.

In any one year, the Board may wish the Director to emphasize certain accountabilities. These are designated below by showing the year of emphasis after the accountability. For example, [2003] would designate emphasis for the year 2003.

A. *Objectives and results* (25% of Director's time input):

1. Develop measurable input and output objectives for OPL that can be compared to objective results achieved by other public libraries. Review and adjust as needed. (A)

2. Distribute the above objectives throughout the OPL staff and assign appropriate responsibilities so that the largest possible number of employees are involved in working to achieve them. (P) [2003]

3. Measure results regularly against objectives and motivate all contributing parties toward achieving them. (M)

4. Maintain ongoing contact with directors of other well-run libraries in order to learn ways to better achieve goals that improve OPL services; then implement them. (P)

5. Regularly measure community opinions regarding library needs and how OPL is doing. Use results to improve. (M)

B. *Planning* (20% of Director's time input)

1. Maintain an ongoing knowledge of current library trends and improved service ideas. Communicate resulting recommendations to the OPL Board and staff. (P)

2. Facilitate the development, approval, and achievement of an ongoing long-term strategic plan. See that the long-term plan is reviewed and updated annually, without destroying the ongoing nature and value of previous plans. (A)

3. Facilitate the development of capital expenditure plans and their coordination with City officials. (A)

4. Lead development and implementation of annual plans for library operations. Ensure that Board priorities are emphasized appropriately in these plans. (P)

5. Organize efforts to ensure that staff members have specific current assignments aimed at achieving both long-term and short-term plans. (P) [2003]

C. *Library operations and facilities* (20% of time input)

1. Organize the OPL staff so as to optimize human resource utilization. (P) [2003]

2. Establish through personal example and sound leadership a motivated, can-do, service-oriented culture and attitude throughout the OPL staff. (P)

3. Ensure that the OPL staff is competent and well trained to manage libraries and serve public library needs. (M)

4. Control library operations so that expenditures remain within budgeted amounts. (M)

5. Control library material expenditures in order to optimize resources and best serve customer needs. (M)

6. Coordinate the construction, renovation, and maintenance of library buildings and equipment with staff and City depts. to ensure that quality ongoing service is provided. (M)

7. Monitor library service levels and make all necessary corrections to provide high-quality public service. (M)

8. Keep the OPL Board regularly informed about current operations, opportunities, problems, and proposed solutions thereto. (P)

D. *Financial management* (15% of Director's time input)

1. Direct preparation of the annual operating budget for review and approval by the OPL Board, City administration, and the City Council. Ensure estimates are as cost efficient and accurate as possible and resources are allocated to the highest and best uses. (M)

2. Lead staff efforts to identify and implement sound means of cost control and reduction. (M)

3. Seek out and strive to secure funding from sources that will complement and expand upon services that are and should be paid for by the City of Omaha. These efforts should be coordinated with those of the Omaha Public Library Foundation. (P) [2003]

4. Direct coordination of OPL financial management with all required governmental and private organizations. (M)

5. Keep the OPL Board well informed on all significant financial matters. (M)

E. *Government and community relations* (20% of time)

1. Direct efforts to maintain open and constructive communications with the State, City, County, other libraries in the metropolitan area, and community groups, in order to support improved library services. (M)

2. Seek out and develop with other organizations possible joint ventures that will provide synergies that lead to more cost-efficient and better library services. (P) [2003]

3. Develop customer-focused library services that increase public library use and market them effectively. (M)

4. Represent the OPL on the Mayor's Cabinet, if requested to do so. (P)

5. Lead staff efforts to implement OPL Board policies relating to community relations and marketing. (M)

VII. Compensation: Compensation for the Director of OPL is set by the OPL Board of Trustees and will be confirmed to the Director in writing. The Director will participate in the City's fringe benefit programs and follow City vacation and holiday schedules. The OPL Board may implement performance bonus programs for the Director if it determines their use can result in improving measurable library results.

VIII. Performance Review:

A. The Board will review job performance with the Director in November of each year, give the Director a written evaluation, and highlight areas the Board wishes to emphasize in the new year.

B. The Board's Executive Committee and the Library Director will discuss job performance issues at least quarterly.

C. The Director will submit a written status report before each monthly Board meeting.

IX. Amendments: This Position Description for the Library Director may be changed only by a majority vote of the OPL Board of Trustees.

Source: Used by permission of Rivkah Sass, Director, Omaha Public Library.

APPENDIX 6.3

Director Search Promotional Piece, Santa Cruz Public Libraries

S A N T A   C R U Z

Santa Cruz
Public Libraries
Library Director Search 2009

About the City & County Page 1	About the Library Page 2	Numbers Snapshot Page 2	Job Description Page 3	Compensation & Benefits Page 4	How to Apply Page 4

The City and the County

Santa Cruz County is located on the California coast at the north end of Monterey Bay, 65 miles south of San Francisco and 35 miles from Silicon Valley. Its natural beauty is present in pristine beaches, lush redwood forests, and rich farmland. It has an ideal Mediterranean climate with low humidity and sunshine 300 days a year. Residents and tourists alike enjoy 29 miles of beaches and six state parks providing opportunities for a multitude of recreational activities such as sailing, fishing, golf, tennis, hiking, and surfing. The Monterey Bay is part of the Monterey Bay National Marine Sanctuary, which extends from Marin County down the Big Sur Coast to Cambria. Cultural amenities include the Santa Cruz County Symphony, the Cabrillo Music Festival, Shakespeare Santa Cruz, the McPherson Museum of Art and History, and a host of other venues.

The area benefits from a diversified economy that is anchored by vibrant high technology, manufacturing, agriculture, education, and tourism. The high-quality school system includes Cabrillo Community College and the University of California at Santa Cruz.

Santa Cruz County has over 250,000 residents and includes four incorporated cities. The largest is the City of Santa Cruz, with a population of approximately 60,000. The other incorporated cities are Capitola, Scotts Valley, and Watsonville. The Santa Cruz Beach Boardwalk draws tourists, and the pedestrian-friendly downtown is filled with tree-lined streets, quaint shops, and outdoor bistros. The library's administrative offices are located in the Santa Cruz downtown in a newly renovated green commercial building, Santa Cruz' first.

The great natural beauty of the area, the temperate climate, and the vast and varied cultural resources combine to make Santa Cruz County a very desirable place to live and work.

Learn more at:

http://www.santacruz.org/index.shtml

http://www.co.santa-cruz.ca.us

http://www.ci.santa-cruz.ca.us

http://www.ci.capitola.ca.us

http://www.scottsvalley.org

(cont.)

The Library

Santa Cruz Public Libraries is a city-county library system providing the widest range of services to all county residents with the exception of residents in the City of Watsonville, who are served by an independent library. Ten libraries serve more than 200,000 residents, utilizing a budget of almost $12,500,000 to circulate over 2,000,000 items a year. Collections include materials in the usual broad range of formats, special collections of musical scores and sheet music, Californiana, and genealogical items, all to fulfill the mission of helping community residents meet their needs. Outreach is provided through a bookmobile serving preschoolers and seniors.

A staff of 134 handles about 300,000 reference questions a year, providing service six days a week in most branches. An active Friends organization recruits volunteers who donate more than 16,000 hours of service each year. These volunteers assist staff in providing over 2,000 programs from preschool story times and class visits, to "Munching with Mozart" and book discussions with author visits for adults. The Summer Reading Program features the popular Festival of the Book, as well as a kids-only book sale.

In striving to meet community needs, recent grants have focused on preschool literacy and teens. "First 5 Family Place" provides service to home care providers and day care centers, as well as special programs for preschoolers and their parents followed by meetings with professionals who coach on topics such as nutrition and reading readiness. A previous grant titled "A Place of Our Own" helped develop effective library service for young adults through switching the primary service focus of a small neighborhood library to young people.

The library system operates pursuant to a Joint Powers Agreement that includes the County of Santa Cruz and the cities of Santa Cruz, Capitola, and Scotts Valley. The governing body of the library system includes elected officials from each member jurisdiction, as well as three citizens.

Relationships among member jurisdictions are excellent, as is the relationship between the Library Board and the City of Santa Cruz. Formally, the Santa Cruz City Manager is the hiring authority for the position of Library Director, subject to the consent of the Library Board. In fact, the Library Board and City of Santa Cruz administration are working together to conduct the recruitment and select the next Library Director. This reporting and governing structure has worked very well for all parties. The larger community is highly supportive of library services, so the overall environment is positive and forward-looking.

BY THE NUMBERS: FY08/09

Facilities: 10 branches

Budget: $12.5 million

Expenditures per capita: $60.64

Staff: 134

Active borrowers: 60,589

Registered borrowers: 127,078

Registrations as % of population: 61%

Materials budget per capita: $4.01

Materials budget: $832,000

Holdings: 560,439

Circulation (FY07/08): 2,159,868

Circulation per capita: 10.5

Number of programs: 2,221

Program attendance: 41,874

Future plans include migrating to an open source integrated library system and capital projects such as expanding a branch parking lot, building a replacement branch, and assisting in the construction of two new facilities.

These are exciting times for this ambitious library system.

Learn more about the library by visiting us at http://www.santacruzpl.org

S A N T A   C R U Z

The Job

The Library Director is responsible for the strategic and day-to-day operations of the library system in accordance with the policies and regulations established by the Joint Powers Board and the City of Santa Cruz.

The Library Director:

◉ Is responsible for planning, organizing, implementing, and evaluating systemwide library and related information services to meet the needs of the community, both immediate and long range.

◉ Prepares the library's annual budget for submission to the Library Board and the City of Santa Cruz. Implements the adopted budget.

◉ Conducts the personnel administration, financial affairs, and general administration of the library system in accordance with adopted policies and procedures.

◉ Hires and supervises library employees.

◉ Maintains effective public relations with public officials, civic groups, the media, and the community.

◉ Serves as a city department head and participates in the work of the city's executive group.

Education and Experience

Qualified candidates will have:

◉ A Master's degree in Library Science from a library school accredited by the American Library Association.

◉ Five years increasingly responsible professional library experience, including three years in an administrative capacity.

The Ideal Candidate

◉ Is able to work collaboratively and harmoniously with the Library Joint Powers Board, the Friends of the Library, the staff, and other key stakeholders throughout the county in achieving library goals and objectives.

◉ Works successfully with elected and appointed government officials.

◉ Is a valuable city department head.

◉ Effectively advocates for the library and its services.

◉ Is willing and able to be an effective, visible library leader in the community.

◉ Is able to develop and communicate a shared vision of future library services.

◉ Communicates openly, clearly and concisely.

◉ Excels in developing, leading, and motivating staff.

◉ Is skilled in strategic planning and plan implementation.

◉ Empowers staff with the authority and resources to carry out delegated responsibilities.

◉ Has a demonstrated record of effective fiscal management.

◉ Has excellent project management skills.

◉ Is a creative problem solver.

◉ Makes wise and fair judgments.

◉ Is customer service oriented.

◉ Acts with a high level of integrity.

◉ Develops relationships based on dependability and honesty.

◉ Is active in professional and civic organizations.

(cont.)

SANTA CRUZ

Compensation and Benefits

The salary is negotiable from $10,747 to $13,714 per month. The City also offers an attractive benefits package including:

◉ 80 hours vacation per year for up to 5 years of service, 120 hours vacation per year for 5 to 10 years of service, and 120 hours vacation per year plus 8 hours for each year of service after 10 years to a maximum of 160 hours.

◉ 8 hours of sick leave per month.

◉ Up to 11 specific paid holidays and 24 hours of floating holidays per year.

◉ 40 hours of paid birth/adoptive leave.

◉ 80 hours of management leave per year, with the option to convert up to 60 hours to cash.

◉ $1,300 annual optional benefit for purchase of additional vacation, placement in a deferred compensation account, or cash payment.

◉ PERS medical plan, family dental, family vision, and employee assistance program.

◉ Optional benefits including: Medical and Dependent Care Reimbursement Accounts, Voluntary Life Insurance, Accident Protection, and Cancer and Critical Illness Protection.

◉ PERS 2% at 55 plan with participation in an IRS 414 (H)(2) plan. No Social Security is withheld.

◉ Deferred compensation program.

◉ $480 per month car allowance.

◉ Long-term disability insurance.

◉ $25,000 term life insurance.

◉ $500 tuition reimbursement per year.

For more details, go to www.ci.santa-cruz.ca.us/hr/specs/benefitstable.pdf

How to apply

To be considered for this exceptional opportunity, please submit a cover letter, resume, and contact information for a minimum of three references by February 25, 2009 to:

June Garcia
1195 South Harrison Street
Denver, CO 80210

Applications received by February 25, 2009 will receive first consideration. This position is open until filled.

Inquiries are welcome. Please contact June Garcia at 303-522-2225 or June@JuneGarcia.com

Photo Credits: Jim Bourne, Kyer Wiltshire, and the Santa Cruz Conference & Visitors Council

Notes

1. Typically members of a board of trustees bring expertise needed by the library. Examples may include professionals in the fields of law, marketing, fund-raising, finance, human resources, construction management (if building), information technology, and organization development. In addition, members of the board can "open the doors" to the library executive for fund-raising and community opportunities.

2. Thomas N. Gilmore, *Finding and Retaining Your Next Chief Executive: Making the Training Work* (Washington, D.C.: BoardSource, 1992), 18.

ADDITIONAL STORIES OF LIBRARY SUCCESSION PLANNING AND DEVELOPMENT PROGRAMS

FORWARD-THINKING LIBRARIES around the country are engaged in a variety of succession planning and development activities. Library directors and HR directors from eleven libraries, as well as a vice president of OCLC, generously shared some of their experiences with us, and we in turn share their stories with you. We use illustrations from Baltimore County (Md.) Public Library, Columbus (Ohio) Metropolitan Library, County of Los Angeles (Calif.) Public Library, Cuyahoga County (Ohio) Public Library, Harford County (Md.) Public Library, and the Public Library of Charlotte and Mecklenburg County (N.C.) throughout earlier chapters of the book. In this chapter we present seven more stories.

We think each organization's story is unique and will be valuable as you think about how to begin or strengthen your own succession planning and development activities. Each library is trying to grow the next generation of library leadership. Each is doing so in a way that fits its own culture and in some cases to meet very specific needs. And as you can tell from reading the stories, there is no one right way to build and implement a plan. The thing is to begin.

/// FRESNO COUNTY PUBLIC LIBRARY

The Vision of the library is that Fresno County residents of all ages will have free access to library services and materials to enhance the quality of their lives and further life-long learning.

This vision from the mission statement of Fresno County (Calif.) Public Library (FCPL) is to be taken seriously; Fresno's population is expected to experience tremendous growth. To support this increase, most of the county's branch libraries as well as central will need to expand. Libraries will need more materials, computers, and meeting rooms to better serve their communities and experienced, competent staff to support them.

Karen Bosch Cobb, county librarian, joined FCPL in 1972 and has served as director since 2003. Like so many library directors and county librarians, she looked around at the management team and saw that many could be retiring within close proximity of each other—and perhaps sooner rather than later.

The FCPL succession management and talent development experience has been colored by past good fortune. In 1998 a sales tax measure resulted in amazing growth for the library. New positions were created, new services and programs offered. The library grew from 143 to 320 staff members in a relatively short time. Prior to 1998 many of these positions were filled by baby boomers, who are a large group of the library's formal and informal leaders. After 1998 new entry-level librarians filled many new positions.

Bosch Cobb spoke of a variety of strategies the library utilizes to develop leaders, including executive training through Infopeople, the Urban Libraries Council Executive Leadership Institute, and California State Library Eureka Leadership Institute; special salary upgrades during leaves of absences; responsibility charting; serving on task forces and committees; shadowing managers; taking on lead responsibilities; growing its own librarians through the use of librarian trainee classification; participation in community leadership opportunities; one-on-one coaching to help staff seeking a promotion develop a résumé and prepare for interviews; and staff forums. Several of these initiatives are described below.

Staff Development

Bosch Cobb believes in committing time, energy, and money to continuous staff development. Opportunities were identified that would develop competencies in FCPL staff, with the California Library Association's (CLA) personal and professional competencies used as a starting point.[1]

Training is one of the ways to develop these and other competencies; both internal and external training opportunities are available. FCPL employs a full-time training coordinator librarian, Camille Turner, who both offers programs and helps staff find the appropriate learning forums. Turner graduated from Infopeople's Master Trainer Program, which added skills to her repertoire of facilitating staff development. Four librarians have completed Urban Libraries Council's (ULC) Executive Leadership Institute (ELI) program. Their projects included supporting the rural community and working with the business community to create an awareness of how the library can support economic development; developing homework centers; and expanding world language services. Two fellows of the ELI program are currently members of the library's management team. In addition, two other librarians attended the Eureka (Calif.) Leadership program, completing a joint customer service and culture-altering project now called "People First!" Staff members regularly attend workshops and webinars sponsored by the statewide Infopeople library staff training initiative. Over twenty employees participated in Infopeople's Building Leadership series of monthly classes, and many learn from OCLC and ULC conferences, webinars, and materials. ULC provided a grant to allow seven employees to attend library school.

Growing Our Own

One example of growing your own is a librarian trainee program in which paraprofessionals (library assistants) who have a bachelor's degree are selected to work under the direction of a librarian as they attend library school. Librarian Trainee is a provisional classification and incumbents must complete eligibility requirements for a Librarian I within three years to retain employment with Fresno County. These employees receive preprofessional training, mentoring, and work experience while in the program. The goal is to promote trainees to the Librarian class when they have successfully completed an MLIS or MLS program. The Friends of the Library supports the program by offering scholarships of up to $2,500 for those attending library school.

Fresno also promotes staff development by encouraging involvement with committees and projects in the CLA and ALA as well as attending conferences. Not only does this help build staff members' professional development, the library generally benefits from the knowledge and experiences gained through participation.

Bosch Cobb talked about outreach as an important component of the library's mission and sees not one but three libraries: the physical branches, the virtual library, and the library in the community. Because the library in the community is so vital, staff members are encouraged not only to take library services to the community but to take on leadership positions in local nonprofit and other agencies as well as attend local leadership programs (such as Fresno Leadership).

FCPL's tactic for filling promotions is a bit unusual. In this system, by library practice, all vacancies are offered internally first. Most transfers and promotions are viewed as opportunities for staff to grow. If an employee wants to, the training and development activities are available—as are the vacancies—to make it happen. The ability to move up into leadership positions is touted as a benefit of working at FCPL when recruiting. It has been a successful marketing tool.

A Tool: Responsibility Charting

An important tool Fresno began using some years ago that has served to develop leaders is responsibility charting (see figure 7.1). Bosch Cobb recommends this tool—long used by organization development practitioners to help clarify roles and responsibilities—to managers and supervisors for major or complex projects throughout the library. She has found it to be very useful in clarifying who is responsible for what and to what degree. Outcomes of using this tool have been quicker goal attainment, increased accountability of staff, less time wasted in meetings, less duplication of effort, and staff who are clear about responsibilities.

As can be seen in the example chart, for each project all tasks and decisions to be made are listed along the vertical axis and key stakeholders are listed horizontally. Key stakeholders are anyone touched by the project.

In each box one of the following codes should be entered: A (approve), R (responsible), C (consulted), I (informed), DK (don't know, and need to determine), Blank (no relationship to task).

There are several tips useful to completing the chart:

- Define each task and the people involved by both name and title; be very clear.
- Assign one "R" for each task; only one person can be responsible.
- The person assigned the "R" role must understand and accept the conditions of performance on the task, including accountability for budget, time frame, completion dates, and milestones.
- Only the "R" person and the "Cs" need to meet with regard to the task.

As you can see from figure 7.2, Fresno also uses this format to track involvement in system meetings as a way of building and tracking the structure for stakeholders to interact on a regular basis.

Where Is FCPL Now?

Recently the California Library Association and the Fresno County Public Library updated their competencies to include "develop political savvy and awareness," that is, be able to identify and enlist the support of strategic partners to complement strengths and weaknesses of the organization and to obtain key resources and assistance to support the achievement of mutual goals. To gain knowledge in this arena as well as to promote big-picture thinking, a variety of new experiences were suggested. These include attending Fresno and Clovis business conferences, board of supervisor and city council meetings, the State of the County breakfast, and the California Library Association's legislative day; in-house training on how to get items on the board of supervisor's agenda and on the best and worst experiences in the political sphere; attendance at San Joaquin Valley Library System committee meetings as an orientation to local library governing; obtaining experience with elements of urban planning; attending Friends of the Library board, council, and oversight committee meetings; and visiting branches and obtaining an overview of service areas and goals.

I ended my conversations with Bosch Cobb and Turner with two questions: "Is it working?" and "Given budget cuts and hiring freezes, will you continue succession planning and staff development?" Bosch Cobb provided positive answers to both. Many employees (seventeen) have been promoted, and vacancies are successfully filled rather quickly without having to worry about new employees learning their staff, culture, organization, county, software, and so forth. Newly promoted employees are ready to go on day one. "We will continue carrying some things forward that are time-tested and make changes as well," Bosch Cobb said. The program is reviewed and updated every twelve to eighteen months, to ensure that it is relevant and meeting the library's needs. Examples of recent changes are the opportunities to increase political awareness and savvy mentioned above and a move toward e-learning.

Continue? "Yes," said Bosch Cobb. "You can't stop. If we are going to move ahead, there is always a need to engage in staff development."

/// JOHNSON COUNTY LIBRARY

Johnson County (Kans.) Library (JCL) is a busy metropolitan library, as of 2009 serving 370,000 residents via thirteen facilities, supported by 365 employees.[2] For some years, JCL administrators experienced a shortage of qualified candidates for midlevel and senior management positions. Recognizing in addition impending retirements from baby boomers and projections for fewer new graduates from MLS programs, the library decided to develop an internal leadership development program to grow its own leaders and create its own recruitment pool.

FIGURE 7.1

FRESNO COUNTY PUBLIC LIBRARY RESPONSIBILITY CHART

Stakeholders Decisions/Tasks	County Librarian	Assoc. Co. Librarian	Managers	Supervisors	SLA	LA's	Public Service Staff	Aides	Maintenance
1									
2									
3									
4									
5									
6									

Codes

A=Approve	I=Informed
R=Responsible	DK=Don't Know
C=Consulted	Blank=No Relationship

Tips

- Define each task and the people involved by name and position
- Assign only one 'R' for each task
- The 'R' person should understand and accept the conditions of performance: budget, time frame, completion dates, milestones, etc.
- Only the 'R' and the 'C's need to meet in regards to the task.

FIGURE 7.2

EXAMPLE OF FRESNO COUNTY PUBLIC LIBRARY RESPONSIBILITY CHART USED TO TRACK ONGOING MEETINGS

	Stakeholders		County Libn	Assoc. Co. Libn	Bus. Mgr	Adult Svcs	Ref Svcs	Youth Svcs	Support Services	SJVLS Program Manager	PIO	Supervisors	Lib I/II	Lib III	Comm Libs	SLA	Training Libn	LA	Libn Trainee
1	Monday Meeting	Weekly	x	x	x	x	x	x	x	x	x								occasional
2	Assoc. Co. Libn	2 times a month		x	Opt.	Opt.	Rep by RS	x	monthly		Opt	Branch Mandatory / Others / Optional		Opt					occasional
3	Departmental Meetings	varies			x	x	x	x	x	x									x
4	Community Libraries / All one person branches	Quarterly		Opt		Opt		x	Tech			Those in Comm Libs			x			opt	
5	SLA	Every other Month		x				Opt	x							x	x		
6	Central Supervisors	Monthly				x	x	x	x			All Central Supervisors							
7	Librarian I/II/III	Monthly											x	x					x

Then deputy and now library director Donna Lauffer and her leadership team identified the need on two levels. First, there was a need for leadership at every level in making decisions and leading projects to make the library more stable and simultaneously more nimble. In addition, managers and senior leaders interested in advancement needed to build skills in creating, leading, and managing systemwide projects. The library aspired to change—both individual and organizational change—resulting in a culture of leadership development that naturally generated leaders and succession rather than a series of programs or initiatives.

Here is how the program was described in a nomination for the National Association of Counties Achievement Award *it won* in 2009 (prepared by Pat Hassan and modified). The library created a leadership development steering committee that conceived a two-tiered, two-year program to address the two levels of need, utilizing consultants only for the design of the Tier 2 curriculum. Piloting Tier 1 in 2007 and Tier 2 in 2008 was a learning experience that would guide Cycle 2, which began with the second Tier 1 group in January 2009.

First Cycle, Tier 1

After nearly two years of planning that included obtaining partial funding, partners, and a curriculum design, the leadership development steering committee launched Tier 1 in January 2007. Tier 1 was open to all staff, and its twenty-seven participants included a cross section of staff: pages, clerks, paraprofessional and professional librarians, supervisors, and managers.

Tier 1 focused on developing behaviors rather than technical skills. Seven identified behavioral competencies served as the basis for all learning: personal accountability, listening and responding, teamwork and cooperation, initiative, flexibility, customer service orientation, and genuineness. (These same behaviors had been identified in prior years as behavioral competencies that supported the library's values, but because the steering committee members felt that these were not extensive enough for full leadership development, Tier 2 was required.)

Over eleven months, each participant was expected to spend 240 hours in four components:

- Classroom learning including four-hour monthly sessions about library governance, public governance, and the behavioral competencies.

- Independent study initiated with a 360-degree feedback evaluation on the seven behavioral competencies, developing an individual development plan, followed by evaluations.
- Project teamwork (using a Project Runway format but without voting anyone off the show) based on real library needs from the strategic plan, utilizing a budget and parameters within which to work.
- Mentoring by the leadership development steering committee, whose members were trained by external specialists.

Because the partial funding obtained was dedicated to Tier 2, no paid instructors could be used. Instead, former staff development coordinator Tiffany Hentschel and other library managers taught sessions. University of Missouri–Columbia professors and public administration budget experts provided some in-kind support. In addition, the library could not afford to hire substitutes to cover off-desk time that participants spent in the program.

Almost immediately, time constraints forced changes to the program. The first casualty was individual development plans, in favor of the project teamwork that required more immediate attention, team interaction, and revolving deadlines—in addition to tangible results. Lack of off-desk time and uneven support by some managers were added factors. Mentoring was also uneven, working well with some assigned pairs but not with others.

The project teams, however, provided high-impact change to the library and the highest sense of satisfaction among participants. One of the projects, the "Art in the Stacks" public exhibits program, received a new name, logo, and contact list.

First Cycle, Tier 2

To design the curriculum for Tier 2, the library hired Paula Singer and Christi A. Olson as consultants. The intention was that the first Tier 2 graduates would teach Tier 2 in ensuing years, with no further use of consultants. The consultants envisioned that Tier 2 participants would develop helpful and relevant conceptual frameworks, build leadership skills, and learn how to focus on achieving results for strategic initiatives and complex projects.

Tier 2 focused on four key leadership competencies: leads change, influences people, achieves results, and fosters communications. (For more about competencies, including the leadership competencies adopted by Johnson County Library, see chapter 3). The consultants designed a program consisting of eight modules, weekly online sessions, and three consultant-led face-to-face workshops. The three workshops focused on problem diagnosis and resolution, skills development, and group learning. Steering committee members led all other coursework. In addition, participants were expected to spend 1.5 hours per week on reading and written assignments. Tier 2 also utilized self-assessments and individual development plans.

Tier 2 goals included increasing leadership skills in complex project management, organizing and managing systemwide meetings, resolving problems in a group setting, and facilitating public and community forums. Participants also learned to adapt to and manage change at all levels of organizations.

As with Tier 1, the Tier 2 curriculum had to be adjusted midway. By May, the steering committee had dropped individual written assignments and journaling in favor of concentrating on two chief vehicles for learning: (1) monthly breakfast discussions (moderated in turn by steering committee members) of concepts in consultant-identified management/leadership books; and (2) action learning team projects that addressed strategic goals. Each team was given background, a budget, and parameters with which to work intensively over ten months to produce recommendations for solutions to specific issues on materials handling, internal communication, organizational culture, and a new way of thinking. These were already on the library's work agenda, and Tier 2 participants invited other staff members to assist them in intensive investigation and problem solving.

The group read and discussed *Good to Great: Why Some Companies Make the Leap . . . and Others Don't* and *Good to Great and the Social Sectors: A Monograph to Accompany Good to Great*, both by Collins; *The Leadership Challenge*, by Kouzes and Posner; *Winning with Library Leadership: Enhancing Services through Connection, Contribution, and Collaboration*, by Olson and Singer; *Difficult Conversations: How to Discuss What Matters Most*, by Stone, Patton, and Heen; and selections from *The Human Relations Reading Book*, 8th edition, edited by Cooke et al.

The consultants joined the Tier 2 group for three two-day sessions—for a kickoff and introduction to leadership, for lessons about diagnosing and resolving problems and developing skills, and for a concluding session.

Criteria of success:

- Create a culture of ad hoc work teams that come to life and bring everyone's best work forward.
- Bring ideas into the organization and have a "spirit of innovation" on a daily basis.
- Stop saying and acting "You can't do that" and "It's always been done that way."
- Be forward thinking, carry a forward-looking attitude.
- Produce better integration across projects.
- New leaders emerge and are encouraged and mentored.
- Participants develop or hone key competencies required for successful change and growth of themselves and JCL.

Program goals:

- Prepare people for library leadership in a complex environment.
- Engage more people in the organization to work actively on strategic initiatives and community needs.
- Fill the identified leadership gap.
- Foster better communication among a broader group of leaders.
- Create management depth and opportunities to practice skills.
- Increase skills in complex project management, organizing and managing systemwide meetings, resolving problems in a group setting, and facilitating public and community forums.
- Adapt to and manage change at all levels of organization.

The first Tier 2's thirteen graduates included five senior managers, two members of the leadership development steering committee, and six Tier 1 graduates. Tier 2 concluded with a celebratory luncheon at which library board members heard presentations on the team projects.

Second Cycle, Tier 1

As the second two-year cycle began in January 2009, the steering committee made the following adjustments to the existing Tier 1 plan, based on input from the first Tier 1 class and initial feedback from participants in the second Tier 1: (1) All work time for Tier 1 was scheduled in advance and relayed to both participants and their supervisors; this helped supervisors understand the commitment up front and plan schedules. (2) The number of projects was decreased. (3) Reading materials for upcoming lectures are to be provided in advance. (4) All presenters will incorporate more interaction into presentations. (5) More field trips will be part of the agenda. Mentoring will be retained as part of the program.

Results/Success of the Program

The retirement crunch did hit the Johnson County Library in 2007 with eleven retirements, in addition to normal turnover, and Tier 1 resulted almost immediately in movement among staff: seven Tier 1 participants were promoted or transferred during the course of the program, including three to management positions. Many expressed that they applied for jobs they would not have considered prior to the program, as even partway through the program they had gained new confidence and had a better understanding of the organization. By the same token, managers began to notice a better appreciation for the complexity of decision-making processes in the library. Four members of Tier 2 have been promoted to date.

An unintended consequence of Tier 1 was that the library's biennial staff engagement survey at the end of 2007 reflected improved scores of more than 7 percent in two areas—satisfaction, loyalty, and growth and development.

Tier 2

The Tier 2 pilot included members of the steering committee, members of the leadership team, and several others. It was a tumultuous time. The library director retired, the staff development coordinator resigned to take a promotion with the county, and the committee chair resigned. Time was limited, workloads high, and reflection less valued by participants than the consultants.

Outcomes for Tier 2 were evaluated carefully, on the basis of the success criteria and program goals listed above, resulting in a 37-page report by the consultants with tables and a listing of all comments submitted by participants. With one exception, all participants felt that the correct goals for success were identified.

Regarding program success, participants' evaluations revealed that 83 percent felt that the program resulted in creating an organizational culture of ad hoc work teams that bring everyone's best work forward;

66 percent felt that new ideas were brought into the organization with a "spirit of organization" on a daily basis; 85 percent felt that they were empowered to find a new way of doing things; 83 percent felt that they were free to be forward thinking; 59 percent felt that there was better integration across projects; 67 percent felt that new leaders emerged from the process; and 67 percent felt that they developed or honed key competencies for successful change and continued personal and organizational growth.

Regarding overall effectiveness of Tier 2, 83 percent of participants felt that they had increased their leadership skills, 75 percent felt that their new knowledge would be valuable in performing their current jobs, and 75 percent felt that what they learned would be valuable in new senior positions.

After evaluating their experiences with the first cycle of Tier 1 and Tier 2 and their outcomes, library administrators believe the leadership development program has been extremely beneficial for the organization as a whole. So important is this effort to the library's long-term success that administrators asked the entire library staff to support the effort by backfilling for frontline participants' time spent in the program—not for just one year but ongoing since 2007. The entire organization has stretched to ensure the success of this program.

/// ONLINE COMPUTER LIBRARY CENTER

Based in Dublin, Ohio, the Online Computer Library Center (OCLC) is a nonprofit, membership, computer library service and research organization dedicated to the public purposes of furthering access to the world's information and reducing information costs. More than 71,000 libraries in 112 countries and territories around the world use OCLC services to locate, acquire, catalog, lend, and preserve library materials. We include the OCLC story because most libraries are members, the organization knows libraries at a deep level, with 1,250 employees OCLC is larger than most library systems, and OCLC is committed to leadership and career development. It also has a formal succession planning program. I spent some time talking with George Needham, OCLC vice president, Global and Regional Councils, to learn about that program.

Motivated by the graying of vice presidents and directors, succession planning has been a key initiative of OCLC for almost eleven years, since president and CEO Robert L. "Jay" Jordan first joined the organization. Since that time, the talent management and succession planning program has evolved and remains a key senior leadership initiative. Top-level commitment to the program is vital, as is the strong support of HR.

The first iteration of succession planning focused on leadership development, mostly in terms of providing technical business expertise. Sixty or so vice presidents, directors, and others from around the world were invited to attend a program designed for this purpose by Ohio State University's Center for Leadership Development. Focused on business operations, the program was dubbed "Business School in a Box." It was a two-week program, offered one week at a time separated by six months. Topics included how to read spreadsheets and financial reports, mergers and acquisitions, and conducting due diligence. There were also self-assessments designed to identify strengths and weaknesses and build on strengths. In truth, the assessment process did not pass the "smell test," and several participants referred to it as "one step away from voodoo."

Many positive outcomes resulted from this program. Two participants were later promoted to vice president, the commonality of language increased understanding and effectiveness, and the interaction with professors and OCLC staff from all over the world enhanced cohesion and trust, thus improving business outcomes.

Talent management and succession planning is now a far more formal program and includes many of the steps and processes outlined in this book. Leadership reviews key positions and key contributors in the context of OCLC's strategic plan and human resources needs toward talent utilization and competency development. It includes a 360-degree feedback assessment for learning how one is perceived and where skills might be missing. The well-respected Birkman Method (see www.birkman.com) has replaced the "near voodoo" assessment tool. Managers, directors, and vice presidents identify employees in management positions on the basis of performance and potential. Managers and above can self-nominate. Anyone wishing to participate in the program must complete an application, which includes an individual talent development profile of career goals, strengths, and development areas.

Development plans are made for and with participants (key talent candidates), who are also invited to attend special training programs around key leadership competencies with OCLC leadership and participants'

managers. A recent program was "Outcome Thinking—Building Leaders," offered by Impression Management Professionals (www.impressionmanagement .com), described as a program to build on new ways of thinking in order to execute and focus on results as well as on building the plans to achieve them. Offered over two days, the program series includes Managing Your Message, SMART (strategic mindsets and articulate in real time) Leadership, and Conflict Harmonizer.

Mentoring

Internal, informal mentoring is a strong component of OCLC's succession planning processes. These relationships often cross divisions and are cross-hierarchical, with staff and vice presidents exposed to each other. For example, one of his colleague vice presidents asked Needham to mentor a young creative individual. They meet for lunch once a month and discuss libraries, OCLC culture, management style, and other topics. Training is provided, including documents and checklists, to help mentors and mentees successfully negotiate and maximize the relationship. In the OCLC culture, anyone can feel free to ask for mentoring. Outcomes of these relationships include familiarity with the talent in the organization, exposure to difference styles of management and leadership, safe feedback on issues of importance, a perspective on organizational life and politics, and a breakdown of narrow departmental tunnel vision. Needham notes, "I learned at least as much about online community, breaking technology, and blogging from my mentee as he ever learned about libraries from me!"

Individual and Career Development Plans

While OCLC has a strong talent management and succession planning program (see chapter 4), it also has a strong focus on individual career development for *all* employees. It trains managers and employees to develop IDPs and expects every employee to have one. The organization ensures that this happens by including employee IDPs as a factor on which all managers are evaluated.

On its website one can find that OCLC

recognizes the importance of continuous development and training to ensure employees have the knowledge and tools to perform their job responsibilities at the highest level and to meet the challenges of a demanding library environment in a rapidly changing information age. OCLC encourages employees to develop their skills through the various programs and development opportunities provided by the organization, as well as academic offerings through our tuition reimbursement program.[3]

The organization provides development and training opportunities for employees in the areas of individual development planning, management and leadership development, technology training, individual and team assessments and coaching, office automation, quality control, ethics and compliance training, and workforce harassment training. Through WebJunction, it also offers employees online self-paced learning in a variety of genres.[4] Tuition reimbursement (to a maximum of $5,250 per year) is also provided to employees for courses that are relevant to their current position or to one to which the employee might reasonably aspire.

OCLC also supports library staff in developing their skills and knowledge through a series of awards and scholarships for new librarians, established professionals, researchers, librarians in developing countries, and ALA Spectrum scholars.

/// PIERCE COUNTY LIBRARY SYSTEM

The Pierce County Library System (PCLS) is headquartered near Tacoma, Washington. Its seventeen branches, two family bookmobiles, and an Explorers' Kids bookmobile bring people together, enrich lives, and provide children and adults with opportunities to learn. The library is an independent junior taxing district. With a 2009 budget of almost $29 million, it serves 534,000 over 1,600 square miles.

Led by executive director Neel Parikh since 1994, PCLS is funded by a separate property tax levy. County citizens showed their support for the library by reauthorizing the library system's levy, to meet the needs of its growing and changing communities—definitely a blessing, and an obligation to the community, that Parikh does not take lightly. PCLS made four levy promises to the community: new materials and faster service, 20 percent more open hours, additional services for kids and teenagers, and upgraded services and technology for customers by offering more computers with Internet access in libraries for public use and computer classes for adults. The library's customer focus of giving those who responded positively to the levy, and all members of the communities served, what they want is seen in the following statement of services:

The Library System's services and resources bring the world of information and imagination to communities. Customers will find helpful, welcoming staff who:

- Answer questions.
- Help find good books to read.
- Assist with using the Library's many resources, including books, magazines, music, movies, audio books, computers and online resources.

The Library strives to grow and change along with the needs of its customers and constantly reevaluates what and how it offers services.[5]

Parikh and the board of trustees knew that succession planning and the development of leaders would be critical if the system was to grow and change along with the needs of its customers. The board, comprising business executives, requested that a succession plan be developed. The request was supported by PCLS's then new HR director, Holly Gorski, who remarked, "Tumbleweeds will be blowing through this place if we don't do something!"

After much study and dialogue, in 2005 Parikh and her executive team decided not to take the route of determining who was going to retire and identifying succession for particular positions. Instead, like others, they chose a multipronged approach to develop all staff, improve leadership throughout the organization, and create a learning organization. An early step was to evaluate the employee pool to determine who and what percentage of employees could potentially retire within the next ten years (assuming a retirement age of 65). Their analysis led to identifying three different categories of employees:

- Top-level leadership: Executive team and leadership team (department heads and managing librarians).
- Specialty positions: Individuals who do not come from the library profession for whom the library would expect to recruit replacements outside the organization. Generally for individuals who lead these departments, PCLS would not expect their replacement to come from within the library.
- Library professional or clerical: Individuals who develop expertise working in the system and would potentially be eligible for higher-level positions within the organization. This category divides between MLS librarian

career-track and paraprofessional supervisory and specialist positions.

In 2009, Parikh shared the following analysis with the PCLS board:

We have many positions in the organization for which we have no trouble recruiting replacements (e.g., library pages, branch assistants, custodians). Some of them may become supervisors or become librarians. I will describe the situation in various tiers.

Executive Leadership Roles: There are 24 Department Heads and top-level administrators. 37.5% will be eligible to retire in the next 10 years. However, looking more closely at the number, you see a different picture. Of the Executive Team, only 1 out of 6 will be eligible to retire, or 16%. The major impact on the organization would be the retirement of professional librarians in leadership roles. It is important to note that the library system is becoming nationally known for innovative services. It is likely that high-level positions that become vacant will also attract national attention for applicants. PCLS ideally will look for a balance of internal and external.

Mid-level Supervisors and Specialists: Of 58 employees 43% will be eligible for retirement in the next 10 years. The majority of that falls in the branch clerical supervisory role. This area is a target for attention for developing leadership skills or leadership opportunities for individuals in the organizations to move into these positions. We are also looking closely at these positions because of the need to expand the number of opportunities for librarians to develop supervisory experience.

The above analysis covers 82 individuals or approximately 23% of the employees in the library. The other 277 employees are generally entry-level positions (such as pages, branch assistants, librarians) or specialty positions (such as Finance Department, custodians, facilities maintenance, graphic designers). There are high retirement rates in some of those categories, but it also easy to recruit for those positions. For instance, nearly half of the page positions are eligible for retirement. We have no problem recruiting for this position. For example, earlier this year over 100 people applied for a single part-time page vacancy. These individuals are an extremely important core to the learning organization and we will pay attention to their learning and growth, building potential for leadership roles.

In another memo to the board, Parikh summarizes the library's approach to succession planning in the areas of hiring, nurture/growth, and creating opportunities to lead. All, she wrote, "are an important part of assuring that we are growing people and 'potential successors'":

Hiring—Get the Right People on the Bus: Recruit and hire high potential talent and ensure that we are hiring people that share the library's vision and with potential to grow and contribute to the library. A key element is regular evaluation of the organizational structure and job descriptions to ensure the library can meet future goals. This includes recruiting talented new graduates from library school or individuals from libraries across the country, in addition to talent in professions. As PCLS gains a national reputation, we are able to attract talent nationwide.

Nurture/Growth: Create an environment that fosters and supports learning and growth. We must offer opportunities to learn and actively support individual growth. This includes not only formal training within the library or outside, but also creating an environment that encourages experimentation, risk taking and decision-making. This is the core philosophy that led to the creation of the "Learning Organization" and the Learning Department.

Create Opportunities to Lead: This element includes not only the opportunity to lead projects, but also ensuring that our organizational structure allows individuals to develop leadership skills in preparation for higher level positions. This also means evaluating our organizational structure to ensure that it supports future goals and creating career-ladder positions that would lead to positions of increased responsibility.

Parikh is definitely taking a systems approach to succession planning. Several projects were begun to support the succession planning initiative. By category, those completed and those in progress at the time of this writing are noted in figure 7.3.

I wanted to know more about some of these initiatives, and Parikh was happy to share. She knew that a culture change was required to create a succession plan, leaders at all levels, and a truly customer-focused library. One leverage point was through defining leadership, and leadership behaviors, at PCLS. The original list of leadership descriptors was drafted by Parikh and deputy director Georgia Lomax and vetted by the executive team, then introduced to the leadership team (which includes all branch managers and department heads). As part of the rollout and training, managers learned to act and then tell what leadership descriptors they were using. They now ask, and ask themselves, these same questions. In a series of meetings in each branch and five at the main library, Parikh and Lomax introduced them to all staff. The final list of leadership descriptors is found as figure 7.4.

FIGURE 7.3

PIERCE COUNTY LIBRARY SYSTEM SUCCESSION PLANNING INITIATIVES

CATEGORY	PROJECTS COMPLETED	PROJECTS IN PROCESS
Hire the Right People • Hiring process that attracts and selects talent • Clear understanding and expectation of desired skills and qualities • Competitive salaries	• Competency Based Hiring for Leadership Team and Librarians • Skills and Qualities for all employees • Leadership Descriptors • Classification and Compensation Plan: competitive salaries • Improve recruitment for special professions	• Hiring process improvement and improved recruitment • Evaluation/Feedback: Use six-month probationary period effectively • Organizational Structure: What do we need to provide future service and accomplish system goals? • Competency based hiring for all positions
Nurture/Growth Provide opportunities and support individual learning either through formal training or outside experience	• Commitment to Learning Organization and creation of Learning Team • Increase resources devoted to learning • Tuition Assistance Program • Coaching/mentor training for managers	• Working to hold managers and supervisors accountable for supporting learning • Improve coaching skills • Personal learning plans
Creating Leadership Opportunities Creating leadership opportunities for individuals to lead either in a project or through a library position	• Project management • I2P2: Idea Incubator Project: How to grow ideas (develop a process) while modeling the kinds of behaviors that support it (learning organization culture) • Participation in Executive Leadership Institute	• Improving and clarifying the decision-making process • Create effective cross functional teams • Reducing silos between work teams • Evaluating organizational structure to provide more career-track positions/ opportunities to develop skills

FIGURE 7.4
PIERCE COUNTY LIBRARY SYSTEM LEADERSHIP DESCRIPTORS

1. Leadership Team members are the leadership of PCLS. You are critical to the Library's success.

- Leaders model excellence in action and attitude
- Leaders are actively engaged in creating our future
- Leaders empower and engage every employee to be involved in helping the Library achieve its vision
- Leaders create a positive environment based on respect and fun
- Leaders give staff permission and support to grow, contribute and succeed
- Leaders hold themselves responsible and accountable for being the leadership of PCLS

2. Leadership and ideas happen at every level at PCLS. Together we insure that we achieve our vision for library service to PCLS communities. PCLS's leadership culture:

- Creates a customer-focused environment that insures delivering excellent service to every customer
- Values and fosters teamwork and respects the importance of everyone's role in the Library's success
- Fosters an environment where we continually learn, seek improvement, takes risks and accept and learn from failure
- Communicates and shares knowledge effectively and proactively, and expects two-way discussion, and listens to understand
- Encourages and supports innovation and creativity
- Empowers decision making and action at the appropriate level and minimizes top-down control and gate keeping
- Coaches and mentors others and develops leadership and contribution at all levels
- Encourages and supports initiative in problem solving and organizational improvement
- Relies on judgment, not rules
- Is concerned with the entire organization's success

"All staff need to be leaders," was the message Parikh sent. Staff responded to one question: "How can we help you become a leader at PCLS?" The responses led to training, coaching, and I2P2, an idea incubator project. Still in pilot stages, I2P2 is designed to encourage ideas and risk taking as well as incubate ideas of potential services and programs in a safe environment. As in numerous libraries and other organizations, too many employees felt inhibited about putting ideas forward. Parikh and the executive team knew that, for the library to develop a strong culture of customer focus, all ideas would be needed and all staff would need to be accountable.

The leadership descriptors were further operationalized by core skills and qualities required of all staff members along with behavioral dos and don'ts for each. The nine skills/qualities identified are customer focus, teamwork, professional integrity, leadership, communication, problem solving, change and learning, positive attitude, and diversity (see figure 7.5). They had started with competencies, but that just did

not work for them. The dos and don'ts were simply more effective in this culture. In rolling out the skills and qualities, HR director Holly Gorski wrote:

These are the skills and qualities all of us need in order to work together and provide outstanding library service, now and in the future. We are currently working to change the Library System's hiring process to ensure new employees are selected based on these attributes. In 2009 we will be changing the performance appraisals for all positions to focus on these as well.

The learning culture being fostered by PCLS relies heavily on coaching, modeling behavior, and setting expectations. Training is based on an 80:20 model, with only 20 percent classroom based. Much of the rest is in-the-moment, just-in-time training and coaching. The newly created Learning Team developed "Foundations of the PCLS Learning Organization" (figure 7.6). This document articulates the critical elements for PCLS to be a successful learning organization. The

PIERCE COUNTY LIBRARY SYSTEM SKILLS AND QUALITIES

SKILLS/QUALITIES AND DEFINITIONS	WHAT THIS LOOKS LIKE AT WORK (GENERAL DOS AND DON'TS)	
	DO	DON'T
1. Customer Focus We (PCLS staff) strive to understand and exceed our customers' expectations. We treat all people with courtesy and respect and are welcoming and approachable. We are aware of cultural differences that may impact how people prefer to experience the library and take our cues from the customer to adapt our styles accordingly. Note: "Customer" always means both coworkers and the public, including both current and potential library users.	Consistently acknowledge all customers as soon as they enter the building/our work area. Let them know we are available (by greeting, smiling, offering to help—take the cue from the customer). Remember and show that the customer is more important than the rule or the task. Express empathy for customers and offer alternative solutions whenever possible. Save the time of the customer whenever possible. Look for ways to streamline our policies and procedures, to present materials effectively, to encourage customers to use the library successfully on their own. Recognize that, and behave as if, our goal is a successful customer experience, not just the completion of our specific task. Express empathy for the customer and if difficulties arise offer alternative solutions. Follow up by exploring ways to prevent similar difficulties in the future. Anticipate customer needs and provide the right level of service for that customer (customize service). Demonstrate good listening skills. Promote library services and programs by matching them to the customer's interests. Seek ways to help non-English-speaking people and people with reading or learning challenges use our libraries and access our services.	Ignore customers by focusing too intently on the task in front of us. Look up! Be aware! Forget to wear our name tag or other staff identification. Adhere rigidly to rules regardless of the situation. Assume we know what is best for customers. Treat customers' inability to use the library as their problem, instead of ours. Say "that's not my job" or otherwise refuse to help customers. Act or speak in a condescending manner toward customers. Allow personal distractions to compromise our willingness or ability to address customer needs and expectations when we're on the job.

SKILLS/QUALITIES AND DEFINITIONS	WHAT THIS LOOKS LIKE AT WORK (GENERAL DOS AND DON'TS)	
	DO	DON'T
2. Teamwork We work effectively with our team, work group, and across organizational lines to accomplish the library system's goals. We build respectful relationships within and between units and among individuals. We encourage and support other staff.	Offer to help coworkers in all positions as needed. Share information that others might find helpful in performing their own tasks. Contribute to achieving the organization's goals. Build rapport among coworkers and other departments. Respect others' ideas and abilities. Accept and consider suggestions from customers and colleagues for improvements in our work. Be dependable.	Say "that's not my job" or avoid offering assistance to others. Neglect our share of the work. Treat coworkers disrespectfully or dismiss differing opinions. Insist on our own point of view and/or refuse to compromise. Dismiss suggestions from customers or colleagues because "they just don't get it."
3. Professional Integrity We project a professional attitude and image and adhere to a high standard of professional conduct. We value and respect customer confidentiality.	Project a positive image of the library to the community. Effectively explain and uphold the library's policies on customer confidentiality. Show pride in our work, conduct, and appearance.	Complain about the job and/or the workplace. Disseminate information that should be confidential according to library policies. Act or dress in a manner that demonstrates a lack of respect for customers or is not conducive to accomplishing our work. Withhold or ignore information that affects the smooth operation of the library.
4. Leadership We accept responsibility and make decisions appropriate to our position and the situation. We contribute, support, and encourage new ideas. We demonstrate grace under pressure.	Demonstrate a willingness to seek, explore, and accept new ideas. Focus on the future instead of the past. Accept new decisions once they have been made. Stay calm in difficult situations such as handling angry customers and emergencies. Tell the truth and offer hope.	Meet new ideas with disdain or be unwilling to explore new ways of thinking and doing things. Replay or dwell upon past disappointments or difficulties. Defer all decisions to other staff. Lose control in difficult situations. Blame others or refuse to accept responsibility.

(cont.)

FIGURE 7.5 (cont.)

SKILLS/QUALITIES AND DEFINITIONS	WHAT THIS LOOKS LIKE AT WORK (GENERAL DOS AND DON'TS)	
	DO	DON'T
5. Communication We effectively communicate, both verbally and in writing. We listen to understand and use constructive approaches to resolving workplace issues. We freely share new ideas.	Actively listen to others and paraphrase what they say to check for understanding. Tailor our message and its delivery to the audience and situation. Write and speak in a professional manner; convey our expectations clearly so that others are not left to guess. Provide and willingly receive effective feedback: address the situation, behavior, and its impact. Use a pleasant tone of voice appropriate for the situation.	Assume that we understand without listening or asking for clarification. Forget to check our e-mail and the staff web bulletin board every shift.
6. Problem Solving We develop effective approaches to address customer needs and solve problems. We use good judgment to resolve conflicts. We address customer behavior and issues when necessary. We are solution oriented.	Rely on judgment over rules to help customers with special situations; use common sense. Always offer other service options to customers if we are unable to meet their specific need. Seek ways to be able to meet their needs in the future. Use actual data/evidence to support our recommendations and decisions. Look to nonlibrary models as well as other libraries for possible solutions to library challenges.	Rigidly enforce "the rules" even when exceptions are appropriate. Ignore or contribute to problems. Contribute to or ignore a disruptive or dysfunctional workplace.
7. Change and Learning We positively respond to organizational change and show a willingness to learn new ways to accomplish work. We are flexible. We take the initiative to look for ways to develop as individuals and to improve the library system. We are strategic thinkers.	Actively seek opportunities to improve library operations and customer success. Stay current with new library and technology trends and developments that may affect our positions. Readily adopt new policies and procedures. Be open to new ideas from all sources. Take responsibility for pursuing learning opportunities within the organization. Share what we've learned with others.	Assume that things are "good enough" because "no one has complained." Fail to stay current with new library and technology trends and developments that may affect our position. Insist on doing things the old way after being informed of new policies and procedures. Reject new ideas without due consideration. Ignore available learning opportunities.

SKILLS/QUALITIES AND DEFINITIONS	WHAT THIS LOOKS LIKE AT WORK (GENERAL DOS AND DON'TS)	
	DO	**DON'T**
8. Positive Attitude We are enthusiastic about our work and like to have fun. We are positive role models for one another and remember that we represent the library and its mission in the community.	Greet customers (including coworkers) every day. Actively support the library's programs and initiatives. Look for ways to make something work, not reasons why it can't work. Bring concerns to the person who can do something about them in a respectful manner and in the proper setting. Demonstrate enjoyment of our jobs; smile! Strive to make using the library a pleasant and productive experience. Respect the workplace as a "no gossip zone."	Ignore customers or fail to greet them. Refuse to try something just because we might not be good at it. Allow unhappy moods to affect our working environment. Complain about coworkers or job in presence of public or in otherwise inappropriate settings and ways. Act as though customers are bothering or interrupting us. Gossip!
9. Diversity We understand and are committed to the principles of diversity. We strive to understand the needs of all people in our community. We treat all people with courtesy and respect and are welcoming and approachable. We uphold the principles of intellectual freedom.	Know that EVERYONE is our customer and treat ALL people with courtesy and respect. Enable all customers to easily access and enjoy our services. Understand and effectively explain the library's policies and procedures concerning intellectual freedom. Seek ways to help non-English-speaking people and people with reading or learning challenges use our libraries and access our services.	Be discourteous, make disparaging remarks, or otherwise treat anyone with disrespect. Pick and choose who we feel comfortable helping. Contradict library's policies and procedures on intellectual freedom.

team also used this document to develop a work plan with strategies for each of the items listed.

Staff members are retooling their perspectives, looking beyond their immediate actions and behaviors to what the implications of their behavior are regarding internal and external customers alike. Employees are constantly asked, and ask each other, "What is the customer perspective on this action or this policy?" A recent illustration is going beyond making a simple change pertaining to e-mail on the server (good internal customer service) to assessing the implications for staff members working at home or away from the office (great leadership and customer-focused behavior).

I asked Parikh how she would know she was successful. She responded by saying that there would be leaders ready to fill vacancies, all employees would be taking on the role of leader (at their appropriate level), things would be happening and getting done, expectations would be set, and staff would be stepping up with ideas as well as taking responsibility for their decisions and behaviors. Staff would be asking the right questions, retooling their thinking, constantly modeling customer focus. Staff would be living the leadership descriptors.

PCLS is spending a lot of time and money creating a culture and a legacy of staff ready to move into new, different, and higher-level positions. In some ways it is the hard way to create a succession plan; in others, it is the only way. I asked Parikh about the time and money, especially in this economy. With further

FIGURE 7.6

FOUNDATIONS OF THE PCLS LEARNING ORGANIZATION

1. **The burden of learning is on the individual.** It is the right and responsibility of staff to learn and acquire new skills. Learning is necessary and urgent to any successful organization. Everyone knows the difference between learning and training.

2. **Everyone needs to know what the organization's big-picture success looks like and each individual's part in creating that success.** This is a shift from the "my tasks" orientation to more universal knowledge of how an individual's task fits in with the team's task. Everyone is responsible for the team's task, as well as the organization's success. Also need to have a view of what is happening in the library world in general and what that success looks like.

3. **Learning happens at all levels of the organization.** Curiosity is seen as a good thing. Recognition that everyone learns.

4. **Organic communication is encouraged.** Communication is the responsibility of all staff and happens at all levels. Assumes that there is no such thing as too much information and it is the responsibility of the individual to seek out and share information.

5. **There is a consistency of policy implementation and practice.** There are clear boundaries within which staff can operate to help the customer.

6. **Curiosity is encouraged; learning is supported; new skills are actively sought at all levels.** Everyone is responsible for the success of the learning organization and ideas come from anywhere and everyone.

7. **Coaching and mentoring happens at all levels.** This includes peer-to-peer mentoring and includes both formal and informal processes.

8. **Feedback at all levels is an essential ingredient to success.** It must be constructive and well thought-out and everyone must do it.

9. **Mistakes are a learning opportunity for everyone involved.**

developmental plans tied to succession planning, I was curious: was she going to continue this effort? At their current level of intensity? "Yes," she said, "It's essential: we are investing in our future. Staff salaries and benefits comprise 70 percent of the library's budget. We must keep developing staff so they are ready, willing, and able to provide customer-focused service—especially when this generation retires." With some realism and a smile she continued, "We are ballot based, as an independent taxing authority—if we are not relevant, we are toast!"

/// QUEENS BOROUGH PUBLIC LIBRARY

Queens Borough (N.Y.) Public Library (QBPL), *Library Journal*'s 2009 Library of the Year, serves 2.2 million people from sixty-two locations plus seven adult learning centers and two family literacy centers. It circulates the highest number of books and other library materials in the country. The library's budget

is $127.5 million. In fiscal year 2009, QBPL circulated 23 million items, opened its doors to 16 million people, and offered 30,000 programs. It has 6.7 million items in its collections and supports 827,500 active borrowers.

Like the County of Los Angeles Public Library, it is a large and diverse library system with many needs, including that for a strong cadre of potential managers and leaders. Succession planning at QBPL, though not formal, is purposeful. What follows are several initiatives described by Tom Galante, CEO and library director.

Succession Planning for Community Branch Managers: Money and Education

The library recently made some organizational changes to facilitate midmanagement development and succession planning. It took money. Many of the forty assistant community branch manager positions were open. Senior librarians did not want to promote into the position, for there was little salary incentive to do so. To fill the vacancies, the library added $3,000 to the salary. That broke the ice. The assistant manager positions are now filled.

But that was not enough to prepare for the future. Assistant community branch manager is a key feeder position in the community library system, so the need to provide learning and development opportunities for the incumbents was clear. The library contracted with a library school that created and facilitated a management certification program for twenty-five employees. Many were assistant branch managers. The curriculum included the topics of management, budget and finance, technology management, human resource management, building management, and general administration. A course with a rigorous curriculum, it was offered on-site, once a week for six months. Homework was required. After completion of five courses over three years, all participants graduated. "The outcome," said Galante, "has been great. These employees, current and prospective library managers, have been networking, sharing their experiences, and learning from each other. They have begun peer coaching and all have a broader view of the organization. . . . And," he adds proudly, "there have already been a number of promotions."

Dual Career Ladders

To support retention of professional librarians, including its library managers, QBPL restructured its compensation structure, including new positions, enhancing its already existing dual career ladders for librarians and managers. To the positions of senior librarian, supervising librarian, and principal librarian a second level was added. For senior librarian positions, a third level was added to support promotions into select assistant manager positions. (The move from Librarian I to Librarian II is relatively automatic.) In both ladders, after six months of satisfactory performance, jobholders are automatically moved to the next level and receive a salary increase.

Succession Planning at the Senior Level

The library has taken a similar approach to creating a pipeline for systemwide management positions. Because the size of the system justifies it, QBPL has seven associate and assistant director positions reporting to public service department heads (directors). Four of those positions are responsible for supervising community library managers. In addition, various support departments include an assistant director position. All in these positions lead major organizational initiatives as part of their development as senior leaders. All are observed, supported, and developed to be able, at a minimum, to serve in an interim capacity in the event of a department head vacancy.

Knowledge Management and Capitalizing on Retirees

Galante is concerned about losing good people to early (or regular) retirement. To date, knowledge transfer planning has been minimal. To help the system buy some time, and to appeal to those retiring and looking for more flexibility and free time, two policy changes were made. First, QBPL now provides an opportunity for those interested in retiring to work part-time. Second, the library is offering retirees the ability to work at a lower-level position yet keep their seniority when setting the pay rate. For example, if the individual was paid at fifteen-year experience in the salary range of the job she is leaving, her new salary remains at the fifteen-year salary range of the new position. This option has proven attractive to retirees who might have otherwise left the system without transferring their knowledge, mentoring new staff, or supporting programs.

Transfers and Job Rotation

Similar to other libraries, QBPL has been rotating staff into different community branches and central. With over seventy locations, there are many opportunities for job transfer. Because the demographics of this system vary widely, staff transferring often find themselves in a very different environment serving a different community and customer. According to Galante, "This provides a broader view and creates stronger, flexible, customer-oriented staff." For union-represented positions, the labor agreement provides for internal transfers for similar positions based on seniority if QBPL-specified job requirements are met; for union and nonunion supervisory and management positions, interviewing is done to select the best candidate from external and internal applicants.

Rotations and transfers extend to the top of the library system as well. In addition to the COO, whose responsibilities include all public services, a dozen department heads report directly to him. With a few exceptions, half of them trade jobs every year.

On the Lookout

Galante acknowledged that he is always recruiting, always on the lookout for talent. He knows that not all positions can, or should, be filled from within. He has been networking and searching for a new wave of managers: creative individuals who can support the new service model of delivering to customers what they want and need. He also wants to recruit leaders who can deal with City Hall—not a typical competency, or desire, of many senior library managers. Which is why he is always looking.

/// SANTA CLARA COUNTY LIBRARY

According to executive director and county librarian Melinda Cervantes, succession planning at Santa Clara County Library (SCCL) starts at the point of hiring, where a solid job description reflecting the desired skill set and competencies propels the library toward its strategic BHAG (big hairy audacious goal): "Building upon our reputation for service excellence, the Santa Clara County Library will have the highest percentage of library service area cardholders in the nation." The three specific areas the library will focus on in the next five years are convenience, public awareness and marketing, and information literacy.

So how does Cervantes find and develop the leadership that will continually propel the library toward meeting its BHAG? She engages in two distinct processes, one external and the other internal.

External View

One way to locate leadership is by investing years actively watching, waiting, and creating a good reputation for the library. Cervantes keeps her eyes and ears open for the up-and-comers in the library community. She goes out of her way to meet them when their paths cross, reads the articles they write, and watches them present at conferences. Cervantes invests her time so she has a front-row seat as talent rises. When the library's deputy county librarian retired last year, and when several community librarians (managers) retired, several librarians nationwide were invited to participate in the county's recruitment process.

Internal Focus

Cervantes's most important and intense focus is internal. SCCL really works developing internal staff. "This library system," she said, "seeks to prepare staff for their next job and provides the opportunity to develop leadership within their current job." In addition to formal leadership development, she mentioned three targeted strategies: fast teams (see chapter 5), job rotation, and development outside of SCCL.

JOB ROTATION

Job rotation is in its first iteration at SCCL. It is designed to help staff acquire big-picture thinking and deliver districtwide service while supporting staff to grow, stretch, and explore. One facet of job rotation is moving community library staff into other community libraries and into headquarters jobs as well as ensuring that employees assigned to headquarters have experiences in community libraries. At another level, the library is trying out the rotation of three senior management positions among the incumbents for twelve-month periods: systemwide circulation manager, reference librarian (which includes 24/7 virtual reference and assisting with collection development), and services managers (adult, youth).

An opportunity arose when a community librarian took medical leave. To fill the gap, the library interviewed qualified managers to take a temporary assignment at the largest and busiest library in the system (2.5 million annual circulation). This resulted in an experienced community librarian from a much smaller library having the opportunity to take on new challenges, learn, and grow. Consequently, a program librarian (manager) became the acting community librarian, and a librarian became a program librarian (adult or youth services manager) for the same period of time.

Cervantes shares two success stories. One shining star in the organization stepped forward and volunteered on an early version of the library's web page redesign. This star, Allison Parham, is now an electronic resources librarian and leading a formal web redesign project for the library.

Paul Sims, formerly an SCCL librarian, is now the technical services manager for Mountain View Public Library. ("Sometimes our succession planning benefits other libraries!") Sims graduated from the San Jose State University MLIS program and went on to become an adjunct faculty member. Building on his enthusiasm for the SJSU/MLIS program, Sims asked if he could offer an orientation to potential students from SCCL staff ranks. He developed the presentation, including PowerPoint slides, and promoted the workshop to recent graduates, current MLIS students, and potential librarians. Both Cervantes and Sarah Flowers (former deputy county librarian) were invited to speak about their own career paths and the SCCL opportunities afforded to MLIS graduates. At least two of the dozen or so who attended this workshop enrolled in the SJSU/MLIS program, and one or more completed their undergraduate degree requirements with Sims's encouragement. "Succession planning," said Cervantes, "can be viral."

DEVELOPMENT BEYOND BOUNDARIES

This library system goes beyond its own boundaries to develop staff. Staff members at all levels are encouraged to become involved and engaged with the California Library Association, ALA, PLA, and the Urban Libraries Council (and pays institutional membership dues and conference attendance fees). This ensures that the library's name is out there, which results in attracting high-quality candidates when vacancies occur. Of course, library staff and the library gain as well. Involved employees learn from their efforts with CLA and other professional associations, develop technical and leadership skills, and build networks. Because one of its goals is to be involved with the cities and county it serves, SCCL also encourages service on local chambers of commerce, the arts and culture, nonprofits, and other key constituent communities. The library pays the dues of managers and supports involvement and leadership opportunities in local volunteer organizations for all staff.

One manager who stands out to Cervantes is Rosanne Macek, Morgan Hill community librarian. Macek joined the SCCL staff as a children's program librarian in 2001, became community librarian in 2002, completed the Leadership Morgan Hill program sponsored by the Morgan Hill Rotary Club, and is now working on a master's degree in public administration using the library's tuition reimbursement program.

SCCL has been working actively on succession planning since 2005. At the time it was facing several retirements among key library managers. Earlier, deputy county librarian Julie Farnsworth had created a leadership training program for potential leaders and invited employees to self-identify. Participants in the leadership program completed nine classes covering all aspects of management and leadership in the SCCL system. More than fifty emerging leaders completed the program during two series of classes.

SCCL places a premium on developing leaders internally and wisely also pays attention to future leaders nationwide. Cervantes showed us the importance of having a variety of smaller, targeted leadership development programs in addition to formal, large programs.

/// SNO-ISLE LIBRARIES

Located in the north Puget Sound region of Washington State, Sno-Isle Libraries, with twenty-one locations in Snohomish County and Island County, serves as a community doorway to reading, resources, and lifelong learning and a center for people, ideas, and culture. Jonalyn Woolf-Ivory is the library director. Pat Olafson, HR director, explained some of the library's efforts in succession planning.

Olafson and her colleagues have been thinking quite a bit about succession planning in recent years. Familiar with the literature on the graying of the library workforce, and looking (literally) at the members of the Sno-Isle workforce, they decided to identify potential vacancies and to develop a backup plan toward ensuring stability and continuity in providing excellent library service to the communities served. The board of trustees was also interested in having bench strength for senior positions in the organization.

The first step was to identify key jobs. Olafson then matched the key positions with the people in them to ascertain the level of risk of retirement each one might be in—that is, she looked at data on each individual holding these jobs to get a deeper understanding of their age and service and a picture of when retirements might take place. She created a schema of employees: at immediate risk (IR), at risk (AR), and at low risk (LR) for retirement.

Olafson defined these categories in concrete terms based on the retirement eligibility provisions of the pension plans. Those in IR are 60 years of age and above today with an anticipated (for the purpose of this exercise) retirement date in the next five years. AR staff in key positions are ages 55–59 or age 50 with at least ten years of service. It is anticipated that these individuals will move into the IR category in the next five years. LR employees do not fall into either of the other categories by age or experience.[6] Another organization's definitions might differ depending on retirement plan provisions covering its employees.

Olafson then linked those in key positions to their risk of retirement. Among those in key positions, she found four IR and three AR staff members holding key positions. Olafson mentioned some examples, starting with the library director, and included herself. The director, at age 55, has twenty-nine years of pension service credits. She is viewed as AR. Olafson, the HR director, needed to code her own position as IR. At age 63 with more than fifteen years of pension service credits, she is eligible to retire within five years.

Over the years, with encouragement from the board, positions have been installed that not only filled a workload need but also were intended as immediate temporary backup in case of a vacancy in some management positions. For example, several of the larger Sno-Isle community libraries have an assistant managing librarian position, and there is an assistant manager in collection development. Incumbents in these positions could step in until a replacement is hired when someone in a key position and IR retires earlier than anticipated. Such a backup plan, along with the outcome of the analysis of key positions and risk of retirement, is clearly and cleanly shown with fictional data in figure 7.7.

Library leadership took this approach further and realized that some of those designated as "backup until filled" might not take (or even want) the vacant key position or might not be ready to take on the full responsibility long term when the time comes. With encouragement from the board to develop a deeper bench and to work toward "growing their own," Sno-Isle identified "developmental positions" (designated "Dev" on the chart; defined as a position, not a person) that could be a step toward a key position. Here Olafson again looked at service and age, this time for individuals currently holding positions categorized as developmental to determine who might retire and create an opening in one of those jobs. They too were coded as IR, AR, and LR. This analysis indicated that several developmental positions could be open in the next few years due to retirements. This provided a list of potential developmental opportunities.

In addition, Sno-Isle has experimented with creating one developmental position to broaden the experience of those who may be interested in library administration. The facilities manager job was recently created (as a temporary position, for two years only) to provide developmental work experience in facilities management and capital facilities development. The incumbent is acquiring a great deal of experience and exposure working on special assignments such as branch renovation projects and creating a preventive maintenance plan for every building. She is now the key contact for building issues in each branch. In addition, she attends community and board meetings and meets regularly with the library director. Previously she was a manager of a large building and will have the opportunity to return to this position at the end of two years. Of course, by allowing staff to take a temporary job and return to their original job, Sno-Isle created a whole string of temporary positions, creating developmental opportunities for many across the system. At the end of two years the library leadership, with input from the incumbent, will decide whether to retain the facilities job as a temporary developmental position or make it a regular assignment.

Along with creating development opportunities in a variety of jobs, Karri Matau, director of strategic initiatives, is charged with creating a leadership development program for the organization. This program, which will support succession planning efforts, is still in developmental stages.

Many—if not most—libraries find themselves in difficult financial straits because of the recession. Thinking about this, I asked Olafson a question for which she had an interesting and clear answer. "Pat," I asked, "in the beginning of this conversation, you talked about the budget constraints facing Sno-Isle Libraries. You mentioned the potential of a hiring freeze. How much leadership development and succession planning do you plan to continue in these tough times?"

Olafson's answer was not one I often hear. "We know we need to have leadership development initiatives and succession planning in process even when times are bleak. Strong, skilled employees are a key ingredient to facing tough times and to carrying out our strategic plan. The library district cannot afford to put leadership development on the back burner."

Sno-Isle library leadership has made a choice—one that has them working diligently to ensure that knowledge is transferred as long-term employees get ready to move into the next phase of their lives and younger members of the workforce get ready to take the baton and bring the library into the future.

FIGURE 7.7
SAMPLE TRACKING WITH SNO-ISLE LIBRARIES' TEMPLATE

SUCCESSION PLANNING—POTENTIAL RETIREMENT VACANCIES   KEY AND DEVELOPMENTAL POSITIONS

Immediate Risk (IR) = (1) age 60 or older today; (2) age 55 or older with at least 15 years of service; (3) any age with 30 years in Plan 1
  IR is potential retirement in next 5 years
At Risk (AR) = (1) will move into the IR category in the next five years, i.e., ages 55–59; or (2) age 50 with 10 years of service
  AR is potential retirement in next 6–10 years
Low Risk (LR) = all other
Note: PLAN 2 eligibility is age 65 with 5+ years or age 55 with at least 20 years
PLAN 1 eligibility is any age with 30+; or age 55 with 25+; or age 60 with 5+
Retirement service credits may be transferred from previous participating employers (indicated with a + sign)

RISK LEVEL	POSITION	NAME	TITLE	SERVICE	AGE	RET. PLAN	RET. SVC. YRS.	FILL?	BACKUP UNTIL FILLED
IR	Key	AC	Finance Director	20	58	1	20	Y	Grants Analyst
IR	Key	BD	Programming Director	5	57	1	25+	Y	Children's Services Manager (branch)
IR	Key	CE	Marketing Director	27	60	2	27	Y	Marketing Assistant
IR	Key	DF	Branch Manager (largest branch)	15	55	2	26+	Y	Adult Services Manager (branch)
AR	Key	EG	Assistant Director, Public Services	17	54	2	17	Y	Programming Director
AR	Key	FH	Collection Development Manager	22	53	2	22	Y	Collection Development Librarian
AR	Key	ST	Circulation Manager	14	52	2	14	Y	Interlibrary Loan Manager

(cont.)

FIGURE 7.7 (cont.)

RISK LEVEL	POSITION	NAME	TITLE	SERVICE	AGE	RET. PLAN	RET. SVC. YRS.	FILL?	BACKUP UNTIL FILLED
AR	Key	RF	Branch Manager (medium branch)	15	50	2	15	N	regional management experiment
LR	Key	JJ	Training Manager	5	45	2	5	N	outsource training
LR	Key	MS	IT Manager	8	43	2	8	Y	IT Technician
IR	Dev[a]	LB	Grants Analyst/Accountant	21	58	2	21		
IR	Dev	AW	Outreach Librarian	20	65	1	27+		
IR	Dev	FF	Marketing Assistant	17	60	1	17		
IR	Dev	TS	Adult Services Manager (branch)	16	66	2	16		
AR	Dev	IH	Branch Manager (small branch)	11	54	2	14+		
AR	Dev	PM	Collection Development Librarian	1	51	2	10+		
AR	Dev	JL	Assistant Circulation Manager	15	53	2	15		
LR	Dev	RS	Children's Services Manager (branch)	10	42	2	10		
LR	Dev	JS	HR Assistant	7	40	2	7		
LR	Dev	PS	Interlibrary Loan Manager	6	45	2	6		

[a]In this context, *developmental* means the *position* can be a development step toward a key position. The intent is to use this information to identify developmental *positions* that potentially will come open, *not* individuals to be developed.

Note: Because Sno-Isle's original chart did not capture the discussion about whether to fill a vacant position or redistribute or outsource some of its duties, we added a column labeled "Fill?" as a reminder to examine every vacant position for the opportunities it may bring.

Notes

1. Competencies for California Librarians in the 21st Century, http://cla-net.org/resources/articles/r_com petencies.php. Professional competencies relate to the librarian's skills and knowledge in the areas of information resources, information access, technology, management and research, and the ability to use these competencies as a basis for providing library and information services. Personal competencies represent a set of skills, attitudes, and values that enable librarians to provide valuable and valued service, communicate well, survive in the new world of information, and focus on continued learning throughout their careers. These skills, attitudes, and values can be acquired through education and experience the same as professional skills and knowledge.

2. Much of this story is taken from JCL's winning application for the National Association for Counties Leadership Development Award.

3. Online Computer Library Center (OCLC): Career Development, www.oclc.org/us/en/careers/develop ment/default.htm.

4. OCLC: WebJunction, www.oclc.org/us/en/webjunc tion/default.htm.

5. Pierce County Library: Fast Facts, www.piercecounty library.org/about-us/about-overview/fast-facts.htm.

6. As with many states, the State of Washington has two pension plans, one more generous than the other. To keep this discussion simple, we eliminate the dimension that would consider whether the employee is a member of Plan 1 or 2, in which members have different criteria of eligibility for full retirement benefits.

RESURCES ///

General Publications

Barner, Robert. *Bench Strength: Developing the Depth and Versatility of Your Organization's Leadership Talent.* New York: AMACOM, 2006.

Berger, Lance A., and Dorothy R. Berger, eds. *The Talent Management Handbook: Creating Organizational Excellence by Identifying, Developing, and Promoting Your Best People.* New York: McGraw Hill, 2004.

Bryant, Josephine, and Kay Poustie. *Competencies Needed by Public Library Staff.* Gütersloh, Bertelsmann Foundation, 2001. www.public-libraries.net/html/x_media/pdf/competencies.pdf.

Byham, William C., Audrey B. Smith, and Matthew J. Paese. *Grow Your Own Leaders: How to Identify, Develop, and Retain Leadership Talent.* Upper Saddle River, N.J.: Prentice-Hall, 2002.

Cappelli, Peter. *Talent on Demand: Managing Talent in an Age of Uncertainty.* Boston: Harvard Business School Press, 2008.

Charan, Ram. *Leaders at All Levels: Deepening Your Talent Pool to Solve the Succession Crisis.* San Francisco: John Wiley and Sons, 2008.

Charan, Ram, Stephen Drotter, and James Noel. *The Leadership Pipeline: How to Build the Leadership-Powered Company.* San Francisco: John Wiley and Sons, 2001.

Dychtwald, Ken, Tamara J. Erickson, and Robert Morison. *Workforce Crisis: How to Beat the Coming Shortage of Skills and Talent.* Boston: Harvard Business School Press, 2006.

Fegley, S. "Society for Human Resource Management 2006 Succession Planning Survey Report." Alexandria, Va.: Society for Human Resources Management, 2006.

Gay, M., and Doris Sims. *Building Tomorrow's Talent.* Bloomington, Ind.: Authorhouse, 2006.

Goleman, Daniel, Richard Boyatzis, and Annie McKee. *Primal Leadership: Realizing the Power of Emotional Intelligence.* Boston: Harvard Business School Press, 2002.

Goodrich, Jeanne, and Paula Singer. *Human Resources for Results: The Right Person for the Right Job.* Chicago: American Library Association, 2007.

Groysberg, Boris, and Amanda Cowen. *Developing Leaders.* Boston: Harvard Business School Press, 2006.

Laughlin, Sara, Denise Shockley, and Ray Wilson. *The Library's Continuous Improvement Fieldbook.* Chicago: American Library Association, 2003.

Lawler, Edward E., III. *Talent: Making People Your Competitive Advantage.* San Francisco: John Wiley and Sons, 2008.

Managing Your Career. Lessons Learned series. Boston: Harvard Business School Press, 2007.

Mayo, Dianne, and Jeanne Goodrich. *Staffing for Results.* Chicago: American Library Association, 2002.

Mendelsohn, Steve, and Ron Komers. "How to Win the Talent Wars by Understanding Critical Factors." *HR News: The Magazine of the International Public Management Association for Human Resources,* February 2008, 22–26.

Moyers, Robert L. *The Nonprofit Chief Executive's Ten Basic Responsibilities.* Washington, D.C.: BoardSource, 2006.

Neighborhood Reinvestment Corporation. *Managing Executive Transitions.* Washington, D.C.: Community Development Leadership Project, 1999.

Nelson, Sandra. *Strategic Planning for Results.* Chicago: American Library Association, 2008.

Odiorne, George S. *Strategic Management of Human Resources: A Portfolio Approach.* San Francisco: Jossey-Bass, 1984.

Rothwell, William J. *Effective Succession Planning: Ensuring Leadership Continuity and Building Talent from Within,* 3rd ed. New York: AMACOM, 2005.

Rothwell, W. J., J. Alexander, and M. Bernhard, eds. *Case Studies in Government Succession Planning: Action-Oriented Strategies for Public-Sector Human Capital Management, Workforce Planning, Succession Planning, and Talent Management.* Amherst, Mass.: HRD Press, 2008.

Schiemann, William A. *Reinventing Talent Management: How to Maximize Performance in the New Marketplace.* Hoboken, N.J.: John Wiley and Sons, 2009.

Singer, Paula M., and Laura L. Francisco. *Developing a Compensation Plan for Your Library,* 2nd ed. Chicago: American Library Association, 2009.

Thorne, Kaye. *The Essential Guide to Managing Talent: How Top Companies Recruit, Train and Retain the Best Employees.* Philadelphia: Kogan Page, 2007.

Ulrich, David, and Wayne Brockbank. *The HR Value Proposition.* Boston: Harvard Business School Press, 2005.

Young, Mary B. *Building the Leadership Pipeline in the Local, State, and Federal Government.* Sacramento, Calif.: CPS Human Resource Services, 2005. www.workforceplanning.state.pa.us/portal/server.pt/community/workforce_and_succession_planning/1442/resources/267538.

Library Director/CEO Succession Planning

Annie E. Casey Foundation. *Executive Transitions Monograph Series.* 7 vols. Baltimore: Annie E. Casey Foundation, 2004–2008.

———. *Helping Organizations Achieve Successful Leadership Transitions.* Baltimore: Annie E. Casey Foundation and Association of Small Foundations, 2009.

Association of Small Foundations. *Primer Series: Investing in Nonprofit Leaders.* Washington, D.C.: Association of Small Foundations, 2009.

Axelrod, Nancy. *Chief Executive Succession Planning: The Board's Role in Securing Your Organization's Future.* Washington, D.C.: BoardSource, 2002.

Bell, Jeanne, Richard Moyers, and Timothy Wolfred. *Daring to Lead 2006.* CompassPoint Nonprofit Services and the Meyer Foundation, 2006. www.compasspoint.org/assets/194_daringtolead06final.pdf.

Cornelius, Marla, Patrick Corvington, and Albert Ruesga. *Ready to Lead? Next Generation Leaders Speak Out.* Baltimore: Annie E. Casey Foundation, Meyer Foundation, CompassPoint Nonprofit Services, and idealist.org, 2008.

Gilmore, Tom N. *Making a Leadership Change: How Organizations and Leaders Can Handle Leadership Transitions Successfully.* San Francisco: Jossey-Bass, 1988.

Kets de Vries, Manfred. "The Dark Side of CEO Succession." *Harvard Business Review* 88, no. 1 (1988): 56–60.

Neighborhood Reinvestment Corporation. *Managing Executive Transitions.* Washington, D.C.: Community Development Leadership Project, 1999.

Peters, Jeanne, and Timothy Wolfred. *Daring to Lead.* CompassPoint Nonprofit Services and the Meyer Foundation, 2001. www.compasspoint.org/assets/5_daring.pdf.

Tebbe, Don. *Chief Executive Transitions: How to Hire and Support a Nonprofit CEO.* Washington, D.C.: BoardSource, 2009.

Tierney, Thomas J. *The Nonprofit Sector's Leadership Deficit White Paper.* Bridgespan Group, 2006. www.bridgespan.org/nonprofit-leadership-deficit.aspx?resource=Articles.

Internet Resources

BoardSource. www.boardsource.org.

Building Successful Organizations: Workforce Planning in HHS. www.hhs.gov/ohr/workforce/wfpguide.html.
Model used by the federal Department of Health and Human Services.

Center for Continuing Study of the California Economy. California's Coming Retirement Wave. www.ccsce.com/PDF/Numbers_CA_Ret_Wave.pdf.
Insights on current retirement projections within the state of California.

Consortium for Research on Emotional Intelligence in Organizations. Bar-On Emotional Intelligence Inventory. www.eiconsortium.org/measures/eqi.html.

Georgia Merit System. Georgia's Flexible Succession Planning Model. www.gms.state.ga.us/pdfs/sp/sp.ga_sp_model_manual.pdf.
Best practices in succession planning for State of Georgia. Includes model training materials.

International Public Management Association for Human Resources. www.IPMA-HR.org.

New York State Department of Civil Service. Workforce and Succession Planning. www.cs.state.ny.us/successionplanning/.
Extensive information related to workforce planning and succession planning best practices.

Pew Center on the States. Management Lab Manual. www.pewcenteronthestates.org/initiatives_detail.aspx?initiativeID=54240.

———. Training and Employee Development. www.pewcenteronthestates.org/initiatives_detail.aspx?initiativeID=51226.

Society for Human Resource Management. www.shrm.org.

State of California. Leadership Challenge. http://cpr.ca.gov/CPR_Report/Issues_and_Recommendations/Chapter_7_Statewide_Operations/Personnel_Management/SO42.html.
Information related to a study of public employees in California, Spring 2004.

State of Colorado. Succession Planning Strategy. www.colorado.gov/cs/Satellite/DPA-DHR/DHR/1248577225227.
Best practices in workforce planning.

State of Texas Human Resources. Workforce Planning Guide. http://sao.hr.state.tx.us/Workforce/guide.html.
Best-practice information in workforce development.

United States Office of Personnel Management. Retirement Statistics. www.opm.gov/feddata/retire/rs-projections.pdf.
Research related to retirement projections in the federal government.

———. Workforce Planning Model. www.opm.gov/hcaaf_resource_center/assets/Sa_tool4.pdf.
Model used by the federal government's Office of Personnel Management.

Washington State Department of Personnel. Workforce Planning. www.dop.wa.gov/strategichr/WorkforcePlanning/Pages/default.aspx.
Workforce planning guide, including tools.

Workforce Planning for Wisconsin State Government. www.workforceplanning.wi.gov.
Best-practice information in workforce development for the State of Wisconsin.

INDEX ///

You may also be interested in